P9-DVF-171

25 May 88of

RICKS COLLEGE
DAVID O. McKAY LIBRARY
REXBURG, IDAHO 83440

WITHDRAWN

JUN 03 2024

DAVID O. McKAY LIBRARY
BYU-IDAHO

Trees in Urban Design

Trees in Urban Design

Henry F. Arnold

VNR VAN NOSTRAND REINHOLD COMPANY
NEW YORK   CINCINNATI   ATLANTA   DALLAS   SAN FRANCISCO
LONDON   TORONTO   MELBOURNE

Van Nostrand Reinhold Company Regional Offices:
New York Cincinnati Atlanta Dallas San Francisco

Van Nostrand Reinhold Company International Offices:
London Toronto Melbourne

Copyright © 1980 by Litton Educational Publishing, Inc.

Library of Congress Catalog Card Number: 79-20497
ISBN: 0-442-20336- 5
ISBN: 0-442-20340-3 pbk.

All rights reserved. No part of this work covered by the copyright
hereon may be reproduced or used in any form or by any
means—graphic, electronic, or mechanical, including photocopying,
recording, taping, or information storage and retrieval
systems—without permission of the publisher.

This book was set in Cheltenham, Primer, and Helvetica.
The designer was Alan Goodheart.

Manufactured in the United States of America

Published by Van Nostrand Reinhold Company
135 West 50th Street, New York, N.Y. 10020

Published simultaneously in Canada by Van Nostrand Reinhold Ltd.

15 14 13 12 11 10 9 8 7 6 5 4 3 2 1

Library of Congress Cataloging in Publication Data

Arnold, Henry F
  Trees in urban design.

  Includes index.
  1. Urban beautification.   2. Trees in cities.
I. Title.
NA9052.A76   715'.2   79-20497
ISBN 0-442-20336-5
ISBN 0-442-20340-3 pbk.

Contents

Preface

The debate over what place people occupy in nature is prominently expressed in the way we build cities. In modern American cities there is an ambivalent attitude about the use of bold man-made forms. The skyscraper is admired for its soaring grace yet condemned for its impact on the landscape. In a similar way urban design has been handicapped by a deeply held common belief that even influences how trees are deployed in our cities. Like many forces that have a profound social influence this one is not easily explained. The nature of this common belief is perhaps best described through the attitudes that it engenders.

The view expressed by Thomas Jefferson, that cities represent a social evil and agrarian villages are more virtuous, still prevails. Our identification of cities with corruption and small rural towns with moral superiority is a sentimental manifestation of the enduring myth. The act of building "romantic garden" parks in all of our large cities provides persistent evidence for this concept. The pastoral philosophy of urban park design calls for making the park an escape from the city rather than part of the city. As an urban antidote, the large park displays scattered trees in an imitation pastoral landscape.

This idea of rural nature set into the city extends beyond the large city park everywhere permeating civic spaces. For example individual specimens are favored over groves or rows, random arrangements of trees displace symmetrical groups and formal pruning is eschewed. The opportunities afforded by geometric arrangement are avoided in favor of naturalistic designs. The belief that the city can be redeemed by introducing fragments of the agrarian landscape has never subsided since Frederick Law Olmsted planned Central Park.

The message of this book runs counter to the pastoral ideal in three essential propositions. The first is that human artistry can improve on rural nature by shaping the materials of the city, including trees, to create a better urban habitat than now exists, without copying "nature". The second calls for the general practice of planting trees as groups in accordance with their intrinsic nature and evolutionary requirements, not as scattered individual specimens. The third is a belief in the value and importance of the city as a nucleus of culture where human life can be nurtured and perfected. The city is an indispensable expression of our scientific and artistic achievements. Urban design must be strongly influenced by the biological requirements of people and plants.

The book is organized so that the first two chapters define the problem, the third chapter states the philosophical design basis and the last four chapters are concerned with ways of applying the design principles that are developed in the early chapters. Illustrations and examples are used to arrive at principles and demonstrate their application. Repetition of the same example to demonstrate different design precepts is intended to contain the broad subject within a familiar context.

A sincere expression of appreciation and recognition for their contributions to this book are due: Louise Schiller for her review, editing and crucial suggestions, Jane Groth and my daughter Joan for their relentless typing, editing and correcting, Jules Gregory and William Flemer III for their review and valued advice, Phyllis Frakt for her perspicacious comments, Alan Goodheart for his assiduous attention to graphics and my daughters Louise for her drafting and Helene for her proof reading. Mirriam Klipper is due special thanks for initiating and encouraging the idea of writing this book.

Henry F. Arnold
Princeton, New Jersey

Today and yesterday

A view of the problem

Trees in design. The most persistent problem confronting every designer who works with trees is their seductive appeal. The remarkable aesthetic power of trees distracts artists so much that their potential for building dense organic compositions has been replaced by an over-refined, precious reverence for individual trees. Trees are the most exquisite and the most sparingly apportioned raw material of urban design. Our cities display a mere dollop of their sensual color and form. There are exceptions both in North America and Europe to this general rule. Yet the paradox remains—we fail to design with our most humane raw material.

1-1 Brooklyn, New York: Cadman Plaza Park. An exceptional example.

The coherence achieved by planting a dense grove of a single species can be viewed along the Parkway in Philadelphia, in Bryant Park in Manhattan, in Grant Park in Chicago, and in Paris, France. In fact the memorable quality of Savannah, Paris and Old Philadelphia can be attributed as much to the organized patterns of trees as to the architecture and urban design. Europeans began to manipulate trees for urban design many centuries ago. Europe provides many examples of trees used in sympathy with the geometry of the city. They create patterns that are woven into the fabric of the city, just like well designed buildings. European streets, squares and parks are often linked together by an intricate ceiling of tree branches. The visual poetry created with trees, stone and water was deliberately achieved by designers who understood the nature of the materials. Although we have been able to enjoy European urban design, we have not yet fully perceived and interpreted the experience for our own urban centers.

Trees in American cities. Trees in North America tend to be exploited as individual specimens that do not form a roof of foliage and branches. The Plane trees in Cadman Plaza Park in Brooklyn are an exception.

In downtown areas, trees are usually insignificant compared to trees along older residential streets. There are notable, though usually isolated exceptions which will be cited in later chapters. The contrast of Philadelphia's Benjamin Franklin Parkway with North Broad Street illustrates the dichotomy—the Parkway is experienced with trees, while North Broad Street is starkly treeless.

1-3   Philadelphia, Pennsylvania: North Broad Street.

1-2   Philadelphia, Pennsylvania: Benjamin Franklin Parkway.

The following aerial views show how our cities have neglected a prime opportunity for improving urban life with trees. These central districts are not only functional and symbolic centers of our metropolitan areas, but they are also the locations of most intensive human activity. Our civilization is mirrored in the way we treat these central public open spaces.

West Palm Beach, Florida, has made an important gesture toward preserving the waterfront with a pedestrian promenade at the water's edge. Trees are used sparingly near the waterfront and are abruptly discontinued at the edge of the downtown shopping area. Clematis Street is the spine of this retail center that terminates at the Public Library where the trees stop.

The Inner Harbor Area of Baltimore remains without trees—its demolished landscape is a gaping hole in an industrial waterfront—signifying progress?

Tulsa, Oklahoma, epitomizes the parking lot city. Buildings stand in acres of treeless pavement. In Lexington, Kentucky, trees in the older residential neighborhoods flank the downtown. Extension of this tree pattern into the central area could be hastened by measures to curtail automobile traffic within the

1-4

1-5

1-6

Today and yesterday

1-4   West Palm Beach, Florida: Downtown.

1-5   Baltimore, Maryland: Inner Harbor.

1-6   Tulsa, Oklahoma.

downtown loop so that pedestrian space could be increased and made more hospitable.

Small towns like Princeton, New Jersey, can sterilize acres of ground for vehicular storage in the same manner and to the same detriment as in large cities. The view of State Street in Trenton, New Jersey, has only slightly fewer trees and comparable surface parking. The State Office building development in Trenton typifies the crass insensitivity of most recent large scale construction in cities. Providing shade and visual relief in parking areas should be the typical solution in civilized societies. Here the government agencies responsible for environmental monitoring have indirectly collaborated in assaulting human sensitivity and eroding the city environment.

The improvement that could be made to these ravished landscapes with groves of trees is staggering. Despite the immense scale of such sites, it is possible to plant trees in a way that will provide the immediate benefits of summer shade, seasonal color and winter texture. The economic cost of such extensive large scale tree planting is justified by the magnitude of the public values attained. Indeed the cost of keeping our cities ugly and inhospitable is one that we cannot afford.

1-7

1-8

1-9

1-10

1-7   Lexington, Kentucky.

1-8   Princeton, New Jersey: Town Center.

1-9   Trenton, New Jersey: State Street

1-10   Trenton, New Jersey: State Office Buildings.

1-11
1-12

Wilmington, Delaware and Newark, New Jersey views typify the attitude of disinterest in urban waterfront potential. This segment of Wilmington's riverfront could be linked with the central area of the city by treelined streets. Both cities would benefit from extensive shade tree planting even at the expense of a few parking spaces. Having a tree shaded waterfront promenade next to the train station provides a relaxing atmosphere for the waiting traveler that no airport in the country can match. The benefit of such an amenity is not difficult to imagine for anyone who has waited an hour or longer in a dreary railroad terminal.

Train stations in major cities between Boston and Washington are particularly barren. In New York, Boston, Baltimore, Philadelphia, and Wilmington, there is simply no space left near the railroad station that is not totally preempted by motor vehicles. A major redesign of the Baltimore, Philadephia and Wilmington station sites would allow highly beneficial tree plantings giving the railway visitors to these cities a completely different first impression. With some minor redesign of the surrounding space, the train stations at New London, New Haven, Stamford, Providence, and Trenton, could benefit from massive tree plantings to shade and accentuate the public entry zone. Union Station in Washington, D.C. is perhaps the most conspicuous example in the United States of a prominent public building that cries out for formal tree groves. In the five acre space in front of the station, the heat, glare, exhaust fumes and noise, are a genuine test of human physical endurance. The visual and functional need for massive groves of large shade trees in this sprawling semi-circular plaza is exceeded only by the need to reroute the automobile and bus traffic that crowds the handsome entry portal. Successive redesigns of this space have only increased the vehicular traffic at the expense of pedestrian comfort and security. The plaza itself is a clutter of steps, flag poles, flower beds, statuary and signs that exacerbate the problem of pedestrian use and enjoyment.

Viewing cities of the United States from the air reveals that the central areas are deficient in shade trees regardless of the size of the city or its location. In every city, automobile parking lots occupy large treeless paved areas even though trees would make an ideal sun screen for such a land use. Lack of trees does not correlate directly with building height, but does reflect the intensity of use. Waterfront sites are almost universally treeless even when they are not being employed for any active use. The density of tree planting commonly increases in direct proportion to distance from the urban center. The aerial photograph text illustration of Lexington, Kentucky, Figure 1-7, illustrates this typical vegetative pattern of our cities. Random planting of trees is more common than organized or regular patterns even in the less dense areas. There is little or no evidence that tree planting was a deliberate design consideration in planning the geometry of any districts of our cities. Rather, it is apparent that trees were used to fill in the left over spaces that resulted from building and circulation demands. Spaces generally were not planned for trees. Parks and public squares are, of course, the major exception.

1-13

1-14
1-15

1-7

1-11 Wilmington, Delaware: Train Station.

1-12 Newark, New Jersey: Train Station.

1-13 Washington, D.C.: Union Station.

1-14 Washington, D.C.: Union Station.

1-15 Washington, D.C.: Union Station.

Important public buildings are not often enhanced with trees, even when surrounded by substantial open space.

A more detailed look at urban streetscapes amplifies the same conclusion—the opportunity to enrich public spaces with trees has seldom been addressed. In Newark, New Jersey, for instance, the 130 foot wide space between buildings on Broad Street is dominated by the sight, sound and smell of eight lanes of vehicular traffic unrelieved for most of its length by street trees. One small corner space is occupied by ten foot square planters containing Honeylocust trees. This little grove of six trees creates a welcome pocket of visual relief. Imagine trees of this scale lining both sides of the street and the median strip.

In Charlotte, North Carolina, the streets in the older single family house neighborhoods have magnificent arching canopies formed by 90 foot tall Willow Oak trees. In contrast, many of the bare streets in the center of the city have been planted with young trees. Along Tryon Street, a major traffic artery, small Cherry Laurel trees were planted 40 feet apart in a single row on both sides of this 120 foot wide right-of-way. Despite the city's good intentions and modest in-

1-16

1-17

1-18

1-16 Newark, New Jersey: Broad Street.

1-17 Newark, New Jersey: Broad Street.

7

vestment, those trees will make an insufficient impact on the scale of this street even in fifty years if all the trees grow. These trees are too few, too far apart and too small at maturity.

In Philadelphia, a city memorable for its majestic avenues of Plane Trees, the new Chestnut Street Mall has two blocks cluttered with bulky raised granite planters containing small Callery Pear trees. These trees will never grow large enough to match their containers in visual impact. By contrast, the city's tree-lined alleys and side streets are handsomely detailed and inviting. The trees in containers will never grow to half the size of the Plane trees shown in the illustration. Even if the trees could grow large enough in these planters to meet the scale requirements of the street, the clumsy street furniture dismembers the ground level and visually detracts from the street space.

1-18 Charlotte, North Carolina.

1-19 Philadelphia, Pennsylvania: Chestnut Street.

1-20 Philadelphia, Pennsylvania: Delancey Street.

Houston, Texas, has one of the most luxurious treelined streets in the southwest. This arterial street with its broad median is clothed with four continuous
rows of sculptural Live Oak trees that terminate abruptly in what is ostensibly
Houston's downtown area. From that point on, this central city node is unrelieved by trees, as one views the tall buildings set in hundreds of acres of parked
and moving vehicles. The illustration, Figure 1-22, shows one small segment of
this "tree limit line" beyond which few living organisms appear to survive.

In Minneapolis, Nicolette Avenue was converted to a pedestrian oriented
shopping street with a cartway limited to bus traffic that meanders within the
right-of-way. The wiggles in the street result in more vehicular pavement than
necessary and prevent the street from having a unifying canopy of trees. Instead
there are isolated groups of trees that do not seem to bear any relationship to the
surroundings or to the circulation pattern. The pavement pattern was given
more attention than space-defining trees.

In Alabama, the Birmingham Green is a kind of glorified median strip with a
hodge podge of little plants and inert materials that look pathetic in the scale of
the broad street space. In this case there was obviously room for a unifying

1-21

1-22

1-21   Houston, Texas: Main Street.

1-22   Houston, Texas: The edge of the
"center".

9

canopy of trees that could complement and extend the delightful character of the nearby City Square with its large Live Oak trees. Large, significant trees would have cost no more than the doodling that was done with expensive ground materials. The concept of designing ground patterns without trees suggests that there is nothing worthwhile in the landscape to elevate our eyes. It would be much more inspiring to look up at tree branches that also enrich the ground with ever changing patterns of light and shadow.

The list is endless. Dayton, Ohio, with its undeveloped river banks in the downtown could be a city of distinction. Its virtually treeless center and wide congested streets seem to defy the unusual opportunity that its broad green levees suggest. The river banks may be more fortunate since the work of Dayton's River Corridor Committee includes proposals for many trees along the urban edges of the Miami River. A study by Landscape Architect, Dan Kiley in 1971 recommended new tree plantings of major significance. (Kiley)

1-23

Salt Lake City has some of the widest streets of any city in the country. There is room for a double row of large shade trees on each side of the main streets. The central area lacks even one intact single row of appropriately scaled street trees. Lexington, Kentucky, has beautiful treelined streets everywhere but in the downtown loop. Burlington, Vermont's business district is without trees. There the Dutch elm disease has claimed most of the old trees on streets immediately adjacent to the downtown, the treeless area spreads out over a large part of the town.

1-23 Dayton, Ohio: A potential tree lined river edge.

1-24

1-24 Salt Lake City, Uah.

Today and yesterday

The treeless streets, and moreover the feeble gesture to restore trees in most of our cities and towns are depressing to witness. In many instances where improvements were undertaken, an effective treescape could have been achieved for no more than the cost of the landscape elements that were installed. In most of our downtown areas we cannot rely on an architectural richness for unity and scale. The typical pedestrian mall is an abomination of signs and plastic furniture with a few undersize trees added for decoration. Trenton, New Jersey's Commons competes with Nicolette Avenue, Minneapolis, for sparing use of trees set in elaborate paving designs. The "greening" of Trenton was one of many exterior decorating projects that missed an important chance to reshape the space between buildings with trees. The flowering trees will never grow large enough to create the kind of shading canopy that all of this paved area needs for comfort and scale.

1-25
1-26

In the past three decades, planners and urban designers have shown increasing concern for urban improvement, human scale, and bringing life back to city streets. There is no lack of professional design interest and there has been money to improve cities. Yet there is not one city in the United States where a pedestrian can experience a visual or environmental plan that adequately exploits design with trees.

The literature. The literature on trees and tree use treats the subject in a romanticized suburban context. Even scientific works about trees begin with a number of unproven aesthetic assumptions and use these as a basis for research and conjecture. The most common preconceptions occur in five categories stated in simple form as follows:

1. Density: Trees should be widely spaced when planted so that they can develop a symmetrical spreading crown form. When planted close together, they are less healthy than when grown as single trees standing alone.

2. Order: Trees grow naturally in random arrangements of different species. Planted in straight rows or geometric patterns, they are visually less interesting than unordered, "natural" arrangements.

3. Diversity: Planting a large variety of different tree species in each area of the city is a sound practice based on principles of ecology.

4. Scale: It is better to use small trees with limited growth on narrow streets than large types of trees.

5. Form and Detail: The typical crown shape of an open grown tree and seasonal color are important determinants in selecting a tree type for city planting. In general, street trees are better planted back away from the curb where they will have more room to grow.

Each of the foregoing statements contradicts experienced observations, and is unsupported or easily disproved by scientific data. These aesthetic preconceptions are of central importance in the use of trees for urban design. Subsequent chapters of this book will deal with each topic in more detail.

1-25 Trenton, New Jersey: The Commons.

1-26 Trenton, New Jersey: The Commons.

In urban situations, trees are most effective and healthy if grown close enough together for the branches to intermingle and create a continuous network of branches as they do in the forest. Open grown tree specimens are uncommon in nature and are probably more susceptible to injury and disease, since genetic evolution favors trees in close groups.* Trees seem to have evolved more by cooperation than by competition. The forest is a profound expression of the organic cooperation of individual trees adapted to a plant community in which trees exist in highly organized arrangements.

Plant ecology, as presently understood, cannot be directly applied to cities. Ecologists cite the diversity of natural organisms that grow together in the forest, creating an interdependent community of plants and animals. Under the evolutionary conditions of a natural site, organisms that are mutually dependent range in size from the submicroscopic to the giant forest tree. Many, perhaps most, of these forest organisms cannot survive in an urban habitat. Therefore the trees that grow in cities do so independently of many smaller natural woodland associates. Providing a greater diversity of tree types will not compensate for the natural forest diversity that is unattainable in the city. Yet many recently published articles and books on planting design claim that a diversity of tree types planted in the city is in accord with sound ecological principles. Furthermore, since many urban habitats are unsuitable for more than two or three different tree types, forced diversity results in planting unsuitable species of trees.

Planting small scale trees in the city is part of a popular movement given impetus by utility companies to reduce maintenance pruning. It is based on a misunderstanding of what trees in the city could and should be. Most of the tree species that are classed as small or medium sized do not meet the inherent scale requirements for city streets. They are too small to create an arching roof of branches and foliage. As a result, their use in public urban spaces is at best self-consciously decorative and more often distractingly inappropriate.

Contemporary attitudes. The notion that trees and smaller plants are used as furniture or sculpture to decorate exterior spaces summarizes the popular view of what landscape architecture is about. The antithesis of the decorative approach to landscape design focuses upon creating or reinforcing spaces with trees. In this view, scale and spatial proportion are the fundamental design concerns, not embellishment. This fact is of such profound importance that cosmetic efforts to embellish the city with trees are irrelevant to urban design.

Attitudes about the use of trees in cities are influenced by a resurgent interest in designing "with nature," even though the city is the wrong focus for many of these ideas. Guidelines for tree planting based on the incipient science of plant ecology may be logically applied on a regional basis in rural areas. The same rules may have no application in the city where a different order of nature exists. For example, the idea of the farm monoculture and the need for plant species diversity on a regional basis has been applied to the city block as if it were a square mile of farm land. This misapplication of a rural conservation idea to the city is indicative of the dominant influence of agricultural science on urban landscape design at the present time. The effects of this misorientation of ideas—this pastoral view of the city—have serious implications for the quality of urban design.

In large measure our central city areas reflect these attitudes and preconceptions. Large city parks are almost universally laid out in the romantic tradition. Trees are planted most frequently as individual specimens, rather than in lines or groups. The species most frequently favored are those considered clean because they drop the least litter. Sparse city tree patterns reflect the concern about planting trees "too close" together because they need space to attain the mature form of the typical "open grown crown." Collectively, these attitudes represent an obstacle to good urban design because they seriously constrict aesthetic choices in creating tree patterns. The resulting designs are praised be-

* The shape of a tree is greatly altered by the space in which it has grown. Trees planted far apart as on most suburban lawns have a wide spreading low-branched crown. Trees in a forest develop a tall straight trunk with a narrow high crown. Throughout this book the former will be referred to as the "open grown" tree form.

cause trees are intrinsically beautiful, and the materials are mistaken for the design.

Our ambivalent attitude toward the complete urban environment is contained within another attitude toward trees in cities. We accept certain levels of technological abuse when we tolerate smog and ozone in our air. Trees are indicators of both the allowable abuse and our ineptness at correcting it. We do not plant extensively enough in central city areas partly because of the toxic conditions that abound there. We fear that the trees will not survive. Ironically, atmospheric conditions that will not support trees are even more destructive of human life. Therefore, the emergence of trees in our downtown areas is essential as a positive symbol of the renewed fitness of the urban environment for all forms of life.

A glance at the past

Today's scarcity of vegetation in cities of the United States is more noticeable and consequential than it was centuries ago here and abroad. Cities are larger, more distant from agrarian land, and more formidable in vertical scale than they were in the past. The machine, particularly in transportation and communication, has lessened the intimacy of human social contact. The state of modern cities is a departure from historic precedent in the way that trees are thought about and deployed. Today, in our cities, the use of trees is less rational than it was in seventeenth century France. These historic trends may provide clues to help in understanding our modern predicament.

The reconstruction of gardens from paintings found in tombs, such as the tomb of Amenhotep III, tells us that early Egyptians used trees in the same regular symmetrical way that they built their temples. (Newton) It is interesting to observe that one of the tree types used in these ancient gardens has been identified as the Sycamore, one of our most durable city trees today. The Assyrians planted trees in regularly spaced rows to create the world's first known parks in 700 B.C. The great royal parks built by the Persians at about 480 B.C. were characterized by the same regular geometry. (Tobey) These early hunting parks provide the first historical evidence of trees planted in cities. Trees were arranged in rows, aligned both ways as described by Lysander. Early planners expressed man's evolving mathematical knowledge through the geometry of their designs. They were not yet touched by the modern notion that man is apart from nature, and therefore man-made regular forms were not considered unnatural. Trees were not scattered in random arrangements, but they were deliberately placed in lines as an expression of nature. Our way of seeing and expressing nature, which emphasizes the irregular aspects of natural forms, may be more complex, but it is still only an incomplete abstraction. Straight lines, bilateral symmetry and rectilinear geometry are found in the universe along with random forms of order. That man recognized and used this simple geometry from ancient times up to present day in the basic layout of urban centers, shows the intrinsic practicality of the rectangle and the square.

We lack evidence that there were trees planted in any significant way in Mediterranean cities at the time of the early Roman Empire. These cities lacked the functional necessity for shade that exists in most temperate climate inland cities. Even today, a densely built city in a Mediterranean climate has little functional need of shade trees. The buildings give shade and the sea breezes cool. In ancient Rome, public squares were built for large crowds and tree planting was restricted to private gardens. Today's designers who copy Italian piazzas would do well to understand the climatic basis for Italy's treeless urban areas when planning city spaces in more varied and hostile climates.

In later centuries, the Romans learned the value of street trees for spatial enhancement even though shade was also provided by porticoes. A row of ancient

Plane trees along the Tiber River in Rome transforms the walk into a delightful pedestrian way. Other wide streets in modern Rome are planted with trees that are sometimes clipped to create a more dense, uniform canopy, like a living arcade.

1-27

1-28

The medieval city did not lend itself to trees because of its very narrow, organic street pattern. Secular and sacred gardens were small, private, walled-in spaces with raised planters for low species, principally herbs, that required full sunlight; hence, there were seldom trees. Large vegetable gardens were also typical of the period nourishing self-sufficient communities.

Italian villas of the Renaissance exploited water, hedges, and low plantings much more than trees in framing their principle spaces. Here again one reason is climate. Villas were located on hillsides where breezes cooled interior and outdoor space, making shade in the gardens less important. The sites were often carved out of wooded hillsides emphasizing the spatial contrast between forest and garden. Where trees were planted, it was usually to frame a view, often with Cypress. Plantings were regular in the formal gardens of the villa. Sometimes the surrounding hillsides were planted with olive orchards on a square grid. To the extent that trees were planted in villa gardens, they characteristically appear regular and organized. The Renaissance villa garden was an expression of nature tamed.

1-27 Rome, Italy.

1-28 Rome, Italy.

1-29 Paris, France.

The truly spatial use of trees in cities reached its full expression in seventeenth century Paris. The development of the Tuilleries Garden, and its later expansion by André Le Notre to form the green Champs Elysées, illustrates the great spatial value of trees in large scale urban design. The city of Paris was unified by a network of treelined boulevards and avenues connecting the many pleasant parks and squares. The wonderful formal geometry of this open space system, with its highly organized rows of trees, helps to make Paris the universally admired city that it is today.

1-29

The design principles underlying the geometric tree patterns of Paris were developed by André Le Notre at Vaux-le-Vicomte and were best expressed later in the layout of the garden of Versailles. Though not in an urban setting, it is in Versailles that one can best experience the spatial use of trees at a scale congenial to the city. This design also illustrates a highly successful way of integrat-

1-30
1-31

15

ing the man-made with the natural landscape, a basic and difficult problem of landscape architecture today. Nonetheless, conventional thinking holds that Versailles represents an unnatural exploitation of natural materials. Twentieth century writers of landscape history tend to see Versailles primarily as a symbol of mankind's dominance of "Nature" as if man were completely apart from nature. Curiously the separation of man from "Nature" was more profoundly expressed in the ensuing English park and garden style.

1-30   Versailles, France.

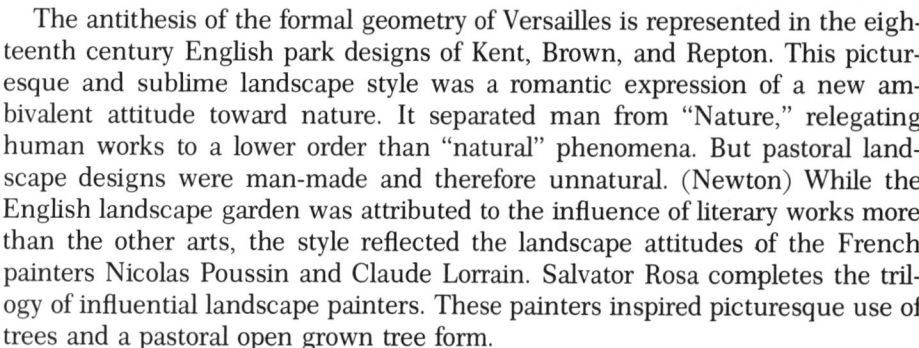

1-31   Versailles, France.

The antithesis of the formal geometry of Versailles is represented in the eighteenth century English park designs of Kent, Brown, and Repton. This picturesque and sublime landscape style was a romantic expression of a new ambivalent attitude toward nature. It separated man from "Nature," relegating human works to a lower order than "natural" phenomena. But pastoral landscape designs were man-made and therefore unnatural. (Newton) While the English landscape garden was attributed to the influence of literary works more than the other arts, the style reflected the landscape attitudes of the French painters Nicolas Poussin and Claude Lorrain. Salvator Rosa completes the trilogy of influential landscape painters. These painters inspired picturesque use of trees and a pastoral open grown tree form.

The English landscape style developed from the early pictorial and less space conscious works of Brown, to the more practical adaptations of Sir Humphrey Repton by the end of the eighteenth century. The most utilitarian expression of this design form came about in the English "Country Parks." Among the first of these new public parks was Birkenhead near Liverpool designed by Joseph Paxton. It is here that Fredric Law Olmsted first observed the use of curving roads, irregular pastoral groupings of trees and lakes that were later employed in Central Park. (Barlow)

The translation of the English landscape style into designs for Central Park and Prospect Park in New York by Olmsted and Vaux was to produce a major impact on the urban landscapes of the United States. The influence of this style set the character of virtually every large city park in America. Indeed the influence has been pervasive in reinforcing pastoral attitudes towards the use of trees throughout the urban areas of this country. Knowledge of the impact of the early park movement in America is crucial to understanding contemporary issues in urban design.

The inappropriateness of the English "Country Park" form for large open spaces in today's American cities is dramatized by the increasing problems of sanitation, policing and use that are being experienced. However, when New

York's Central Park was designed in 1857, both the physical and social conditions were very different from our own. The poor were crowded into tenements far worse than those we see today. Olmsted's pronouncements about providing an escape from the city for the working man who was beleaguered by the pressures of an industrial city reflected social currents of the time. It may be argued that Central Park provided an upper middle class solution to meet the needs of the workingman with its meandering carriage roads and picturesque scenery. However, the well intentioned purpose of closing off the city to create an accessible idyllic setting for rejuvenation is consistent with that prevailing attitude that the city itself was responsible for most social ills.

It was far less expensive and environmentally more sound to adapt the irregular site to free flowing picturesque form, than it would have been to make it level. Had the site been flat it would simply not have been feasible to produce a convincing and successful romantic landscape. The grading operations would have cost much more than the trees.

Finally we must remember the profound influence of *sentimental pastoralism* on early American thinking. This "pastoral ideal" has continued to influence our cultural development until the present day. Today we still hear about the good, clean, honest rural life while we view cities as the centers of corruption and vice. In Olmsted's time the connection of pastoral nature with the "good life" was derived from the social and political ideas influenced by Jean-Jacques Rousseau. (Mumford, 1944) Native American writers like Henry David Thoreau and George Perkins Marsh focused interest for the first time on ecology and natural resources. (Mumford, 1955) It is not surprising that a park designed in the middle of the nineteenth century would reflect both the romantic view of nature and the nature preserve idea. Central Park incorporates both ideas.

Before considering the contemporary design relevance of Central Park, there is an historic example that is important to the development of our ideas about the use of trees in urban design. Biltmore in Asheville, North Carolina was constructed about 1890. It represents a fruitful collaboration between Richard Morris Hunt, the architect, and Fredric Law Olmsted, Sr., the landscape architect. Though it was built after Central Park, the planning is discussed here because of the light it sheds on Olmsted as a designer. Criticisms of the historical accuracy of the overall stylistic composition aside, the landscape design for the house at Biltmore is well handled. The restraint in designing the entry area and the bold simplicity of the esplanade are better illustrations of Olmsted's understanding of scale than any element in Central Park. The composition of house and grounds also shows recognition of the need to organize the space

1-32

1-32 Ashville, North Carolina: Biltmore.

17

around a building for active use. The photographs show the design when it is mature enough to demonstrate the value of trees in organizing architectural space. The three views show how the double rows of Tulip trees are arranged to, in effect, create an enormous arcade on each side of the esplanade. There is no clutter of little plantings to dilute the strength of this handsomely scaled composition. By contrast Central Park lacks a single space of similar inspiring clarity. The best spatial design with trees, the formal esplanade called "the Mall" in Central Park is irresolute in scale. Trees are spaced too far apart both longitudinally and transversely to produce the noble clarity that is exhibited so well at Biltmore. The only other clearly space-forming use of trees in Central Park is found in a few small random groves where individual trees were planted closely enough together to develop upright high-branched trunks.

1-33 Ashville, North Carolina: Biltmore.

1-34 Ashville, North Carolina: Biltmore.

1-36 New York: Central Park. Tree grove.

1-35 New York: Central Park. "The Mall".

18

Altering and expanding perceptions

Central Park today. It does no injustice to Olmsted and Vaux and their pro-digious park planning accomplishments to reflect on the inadequacies of this type of park for today's cities. The design of Central Park was conceived as an antidote to the City, rather than as an extension of the City. Its surrounding wall is symbolic of this philosophy—separation rather than linkage and extension. Central Park demonstrates positively that having many large trees in the center of the city cannot help but improve the environment no matter how in-consequentially the trees may be related to human use of the park. The incon-gruous pastoral landscape at the center of a high density city however, does not provide the best setting for today's larger population and our mode of park use. Unless we can justify the under utilization of this critical space in order to preserve an exact replica of the original design—in effect we now have a monu-ment—we need to be concerned with improving and refitting the park for the maximum enjoyment of today's users.

Contemporary use of the park differs from mid-nineteenth century use in two important ways. There are more actives uses now, such as organized team games, bicycling, foot racing and open air performances to mention a few. This greater diversity of use is further reflected in the large variety of ethnic groups who come to the park.

1-38 New York: Central Park. Overused lawn.

1-37 New York: Central Park. Looking north.

The population of New York City has risen from about 600,000 people in 1850 to the present population of over 8,000,000. With this enormous demo-graphic increase, we find certain areas of the park crowded beyond their capac-ity to withstand wear. Areas such as "The Mall" and the terraces around the Bethesda Fountain (which were crowded even in the late nineteenth century) cannot adequately serve the needs imposed today by so many additional users. (Barlow) Large areas of worn out grass, deteriorating paving and abused plant-ings testify to the lack of capacity of the existing facilities to accommodate users now or in decades to come. Yet even on days when the most popular areas of the park are overcrowded, a large portion of Central Park remains unused, except by squirrels, pigeons, and rats.

There is adequate area within this park to make badly needed visual improve-ments and accommodate two to three times the present number of users, with-out sacrificing any of the intrinsic qualities, including historic, that make Cen-

1-39 New York: Central Park. Used by birds.

tral Park delightful. By comfortably accommodating more people while adhering to sound aesthetic principles, the park would gain social vitality. Any design introducing the needed accommodations successfully must recognize three major flaws in the park layout as it relates to contemporary needs. These are in order of urgency:

Lack of accessibility. Both sight lines and pedestrian access into the park are restricted throughout most of the periphery. The relationship of the park to the city is obscured. Within and around the park, masses of unattractive shrubbery block desirable views and damage the essential visual expression of tree trunks clearly rising from the uncluttered ground form. The shrub masses collect trash and interfere with maintenance and safety. Some of these shrubs and small trees bloom and are attractive for only one week each year. During the other 51 weeks, they clutter the park.

Lack of durability. Inadequate detail design of special areas throughout the park make the more intensively used spaces susceptible to damage and decline. As a result organized activities and crowd drawing events produce excessive wear that hurts the park visually for passive users. Trees could be deployed in some areas to define and direct the use.

Lack of clarity. Trees are not used in a strong visual and organized way, with one partial exception of "the Mall." They could clarify the function and articulate spaces and walkways. There is no noble use of trees anywhere that expresses the park's geometric relation to the rest of the city. Instead trees are employed in a uniformly uninspiring, monotonous, random arrangement from one end of the park to the other.

Though simplified here for understanding, these issues are complex and their resolution would undoubtedly involve some compromise with the original Olmsted—Vaux plan. In dealing with the broader issues of trees in urban design, it is necessary that these basic design questions be posed. Each important park design issue will be examined elsewhere in more detail.

1-40
1-41
1-42
1-43
1-44

1-45

1-46

1-47

1-40 New York: Central Park. West side.

1-41 New York: Central Park. East side.

1-42 New York: Central Park. East side.

Today and yesterday

1-43   New York: Central Park. Lack of clarity.

1-44   New York: Central Park. Blocked views.

1-45   New York: Central Park. Clutter.

1-46   New York: Central Park. Use and design.

1-47   New York: Central Park. Random and monotonous.

Spatial use of trees. Trees in the city are living building materials used to establish spatial boundaries. They make the walls and ceilings of outdoor rooms, but with more subtlety than most architectural building materials. They create spatial rhythms to heighten the experience of moving through outdoor spaces. The structure and texture of trees give urban spaces a sense of scale. Deciduous trees express the change of seasons by variations of foliage and by flowering. They record time by their size and meteorological variations by their growth rate.

In addition to actually creating discrete spaces, trees are used to connect and extend the geometry, rhythms, and scale of buildings into the landscape. It is this function much more than any decorative or softening effect that is of primary importance to architecture. When trees are use primarily to "soften" or "decorate", they are being imployed to correct deficiencies that might have been averted to begin with by sensitive design. Used as extensions of architectural and city form, they greatly expand the scope and potential of urban design.

1-48

The spatial use of trees in Rome and Paris provides only two of the many good European examples. London has numerous examples such as "The Mall" and the Embankment along the Thames. Other great urban spaces in Europe, particularly in Mediterranean countries, do not have trees because of the climate and architectural richness. In St. Mark's Square, Venice, trees are not needed for comfort because of the cooling effect of the surrounding water. The rich detailing of the buildings supplies the intricacy and texture that we often seek by planting trees. In the cities of North America, except parts of the Pacific Coastal region, many of the planned large treeless spaces remain vacant because of the heat and glare in summer and the bleak coldness and glare in winter. Boston's City Hall Plaza, notorious for its lack of windbreak and pedestrian safety in winter, Fort Worth's Water Garden and the Waterfront at Penn's Landing in Philadelphia are recently built urban spaces unredeemed by either patterns of shade or architectural richness of the kinds that complement St. Mark's Square or the Piazza Navona in Rome.

1-49

1-50

On our continent, Mexico City exhibited some outstanding tree use in the Paseo de la Reforma where the avenue was transformed into a delightful forest-like promenade. Unfortunately this example may be lost as a result of air pollution from increased traffic. In the last several years these trees have begun to decline.

1-51

1-48 Chicago, Illinois: Oak Park Center Mall. (Photo by Joe Karr)

1-49 London: The Embankment. (Photo by Roger Osbaldeston)

1-50 Rome: Piazza Navona. Richness without trees.

1-51 Mexico City: Paseo de la Reforma. This once magnificent avenue may serve as another kind of example. Trees are being asphyxiated by automobile traffic. People breathe the same air. (Photo by John Cyrus)

Today and yesterday

The more recently planted boulevard running through Chapultepec Park provides another noteworthy example within the city. The Plaza and Fountain of the Trough at Las Arboledas, a suburb of Mexico City designed by Luis Barragan, is a powerful and poetic example of the way trees can create inspiring spaces. A long smooth sheet of water mirrors huge, closely spaced Eucalyptus trees.

The Chinese have begun planting trees along the major streets of the larger cities. Even though small trees are being planted, it will not be long before the trees make a very noticeable change because of their close spacing. In Singapore, the city has experienced a virtual tree revolution. Tropical growing conditions and an extensive tree planting program begun by the Ministry of National Development in 1970 have transformed most of this equatorial city into a pedestrian delight despite the narrow sidewalks and intense sunlight. "Instant trees" were installed at an impressive rate. The remarkable Angsana tree is planted with bare roots and branches removed as if it were a giant rooted cutting. The illustrations show how these trees are established even when they are over eight inches in diameter. On another street, Rain trees are growing. These were planted only five years earlier. Tropical cities show us quickly what can be accomplished in temperate climate cities over a longer time span.

1-52

1-53

1-54

1-55
1-56
1-57

1-52 Mexico City: Young trees appropriately spaced. Will these trees be saved? (Photo by Louise Schiller)

1-53 Canton, China. Tree planting was not inhibited by arbitrary rules about how far apart trees can be planted. Used this way even small trees are effective. (Photo by Amy Wilson)

1-54 Singapore. Angsana Trees for planting are delivered to the site with bare roots.

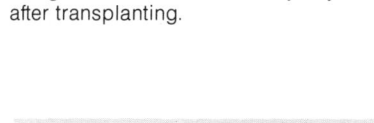

1-55 Singapore: Angsana Tree transplanted. In less than one month this "instant tree" will have leaves and resume its vigorous growth.

1-57 Singapore. Rain Trees growing along a residential street only 5 years after transplanting.

Technology beneficially exploited. Misused technology has been responsible for most of the unsuitable plant growth conditions of the city. It is unlikely that we will correct these abuses by simply adding more technology. Restoring air that is beneficial to plants and human beings is more likely to result from displacing the internal combustion engine from downtown streets, than from more sophisticated anti-pollution devices or planting pollution-tolerant tree species.

Wisely used technology offers the opportunity to grow trees where they would not otherwise survive. We can create ideal growing media to replace poor soils, improve drainage, and provide optimum watering by automatic irrigation systems. The additional energy costs required to make an urban habitat vegeta-

1-56 Singapore. Angsana Tree one year after planting, will grow to the size of a forest tree in 10 more years.

tively productive, even in a dry climate, are insignificant compared with the price that we are paying already by abandoning our cities. We spend at least 25 percent of our annual national energy budget on transportation. (Commoner) A significantly large portion of this prodigious expenditure results directly or indirectly from suburban development. Trees in the city are one positive improvement that can help to restore the desirability of urban living.

This should not be misconstrued as a plea for profligate use of precious resources at a time when some modest efforts are being made toward environmental resource conservation. It is one thing to justify the irrigation of urban tree groves in public spaces that can comfortably accomodate population densities of over 200 persons per acre, and quite another to advocate irrigated lawns in desert areas where the urban population density may be less then 25 persons per acre. The functional and aesthetic benefits of trees in support of high density living are incomparably greater than the benefits of grass, taking into account maintenance cost and human value derived from each.

The amelioration of the urban habitat made by scientific improvements include roof gardens, indoor garden technology, and improved plant feeding systems. Plant breeding offers some promise of improving city-tolerant tree species, though this may simply be another means to delay solving the basic problems causing the unsuitable habitat. The promise of technology in the service of the urban designer has been demonstrated on a limited scale by three urban projects built during the past ten years—the Oakland Museum in California, the Ford Foundation Building in New York and more recently the Winter Garden in Niagara Falls, New York. The first is an example of an extensive roof garden made possible in an arid climate by the use of special growing media and an automatic watering and feeding system. The Ford Foundation Building, and the Winter Garden show potential for growing trees inside of buildings by providing the right mechanical systems and architectural design. All three buildings are accessible to the public and provide beneficial precedents in the exploration of new ways to improve cities.

References

Kiley, Dan et al. *The Great Miami River Corridor Study,* Charlotte, Vermont: Dan Kiley and Partners—Planners and Landscape Architects, 1971.

Newton, Norman T. *Design on the Land.* Massachusetts: Harvard University Press, 1971.

Tobey, George B., Jr. *A History of Landscape Architecture.* New York: American Elsevier Publishing Co., 1973.

Barlow, Elizabeth. *Frederick Law Olmsted's New York.* New York: Praeger Publishers, Inc., 1972.

Mumford, Lewis. *The Condition of Man.* New York: Harcourt, Brace and World, Inc., 1944.

Mumford, Lewis. *The Brown Decades,* Second Ed. New York: Dover Publications, 1955.

Commoner, Barry. *The Poverty of Power, Energy and the Economic Crisis.* New York: Alfred A. Knopf, 1976.

2

A selective view

Choosing examples

Apt examples are indispensable in attempting to describe a philosophy and approach to design. Finding appropriate models to illustrate each proposition correctly is difficult. There are relatively few examples in the world of trees purposefully arranged in cities to create significant spaces. Each species will develop it own unique form when planted at a certain spacing. Even though the spacing drastically effects the character of a tree mass, very few different spacings have been tried in urban tree planting. Examples simply have not been found to illustrate some of the many possible aesthetic choices. A second difficulty lies in obtaining photographs that will communicate the complex subtleties of a multi-dimensional experience. The reader must be called upon to make an imaginary leap from a two-dimensional monochromatic picture to a three-dimensional multicolored experience that is continually changing in light, season, weather, and time of day and is actually viewed sequentially with the observer's movement. There is, however, one positive consequence to using black and white photographs. The crucial aspects of tree use in design are structure, light, shade, mass, void, and scale. Color, with its emotional appeal would distract attention from these more important characteristics of the design. Without the reinforcement of true color, the illustrations convey a more sober and direct message concerning fundamentals.

The examples of urban tree use that follow in this chapter are not intended to provide a representative selection to illustrate conventional practice in planting trees. Rather they are presented as evidence in support of the design principles that are advocated in later chapters. Several broad categories of trees have been omitted because of their limited usefulness in urban open space design. Notably absent are evergreen trees, small ornamental and flowering trees, fruit trees, and other types not usually used as shade trees or that do not grow well under most urban conditions. There are occasions when small trees or evergreen trees can be effectively used in urban design, most frequently for screening wind and views, private gardens, and in spaces with minimal circulation. However, the main thrust of this book is design with trees that fulfill the requirements of scale, seasonal change, and cultural adaptability required for central public urban spaces.

The illustrations that follow have been selected in order to demonstrate good uses of trees based on both design and site analysis techniques. The categories listed here define six criteria used in choosing the examples.

1. Location: Cities in the United States are used to illustrate growth under the more difficult stress conditions of an urban site.
2. Massing: Trees are shown in groups or lines to illustrate the effect of propinquity on tree form and the effect of massing on scale.

3.   Climate: Examples from a number of different climatic zones are given to show how the same design principles can apply equally to different geographic locations.

4.   Type: Large scale deciduous trees old enough to show their full space potential are illustrated wherever possible.

5.   Species: Given the small range of city-adaptable trees, different species are shown to illustrate the available choices in structure, density, and texture.

6.   Adaptability: Examples are limited to types of trees that have been proven city tolerant over a long period of time.

Thirty-three exemplary urban views

Pertinent statistical information is given for each example in Appendix B. Usually the species, size, location, and spacing are listed. Historical information such as tree age is more difficult to find. In some instances where it was not available, age was estimated by adapting known data about other trees in the vicinity.

Parks. Most of the following examples are of small parks where trees tend to be carefully and purposefully arranged. For reasons discussed in Chapter 1, our large city parks exhibit few examples of deliberate spatial design as opposed to a haphazard version of nature. Some of the spaces illustrated here reappear in later chapters to demonstrate different aspects of the design.

2-1

Avenues, streets, and allées. Considering the benefits that trees confer on urban streets it is surprising how scarce tree planting is along the 648,000 miles of urban roadway in the United States. The examples shown here could be replicated in every city and town in the Nation without any danger of monotony. Indeed, the one humane opportunity that most streets could offer is a canopy of branches to walk under.

2-15

Urban spaces. This category includes both public and quasi-public spaces other than parks serving pedestrians in the city. Among the many types of spaces not illustrated are parking lots, traffic islands, roadway median strips and other residual spaces that are compromised for people's enjoyment by automobile traffic. Trees can mitigate some of the undesirable conditions in these spaces, and should be planted wherever they will survive. However, our examples focus on civic spaces that are shaped for human enjoyment, where trees are more than a palliative for urban ills.

2-28

2-2   New York: Bryant Park. These Oriental Plane trees grew from a 5 inch caliper when planted in 1934 to an average size of 17 inches in diameter. They are now over 45 feet tall with a lower branch height of 25 feet in the center of the grove and branches that droop to 8 feet above the ground at the edges. The effect is a tent-like canopy.

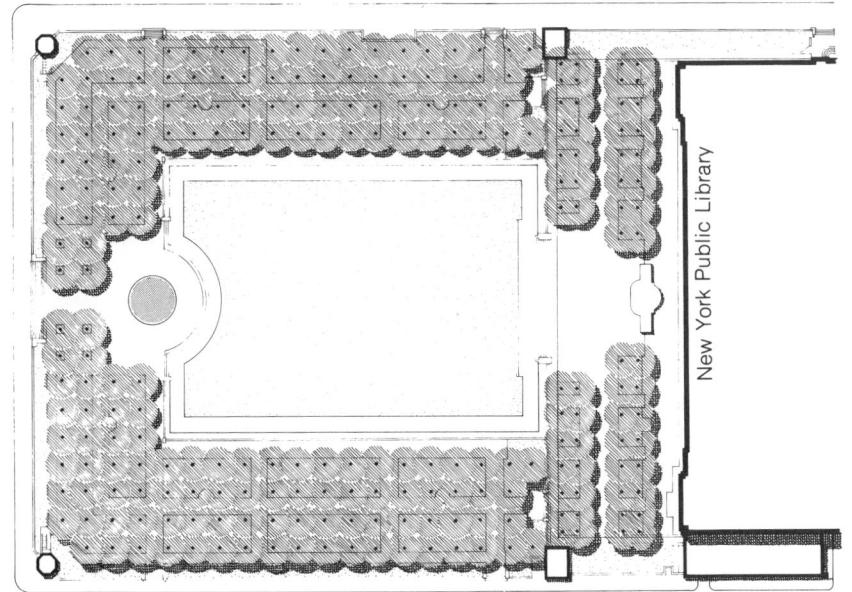

West 42nd Street

Sixth Avenue

West 40th Street

New York Public Library

2-1 Plan: Bryant Park. This 2½ acre site adjoining the Public Library in Manhattan was redesigned as a Park in 1934. The 4 rows of Plane Trees planted 20 feet apart exemplify the spatial qualities that can be achieved with a rectilinear grid planting. The composition is both suitably monumental in size for the Library Building and human scaled in detail. The trees frame a central area within the larger city space and create cathedral-like spaces within the aisles formed by the trees.

2-3 Houston, Texas: City Hall and Park. Live Oak Tree.

2-4 Houston, Texas: City Hall and Park. Live Oak Tree.

A selective view

2-5 Philadelphia, Pennsylvania: Delancey Street Playground. Thornless Honeylocust Trees planted on a 17 x 20 foot grid in 1966. Designed by the Philadelphia Department of Recreation and Collins and Dutot.

2-6 Singapore: Cannaught Drive. Rain Tree.

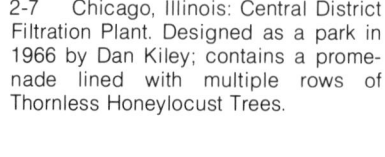

2-7 Chicago, Illinois: Central District Filtration Plant. Designed as a park in 1966 by Dan Kiley; contains a promenade lined with multiple rows of Thornless Honeylocust Trees.

2-8 Philadelphia, Pennsylvania: Independence Mall. Third block contains 700 Thornless Honeylocust Trees. Designed by Dan Kiley, 1961.

A selective view

2-9 Chicago, Illinois: Chicago River Park. Redmond Linden Trees line this water edge park. (Design and photo by Joe Karr)

2-10 Chicago, Illinois: Grant Park. American Elm.

2-11 Bristol, Pennsylvania: Grundy Park. London Plane Trees were planted here in the late 1920's and maintained by a European gardener who kept the trees trimmed in neat rows. In recent years the trees have not been pruned, but they still exhibit the picturesque quality that often occurs with manicured nature.

2-12 Bristol, Pennsylvania: Grundy Park. Clipped Plane Trees. The Park was donated to the Borough by the Joseph Grundy Woolen Mill. Trees are 40 feet tall and create a 9 foot high arcade.

A selective view

2-13 Savannah, Georgia: Park. Live Oak Tree.

2-14 Singapore: Canal Street Park. Madras Thorn Tree. One of the many tropical species that allows filtered light to penetrate the canopy.

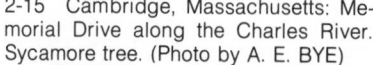

2-15 Cambridge, Massachusetts: Memorial Drive along the Charles River. Sycamore tree. (Photo by A. E. BYE)

A selective view

2-16 London: The Mall. London Plane Tree. Trees that amplify the building arcade. (Photo by Roger Osbaldeston)

2-17 Philadelphia, Pennsylvania: Benjamin Franklin Parkway. Sycamore Trees are large enough to fit the Parkway scale. Small trees on the right fail to extend and complement the avenue scale. Multiple rows of Sycamore Trees further along the Parkway illustrate what this space could be like if the large trees were repeated in additional rows. See Figure 5-53.

2-18 Palm Beach, Florida. Coconut Palms make a distinctive irregular pattern with their whimsical forms when planted in straight lines.

2-19 Palm Beach, Florida. Royal Palms produce formal spaces with their elegant symmetry as shown along Royal Palm Way.

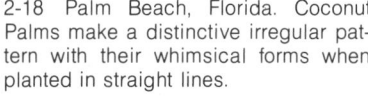

A selective view

2-20 Columbus, Indiana: Hawcreek Boulevard. Plane Trees seen from the road form a band of foliage that subdues the scale of large parking lots and lends visual coherence to the scenery. Part of a landscape design for Cummins Engine Company by Dan Kiley, this exemplifies a sense of civic responsibility uncommon in most industrial towns.

2-21 Columbus, Indiana: Hawcreek Boulevard. Plane Trees. Another view photographed ten years after the trees were planted.

2-23 Trenton, New Jersey: Lamberton Street. Sycamore Trees.

2-22 New York: West 81st Street. Plane Trees on an east/west street.

2-24 Philadelphia, Pennsylvania: De-lancey Street. Plane Trees growing on both sides of this 18 foot wide street at-test to the desirability of planting large tree types on narrow streets. Small Nor-way Maple in foreground is a later ad-dition.

2-26 Tempe, Arizona: Arizona State University. Mexican Fan Palms planted in 1916 as 6 foot tall plants, grown from seedlings, spaced 30 feet apart in rows 30 feet apart, these trees were over 90 feet tall when photographed in 1973.

2-25 Philadelphia, Pennsylvania: Pan-ama Street. Ginkgo Trees. The narrow streets of Philadelphia contradict the conventional idea that only small flo-wering tree types should be planted in confined urban spaces.

2-27 Versailles: Allée. Maple Trees.

2-28 Boston, Massachusetts: The Mar-ket Place. Thornless Honeylocust.

2-29 New York: Lincoln Center. London Plane Trees in 18 foot by 18 foot partially recessed planters that are 42 inches deep. Trees are regularly clipped to keep at a uniform size and shape. Limited space for root growth would keep these trees from growing much larger even without pruning. Landscape design by Dan Kiley.

2-30 New York: Rockefeller University. London Plane are planted throughout this Manhattan campus. The character of the spaces between buildings is greatly enhanced by trees in a pattern that should be typical for cities, not a rare exception. Landscape design by Dan Kiley.

2-31 Berkeley, California: Eucalyptus Grove.

2-32 New York: Stuyvesant Town. Plane Trees growing in a residential area with a gross density of over 100 families per acre shows the important relationship between population density and tree density.

2-33 New York: Stuyvesant Town. Plane Trees. Why are there not more areas like this in New York and in our other large cities?

Design implications

Walking in the tamed nature of a city can be as moving an experience as a trek through the forest. The intertwined relationship of urban man and his ordered wilderness depends for its effectiveness on human artistry. Yet to know what is appealing about a landscape is as elusive as light and shadow. At best we hope to discern a *leitmotif* among many generically similar landscapes. It is this theme of similarity that we seek in the hope that it will provide new insights. The 33 urban views that are illustrated above have certain important qualities in common. The photographs may only hint at some of these shared characteristics. Others may only be accessible by direct experience of the place. Observation of these examples may at least help in understanding the eight important design characteristics of tree use that are described as follows:

1. Transparency at the pedestrian's eye level permits the visual grasp of extensive areas of the city. The emphasis is on spatial continuity that extends and broadens views.

2. In each view, a discrete pattern or rhythm is discernible flowing from the arrangement, spacing and structure of trees, expressing the particular site.

3. Each landscape conveys a scale that is sympathetic to the movement and perception of pedestrians.

4. The great diversity and intricacy of individual trees is subordinated to an established repetitive composition that acts as a counterpoint in unifying the individual parts into a single whole.

5. There is a homogeneity of texture, pattern, light and shade, resulting from the use of a single species that makes the collective impact more important than the individual trees.

6. Trees are related to their surroundings sometimes by bold geometry and sometimes by subtle rhythms. In each case, there is a consistency between tree pattern and the surrounding order.

7. The ground surface, whether flat or undulating, is visually unobstructed to permit a clear expression of trees rising out of the ground. This clarity is amplified when there is a crisp, smooth ground surface.

8. Trees modulate space vertically to create a ceiling with great variability in transparency and height.

After identifying these common design characteristics of tree groups in public open spaces, it is not difficult to develop more detailed generalizations that can be applied to other sites. For example, the need to emphasize transparency and spatial continuity virtually eliminates the use of small trees in most urban contexts. The desirability of establishing a rhythmic order of tree trunks favors the organized placement of trees over random arrangement. The importance of visual clarity of tree trunks joining the ground plant suggests the elimination of most understory planting in shared open spaces of the city. Although the illustrations are divided into three categories of public or quasipublic space—parks, streets and other urban spaces—the eight broad generalizations are appropriate to all three.

3

Principles

Cities and nature

Nature in the city. The great urban spaces of the world owe their existence to artists who have consciously transformed nature. Our enjoyment of these spaces is attributed to the hand of man as much as to the existence of natural materials. Though all of our building materials were extracted from the earth, the use of living materials, trees, best recalls the interdependency of man and the natural systems and gives our cities symbolic significance. The potential of trees in shaping and humanizing cities remains an unperceived amelioration for a civilization that has nearly forgotten the relevance of art in civic design. Paradoxically, the opportunity to use trees as part of the city has been impeded by confusing the intrinsic characteristics of the forest and the city. Current urban planting design is an abstract art in the sense that it represents or symbolizes the way trees grow in nature. This is our inheritance from the nineteenth century and it is unneccessary to repeat the tastes of another age. The proper use of trees in cities should reinforce the structure of the city according to the disciplines of urban design, not plant ecology. Unity, continuity and scale have more consequence than natural history in weaving together the diverse threads of the urban fabric. The civic designer, like the artist and craftsman, expresses his understanding of nature not by copying but by creating an interpretation of our elusive relationship with the organic world.

Parks. We have come to regard parks as a collecting ground for activities rather than as a place to experience the *nature* of the city. In our arguments over what facilities belong in a city park, we have overlooked the obvious fact that none of them may belong there. Ours is a civilization of clutter reflected in the interiors of our homes, our sidewalks, and our city parks which are filled with "things." A cogent example of this clutter is the substitute for creativity that we call playground equipment. The glut of "creatively" designed new play forms that fills American parks should be testimoney enough of this phenomenon. It is hardly surprising that instead of more trees, we get more manufactured objects.

The highest expression of an ecologically sound urban park in our age would be an uncluttered space dominated by a reticulum of tall trees growing through a mantle of crushed stone. Stone, water, trees—all else would be superfluous. A city park with these elemental components could fulfill its highest mission in a setting of inspiring simplicity. Though it is unrealistic to believe that we could build such a park in an age of materialistic consumption, this idealized uncomplicated form is timeless and universal in its human appeal. The closer we can come to this basic simplicity of materials in building urban parks, the more evocative and satisfying will be the result.

Streets. The historical continuity of the gridiron street layout is evidence of its appropriateness for cities. City blocks make regular intervals that give scale. The strong pattern of building walls established by the street system cannot be visually changed in an effective way with trees, especially where the buildings are taller than the trees. Reinforcement of the gridiron pattern with straight rows of trees on both sides of the streets usually achieves greater aesthetic integrity and improves the scale and continuity of pedestrian zones.

Open spaces. Other open spaces in the city—chiefly squares, plazas, institutional grounds, public building sites, roof tops, waterfronts and parking lots—should be planted with large deciduous trees as a matter of biological necessity. Often vacant lots, traffic islands and other residual spaces present a latent opportunity to increase the span of the city forest. Strategies for planting these empty spaces could provide from 10 to 30 percent more trees in our cities. They remain unplanted because their owners or custodians are uncommitted to the enrichment of public areas. In 1934, Robert Moses demonstrated what could be done with unused land in New York City by assembling separate bits of property and turning them into 69 playgrounds and parks. The acquired land included areas such as former construction equipment storage sites, abandoned elementary schools, vacant waterfront property and land left over from street widening procedures. All of these were vacant city owned parcels. (Caro) If all else fails, these spaces can sometimes be planted surreptitiously. Every vacant space in the city without trees represents an unperceived opportunity.*

* There is a group in New York City calling itself the Green Guerrillas!

Cultural constraints

Romantic naturalism. Cultural historians and literary critics have often found it enlightening to view their chosen subjects through the kaleidoscope of attitudes resulting from idealized visions of pastoral life and opaque views of urban experience. The *romantic naturalism* that has influenced urban design in America since the early nineteenth century, reinforced by Olmsted's design philosophy, still presents an obstacle to clear understanding of the nature of the city.* Urban open space in this country and particularly its plantings are still treated in the spirit of romantic naturalism. On the other hand, new urban building is based on the ideal of "technological progress." This dichotomy continues to pose problems for the urban designer and, indeed, is indicative of the conflicts now raging in the post-modernism movement in architecture and urban design.

* Leo Marx's *The Machine in the Garden* describes and evaluates the "pastoral ideal" of American life. His interpretation of the American experience helps in understanding the profound influence of romanticism on our attitudes toward cities. (Marx)

Functional and aesthetic. There is a tendency to give the current aesthetic conceptions about urban trees a rational justification on functional rather than aesthetic grounds. A number of recent publications emphasize the functional values of plants in the city. (Smith, DeChira, Robinette, Hartmann) Yet there is also research which questions these values. (Woodwell) The most vociferous support for continuation of the romantic design tradition in urban parks is based on the notion that species diversity will help stabilize natural plant populations in cities.

Studies have been made to evaluate the functional worth of trees in dollars. (Bernatsky, Pinkard, International Shade Tree Conference) The effort to establish a tree's value on a functional basis shows the difficulty of developing completely objective universal criteria for worth. The most widely accepted method of appraising the worth of trees on residential land in monetary value is based on how trees affect the assessed cost of the land. (Payne) This method does not incorporate an estimate of timber value and therefore suggests that aesthetic value is of greatest significance in our perception of the importance of trees. Despite the substantial functional capabilities of trees in the urban landscape their aesthetic impact is even more dramatic, and provides a compelling justification for extensive tree planting.

40

Plants as a palliative. The main function of planting, particularly trees, is not to hide architectural flaws, yet consistent reference is made to the use of trees to "soften" or "screen" buildings. Curiously, many architects suggest this type of planting treatment for their own buildings. This attitude may arise from the perception of brutalism and lack of rich detail that characterizes much modern architecture. Nonetheless, the pervasiveness of this idea among designers is revealing. Good architecture should not be softened or hidden with plants, but should be reinforced and sometimes embellished. It is not the nature of our cities or urban buildings to be soft. Planting trees to screen views in cities should be limited to masking the less avoidable visual disorder such as automobile parking. Buildings should stand clearly visible as a tribute or admonition to those responsible for their appearance. If flaws are hidden, they are not as likely to be corrected. Trees have a more important positive spatial function, and are used only as a last resort to mask.

Over planting. A curious fear of planting "too many" trees is often expressed by municipal authorities and private clients of landscape architects. It is as likely to come from the municipal forester or arborist as it is from someone totally unfamiliar with plants. While there is still considerable sympathy for the idea that trees are healthier the farther apart they are grown, the reasons given for objecting to closer, more dense planting of trees are usually covertly aesthetic rather than scientific. When confronted by the question, "What do you mean by *too close together?*" the reply usually begins with a technical reason and ends with an observation about the untoward visual effect of close tree spacing. An Arborist of one Eastern United States city, in objecting to the proposed close (20 feet apart) spacing of Red Maple trees near a new courthouse building, based his disagreement on the cost of the additional maintenance that would result from having so *many* trees.

Language

There are three important examples in our language of how landscape architecture and urban open space design, in particular, are hampered by deficiencies in terminology. Several words have had a complex influence on the use of trees in urban design. The word "nature" with all of its subtle nuances and meanings perhaps poses the most difficulty. This problem is compounded by different concepts about man and nature in which man may or may not be considered part of nature. Clear communication requires us to refine our mode of expression and become more precise when we describe man's complex relationship to the landscape. Use of the word "nature" herein means the undisturbed out-of-doors, such as "natural scenery." It is a convenient word for separating the man-influenced landscape (agrarian and urban) from the wild (uncultivated) landscape, even though we recognize human beings and their works as part of the natural environment.

The conventional sense of the word "formal" in referring to a garden or landscape implies a style that is very exact, methodical, orderly, and usually stiff, arranged symmetrically on one or more axes. Landscapes less thoroughly organized, including naturalistic arrangements, are referred to as "informal." The vast majority of urban landscape designs cannot be accurately characterized by either the word formal or informal. They are often eclectic, employing several, more or less organized, styles. Even the romantic English landscape, often referred to as informal, is a highly stylized mode of design incorporating occult balance, exaggerated perspective, and other devices employed by painters to create illusions in depicting three dimensional spaces. Highly organized urban spaces can employ asymmetrical geometry and have apparent random qualities.

As a result of these ambiguities, the words "formal" and "informal" are best avoided in descriptions of open space design.

Another instance of terminology that misleads is the use of the terms "landscaping" and "beautifying." The latter term, which means masking something that is plain or unattractive to make it more attractive, is not characteristic of good urban design. The implication is one of superficial beauty. It was popularized in the 1960's by Lady Bird Johnson, who advised people to go out and plant a tree or shrub in their community. Consequently the word is now written into many of the Federal documents that deal with visual enhancement of cities. The word "landscaping" has taken on a similar cosmetic meaning through the excessive commercialization of the term. The planting of trees should be an intrinsic part of the city's structure, not a mask for inept design.

The need for order

To say that today, most American cities are visually disordered seems to be a truism, yet designers often recommend proposals that further impair the aesthetic coherence of a city. Mechanical order has become associated with industrialism and the dehumanizing effects of industrial production in a capitalist society. We see the response to this everywhere from the superficial diversity of suburban tract houses to the urban planning schemes that introduce variety as an antidote to regimentation. "Variety" and "diversity" have become the catch words for good design. The designer, who is powerless to control technology, attempts to camouflage its visual structure by introducing randomness into the functional order of the city. This is illustrated in the critical reaction to the grid-iron street layout. The construction of streets in a right angle grid pattern has been blamed for almost every shortcoming of the modern city. A common visual expression of this reaction is seen in recent designs for "pedestrian malls" that use trees in deliberately disruptive patterns to counter the basic linear street alignment. The most publicized of these designs is the Nicolette Mall in Minneapolis, where the pavement and trees are wiggled within the straight right-of-way. Since the sinuously disposed elements are visually less emphatic than the strong building lines, the visual effect is to weaken rather than reinforce the sense of space. The spatial quality of the city is sacrificed for the sake of arbitrary diversity in design.

This spurious design approach runs counter to the nature of the city. The error is obscured by a belief that irregularity is a hallmark of nature. Therefore, the new pattern is thought to be more in harmony with "nature." "Art" is limited to the creation of sculptural objects placed in a space. Yet instead of an artistic achievement, the actual design of the open space is a pathetic copy of what nature is mistakenly thought to be.

The largest and most important principle of urban design is spatial order.* Just as building architecture is concerned with forming and ordering spaces, so the urban designer modulates spaces, but in a larger context. Even though the major definition of outdoor space is achieved in most urban places by buildings, the most important function of trees is to define, reinforce or create spaces. The definition of horizontal space by walls, and vertical space by canopies underlies all of the examples and discussions of tree use in this and subsequent chapters. The use of trees as sculpture or decoration is incidental to fundamental spatial arrangement in urban design.

To purposefully produce diversity as an end product of design is to create visual disorder. Diversity that occurs as a result of functional aesthetic purpose is more likely to be visually satisfying. The important contribution of Robert Venturi in writing about complexity and contradiction in architecture has been misconstrued as a plea for arbitrary diversity even though its aims were profoundly

* Bruno Zevi's thesis that space in and around a building should be the basis for judgment of the building is even more applicable to urban design and open space. As in architecture, all other aesthetic criteria must be subordinate to the spatial idea in assessing the urban landscape. (Zevi)

42

different. (Venturi) The city, like the forest, can accommodate great variety and complexity when it is an expression of complex organization. Modern cities lack the unity of consistent materials and homogeneity of scale that characterize cities built prior to this century. The complexity of the architecture or other eras was given coherence by materials, handcrafted details and reflection of human use to a degree that is almost totally absent from today's metropolis. One function of trees in the urban landscape is to restore that rich textural detail missing from modern architecture.

Physical design principles

Coherence. Spatial definition using trees becomes more coherent with repetition and continuity. This important urban design principle, coherence, has been degraded by the greater emphasis given to diversity in recent times. The confusing visual disorganization of most cities in the United States desperately needs to be reorganized by physically linking the disparate parts, including the fragmented open space. Bands of large deciduous shade trees can achieve this coherence by establishing an ordered continuity of trunk spacing and branch texture. Trees are the most prominent design element capable of linking together an entire city.

Organization. In considering the landscape, we can recognize three more or less discrete levels of natural order. Large areas of land relatively undisturbed by human intervention are referred to as wild or *uncultivated nature*. In this kind of landscape, trees interact with the organic surroundings according to certain ecological principles that tend toward stability and continuity.

Where human activities have interrupted natural order, we have established a compromise with nature, as in our New England farms. There human toil and energy have replaced the energy of the natural systems to maintain order that is more or less in harmony with the biosphere. The satisfying visual order of farm land is a result of learning over time how to cooperate with the landscape and adapt our rational intellectual process to the natural order. Rural land is aesthetically pleasing because human artistry had molded and played upon a canvas of natural forms with economy. The contrast of natural and man-made forms is pleasingly expressed by the juxtaposition of pastures, fences, farm buildings, hedgerows and the native topography of forests. In this pastoral or *agrarian nature,* trees are less numerous and are often found growing in open fields where they develop an open grown form.

In the village or city, human intervention is carried quite far and the accommodation with natural order is more likely to occur at the boundaries than in a meshed centralized pattern. When urban development spreads too far—the suburban ring—the accommodation of urban with natural conditions is further compromised, and the visually satisfying contrast between *agrarian nature* and *civilized nature* is lost. In urban space and parks, trees grow under artificially controlled conditions and are not subject to principles of forest ecology. Attempts to recreate an *agrarian* or *uncultivated* natural order within the city are biologically unsound. The growing conditions of the city do not permit the multilayered species diversity that is characteristic of uncultivated natural woodlands.

A haphazard arrangement of trees in an effort to duplicate nature fails because it lacks the complex organization of woodland organisms that gives the forest an inimitable beauty. Each natural plant community is organized by species, composition, horizontal spacing, vertical layering, and the adaptive geometry of the individual plants. Far from being a random planting of different tree types, the forest is a profoundly ordered system of plants.

Geometric pattern. The arrangement of trees in definite purposeful patterns enlivens spaces. Our habit of considering geometric composition as static comes from the limitations of two dimensional representation in drawings. Moving through a space, what appears in plan as static row or grid, becomes a rhythm sprung from tree trunks and provides a visual syncopation that improves human comprehension of the space, just as metrical form in poetry guides measurement and understanding. The effect is also like the shifting scene of a kaleidoscope with each twist compounding a fixed number of elements.

Tree patterns that reflect or amplify the building geometry can improve the connection between indoor and outdoor space. This is an important reason for designing building and landscape together as a single composition inspired by one unified conceptual grasp of the problem. The arrangement of trees at calculated intervals, that can be varied, gives the open space designer a greater freedom than the building architect when it comes to using space forming elements artistically. The opportunities that are latent in the two perfect forms—the circle and the square—for creating spatial patterns with trees are infinite and fascinating.

Abstract design principles

Transitions. An important, though less obvious, responsibility of the open space designer is the creation of transitions between spaces and between buildings and spaces. Trees link and divide human scale spaces and monumental buildings and spaces in a way that allows simultaneous comprehension of both scales. Trees function well as materials for transitional connections because of their transparency, texture, contrast, and size. This linking capacity can be used to form arcades that connect buildings, to separate areas with different scales or geometric configurations, and to create entrance canopies for buildings.

Scale. An aesthetic function of trees is the resolution of conflicting scale demands of the city. Scale implies a relationship, in this instance between the dimensions of the trees and urban spaces as perceived by human beings. Trees establish a lower space that is comfortably sized for human use and still permits people to experience the larger space. Tree branches create a partially transparent tent or canopy that allows awareness of the space beyond, but confers a psychological sense of containment and protection. The intricacy of the branches and foliage provides a foil for the monumentality of the larger space and buildings that appeals to our visual perceptions. Thus, the addition of an arcade of trees in a large space can create a zone that is visually comfortable for the pedestrian without compromising the scale of the larger space. Trees can do this more easily than inert materials because of their unique properties. Their size, irregularity, subtle translucency and psychological impact make them appropriate where no other structure would seem suitable. This is clear to any architect who has struggled with the intractable problem of trying to design a visually suitable pedestrian canopy for a large space in front of a monumental building. There is often no satisfactory way to make the scale transition with architectural building materials. Any structural addition looks tacked on. A grove or arcade of large trees may resolve the problem where there is adequate horizontal space.

Light and shadow. Lights gives life to a space. Manipulation of light and shade gives the urban designer power to transform spaces of stone, bitumen and concrete into tapestries of sunlight and shadow. No medium for accomplishing this modulation of light is more appropriate than the structure of a tree in its seasonally adapted forms. Intricate shadow patterns on pavement and building walls create architectural richness from even the crudest materials.

In most urban spaces, direct sunlight is limited to certain hours of the day. Therefore trees must be arranged in relation to building shadows to give shade and admit light in critical areas at appropriate times. Deciduous trees are indispensable in warm, temperate climates, because they adjust to seasonal light demands and temperatures. Most urban spaces requiring summer shade are equally in need of winter sunlight for warmth and brightness. Evergreen trees, except in the warmest United States climates make spaces cold and dreary in winter. The use of evergreen trees in the city, because of their dense, unchanging foliage in temperate climates, should be limited to wide open areas where their winter shade will not be oppressive. By contrast, seasonal change in deciduous trees provides a continual and infinite variety of colors and textures during the entire year. The least appreciated of seasonal effects, the loss of leaves, provides nature's most welcome bounty—winter sunlight.

References

Caro, Robert. *The Power Broker*. New York: Alfred A. Knopf, 1974.

Marx, Leo. *The Machine in the Garden*. New York: Oxford University Press, 1964.

Smith, William, and Dochinger, Leon. "Capability of Metropolitan Trees to Reduce Atmospheric Contaminants," *Better Trees for Metropolitan Landscapes*, Symposium Proceedings, USDA Forest Service General Technical Report NE-22. Washington, D.C.: U.S. Government Printing Office, 1976. (pp. 49–57).

DeChiara, Joseph, and Koppelman, Lee. *Urban Planning and Design Criteria*, Second Ed. New York: Van Nostrand Reinhold, 1975.

Robinette, Gary O. *Plants, People and Environmental Quality*. Colorado: U.S. National Park Service, 1972.

Hartmann, Frederick, ed. The Metro Forest. *A Natural History Special Supplement,* Nov. 1973.

Woodwell, George. The Carbon Dioxide Question. *Scientific American* 238: 34–43 (1978).

Bernatsky, Aloys. The Performance and Value of Trees. *Anthros* Year 8 No. 1 (1969).

Pinkard, Haques. Trees-Regulators of the Environment. *Soil Conservation* 56 (1970).

International Shade Tree Conference. *Shade Tree Evaluation*. Illinois: International Shade Tree Conference, Inc., 1970.

Payne, Brian, and Strom, Steven. The Contribution of Trees to the Appraised Value of Unimproved Residential Land. *Valuation* 22(2): 36–45 (1975).

Zevi, Bruno. *Architecture as Space*. Translated by Gendel, Milton, Barry, Joseph, ed. New York: Horizon Press, 1957.

Venturi, Robert. *Complexity and Contradiction in Architecture*. New York: Museum of Modern Art, 1966.

Closely observed geometry

Characteristics of tree growth

Purpose and method. The practice of using trees to make urban spaces is, in its most advanced form, inspiring. Urban trees are powerful symbols. Like words, they can be organized to create confusion or poetry. The processes that organize trees into forests—adaptation, genetic selection, symbiosis, and succession—are disrupted by the city. Human intervention, the same agent that dismantled the forest to build the city, can create civilized order and noble meaning by appropriately arranging natural materials. The artist who composes with trees must have the detachment of a surgeon to avoid the sentimental response that has trivialized urban design. It requires looking beyond the individual tree.

The best location, arrangement and spacing for trees must be determined individually to meet the demands of different sites. Every species of tree is unique in its growth habit and adaptability to different spatial conditions. The knowledge of how trees respond to different conditions of the city should be unfettering rather than restrictive. We should establish some iconoclastic rules for tree planting, considering first how the trees are arranged and later, by examples, how the aggregation of trees are used to form spaces in the city. The first illustrations will deal with the small interstitial urban spaces, then we will return to Central Park to test the hypotheses.

Tree form. Most organisms grow in communities or colonies. No animal or plant lives alone or is self-sustaining. (Dobzhansky) For example, species as diverse as bacteria, meadowgrass, deer, seaweed, people and bees all exist as a group or agglomeration and cannot survive for long as solitary creatures. In studying about living things, we usually find that their interrelationships are as important for us to understand as their individual characteristics. It is the evolutionary nature of a tree to be part of a forest or plant community. Trees do not grow as lone individuals under natural conditions. This principle of cooperation referred to by biologists as mutualism appears to have governed organisms from their beginning.

Despite the universal gregarious nature of trees, they are almost always discussed and depicted as solitary specimens. Children's books, technical publications and literature on gardening only illustrate and discuss the atypical form of a tree—the symmetrical, low-branched, open grown form. All of our knowledge about trees is colored by this cultural archetype. We celebrate the singular specimen.

Observe trees growing on a natural woodland site. The tall erect trunks of closely spaced forest trees and branch configurations shaped to admit light are two of the more obvious adaptive responses of trees to forest conditions. Each layer of the forest contains examples of this kind of adaptive geometry. The result is that trees can grow very well in dense forest conditions, and in fact are uniquely suited to what we regard as close spacing. For example, it is not unusual to find northeastern forests growing at densities of 400 trees per acre. This is equivalent to trees ten feet apart in both directions. Much higher and lower densities also occur naturally. It is significant that trees can adapt to such a wide range of conditions. A group of Maple trees growing five feet apart is just as healthy, or at least better able to survive, than a single tree growing in an open meadow. The slower growth rate of trees growing closer together is part of their adaptive response and does not indicate that they are less healthy than faster growing trees.

Popularized by its symmetrical shape, the individual tree has adopted a form that is not of evolutionary derivation. The tree in this situation needs the lower, more spreading branching as a protective measure for survival in the hostile open environment. Its faster growth rate actually produces less sturdy wood.

To retain their vitality when growing close together, trees adjust their form and growth rate. In this way, they are able to share the more limited amount of sunlight and root growth space. Trees of the same species do not kill each other off in a fight for survival. This more dramatic image has greater popular appeal but limited accuracy. In the natural process of forest succession, a certain species will dominate all other trees for a given soil type and climate. This is a long term process that occurs because less tolerant trees tend to grow on a site first and would not occur if the climax species were planted first. It is true that in natural repropagation of a cleared area, a superabundance of seedlings is often produced, later thinned by competitive survival of the stronger individuals. This process is limited for the most part to the seedling and early stages of forest succession and is a minor factor in later development of the forest when the adaptive process assumes a more important role than competition.

It is important to understand this fundamental growth characteristic of trees if they are to be used effectively in design. The open grown form of a tree may be suitable for decorative use where a tree is used as a piece of sculpture. Spatial design requires trees that are similar to forest grown forms. Appropriate spatial manipulation occurs when trees are planted close enough together to make a continuous higher canopy of foliage. It is a fortunate concurrence of growth habitat and design requirements.

Through observation of trees growing in natural habitats, a designer can conclude that there is no biological basis for keeping trees far apart, since they grow at every possible spacing. Tree spacing in urban design is largely an aesthetic question except where functional requirements dictate the ground plan. As such, spacing will vary in relation to specific design requirements in each individual circumstance.

Urban trees. It is often argued that city trees have an unaccommodating habitat, therefore they should be more widely spaced than forest trees to compensate for the restricted growing conditions. This is based on the widely held, but unsubstantiated assumption that trees are healthier when grown in an open (rather than forest) situation. Trees adapt to the space limitations of cities much as they do in forests by fitting their branch and root structures into the available space. This does not make them unhealthy, though it can slow their growth rate as they get larger. The adaptability of deciduous tree root systems is as remarkable as that of their crowns. The results of studies on forest tree roots, done in the towns of Cornwall and Highlands, New York, shows the ratio of the crown spread area to the root spread area varied by as much as five times for the same species on different sites. (Stout) The same study indicated that variations in local conditions, such as soil texture, resulted in impressive differences in root development. It was also learned that some species of trees are more adaptable than others in this respect. It is well known among nursery owners that trees grown in sandy soil develop much more extensive root systems than similar trees grown in clay soil. The general conclusion from investigation and observation is that most city adapted trees are capable of adjusting to vastly different physical conditions for both root and crown development. It explains why trees so often flourish in the most crowded and inhospitable urban spaces.

On the other hand, the urban conditions that pose the greatest stress on trees were not encountered in their phylogenic development, they were brought about by the technology of modern cities. The most damaging among these deleterious influences are toxins from automobile exhaust, concentrated animal excreta, and salts used to melt snow. Each of these has undersirable effects on human beings as well.

Relationships to buildings and streets

Defining and reinforcing space. Most major spaces in cities and villages are defined by buildings. Trees in their best use reinforce, articulate, add scale, and subdivide these spaces. Where very large open areas exist, trees could well become the principal space defining materials. This refers, of course, to a large scale deciduous type of tree that reaches 50 to 70 feet at maturity in the city. The addition of a colonnade of trees within a building quadrangle is a simple idea with easily apparent beneficial impact.

Bryant Park in Manhattan is a good example of trees used to define an outdoor room in a way that complements the architectural mass of the New York Public Library. This space within a space illustrates urban tree planting at its best, despite the inhibiting presence of low walls and hedges that make the space unsafe and under utilized. The two and one-half acre central Manhattan site was at one time used for a reservoir and was first made into a park in 1871. The park was redesigned in a 1934 competition, and the winner was employed by Gilmore Clark to complete the design. The 200 Oriental Plane Trees from the New York Parks Department nursery in Long Island were about 25 feet tall and five to six inches in caliper when they were moved in early 1934. They are now over 50 feet tall and vary from 14 to 18 inches in diameter. The trees are spaced 22 feet apart center to center in both directions. The branch height in the center of the grove is 25 to 30 feet above the ground, though branches at the edges of the grove hang down to within eight feet of the ground.

4-1   Trees forming a colonnade.

4-2   Bryant Park. A space within a larger space defined by buildings.

4-3

4-4

Distance from buildings. Unlike smaller types of plants, trees can be planted as close to buildings as desired without damaging the visual relationship between building and ground. If planted against a building wall, a tree can be grown as an espalier if pruned, or simply develop asymmetrically in response to

4-3   Trees 8 feet from building illustrating crown adaptation.

4-4   Trees close to building showing effects of phototropism. The tendency to grow toward the light gives the trees a picturesque slant, like trees along a canal.

phototropism (attraction to light). Usually the building fenestration restricts this use of trees, requiring that the tree be a minimum of eight to ten feet from the building wall to allow sufficient interior light without regular pruning. The space near the ground is not encroached upon by trees. The designer is free to locate trees in relation to buildings within the constraints of aesthetic and operational requirements. The use of trees on narrow sidewalks can make a pleasant division of the street space.

The diagram governing the planting of trees on the south side of the street to maintain a minimum distance from the building, Figure 4-9, relates to the cultural requirement for midday sunlight and should not be construed as simply a need to keep trees away from buildings.

4-9

Relation to sidewalks. An urban sidewalk without trees is like a building without a roof. Even if the trees had no functional value, such as providing shade, they would be indispensible to give a sense of scale. The street side near the curb is the best location for trees along sidewalks. This is one of the few purely aesthetic judgments that should become a rule in most urban situations.

4-5   Trees in relation to street. Trees planted close to the curb produce valuable spatial enclosure.

It is commonly recommended that where buildings are set back far enough from the street, shade trees should be planted only on the side of the walk away from the street. This does serious harm to the street aesthetics whether or not there are above ground utility lines. Every city and town with overhead wires has streets where utility poles coexist with large shade trees. Except where the trees have been incorrectly pruned, the location of large shade trees close to the curb results in greater visual unity and enclosure for the pedestrian. The purpose of planting trees close to the curb where there are overhead wires is not to mask or screen these functional components of the urban environment. Utility poles with wires can add depth and interest to a street where there are no trees. In some instances they are an aesthetic gain. However, where there is a choice, the trees are far more beneficial in humanizing a street and can be used close to the curb along streets even where there are overhead wires. Where trees are set back in deference to the utility lines, the comfortable sense of street enclosure is weakened or lost.

4-6 Trees and utility lines. No conflict here.

4-7 Utility poles, an alternative view, used as a framing device.

There are four criteria that should be applied when locating city street trees. They are as follows in order of importance:
1. Direct sunlight for tree growth.
2. Aesthetic improvement to the urban environment.
3. Circulation.
4. Obstructions below and above grade.
The implications of these will follow.

Direct Sunlight. Trees growing anywhere should have a minimum of three to four hours of direct sunlight each day of the growing season to remain healthy. Tree leaves are capable of utilizing up to 25 percent of the direct sunlight that falls on them. A tree can be kept alive by harnessing as little as three percent of the direct sunlight that is normally available to it. From these generalized facts, we can analyze urban street conditions in relation to building heights and hours of summer sunlight and arrive at some guidelines for locating trees and designing cities. The street orientation plays an important part in determining where trees should be planted in relation to building height. Because of local variations in building type and difference in latitude, this needs to be examined for each particular city. Figure 4-10 shows the ramifications of available sunlight on streets with four story buildings for planting street trees at the latitude of Philadelphia, Indianapolis, Denver, and Salt Lake City. Zoning regulations, now considered outmoded, that allowed tall buildings to be stepped back could be advantageous to trees. If every city street could be lined with trees, the aesthetic ramifications of the discredited New York City zoning setback principle would deserve reevaluation.*

Aesthetics. Where street trees are planted closely enough together to form a continuous, arched canopy, visual unity is achieved, spatially reinforced by the resulting uninterrupted quality of light and shade. If the trees are spaced too far apart, each tree develops a more dense lower-branched crown. The effect of this wider spacing is to produce an interrupted pattern of contrasting light and shade that emphasizes each individual tree. In most urban situations, it is difficult to achieve a uniform spacing of tree trunks. The discontinuities in spacing

4-8
4-9
4-10

* Prior to the 1961 New York City Zoning Resolution, the bulk allowances for new buildings were controlled by setbacks related to height that resulted in the "ziggurat" building shapes characteristic of older office buildings in Manhattan.

Closely observed geometry

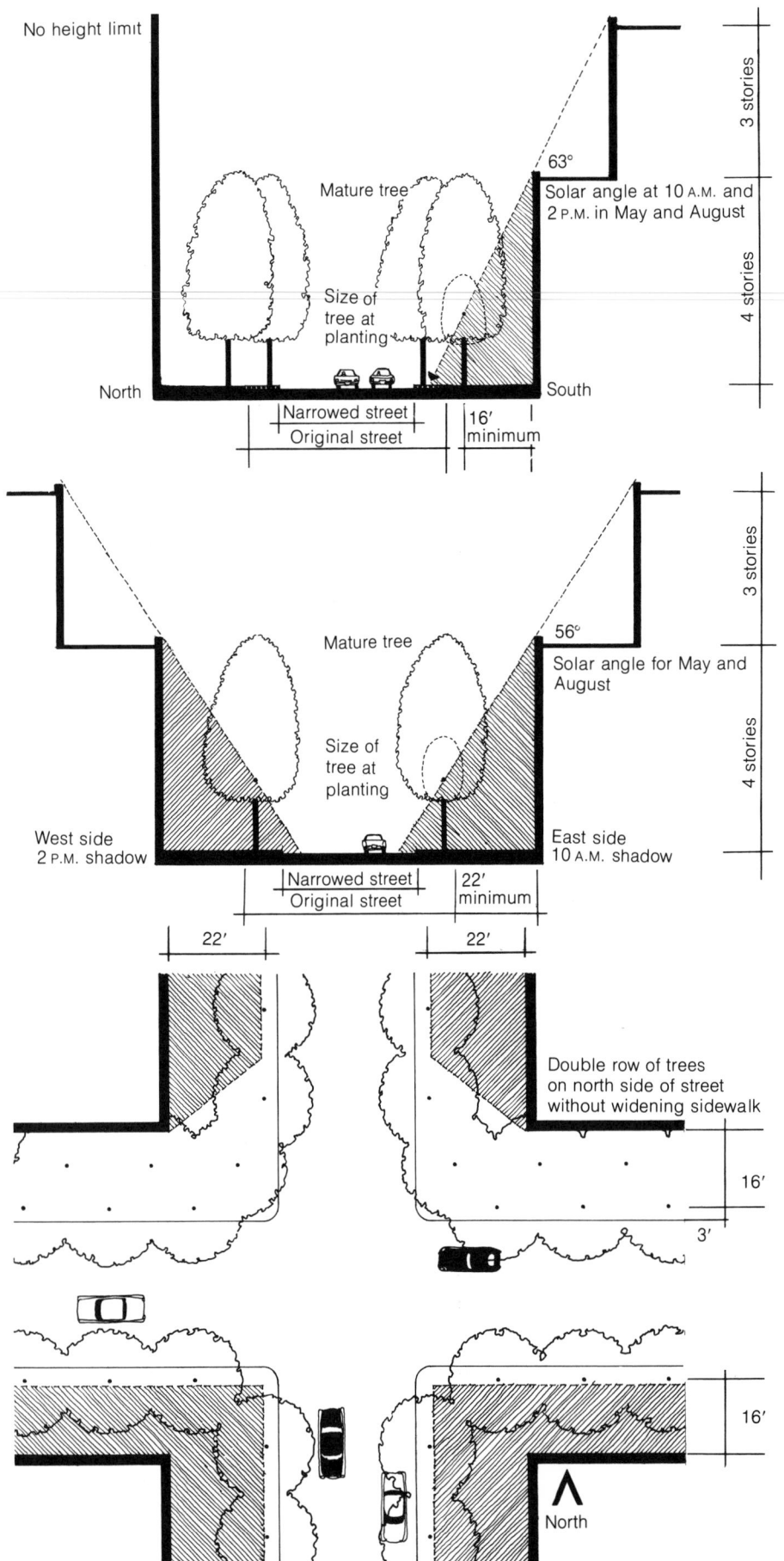

No height limit

Mature tree

63°

Solar angle at 10 A.M. and 2 P.M. in May and August

Size of tree at planting

3 stories

4 stories

North

South

Narrowed street

Original street

16' minimum

4-8 Cross section: East/west street. Tree loctions related to building height allowing 4 hours of midday sunlight during growing season for trees on south side of street at 40 N. latitude. (Philadelphia · Minneapolis · Denver)

Mature tree

56°

Solar angle for May and August

Size of tree at planting

3 stories

4 stories

West side 2 P.M. shadow

East side 10 A.M. shadow

Narrowed street

Original street

22' minimum

4-9 Cross section: North/south street. Tree locations related to building height allowing 4 hours of midday sunlight during growing season for trees on east and west sides of street at 40 N. latitude. (Philadelphia · Minneapolis · Denver)

22'

22'

Double row of trees on north side of street without widening sidewalk

16'

3'

16'

North

4-10 Plan: Tree planting zones. Areas related to 4-story buildings where trees receive less than 4 hours of midday sunlight are shown shaded for cities at 40 N. latitude.

receive greater emphasis as the tree spacing is increased. Used collectively, trees produce a more open, translucent canopy that greatly improves visual continuity.

The most obvious benefit of planting trees close to the curb is their effect on the overall street scale. By extending the branch canopy over the street the immensity of the right-of-way is reduced. Where streets are over 40 feet wide additional rows of trees are needed to satisfy the urban scale requirement before the trees are near full size. The principle of planting trees close to the curb is applicable to all types of streets. When the trees reach maturity, the effect is more spectacular.

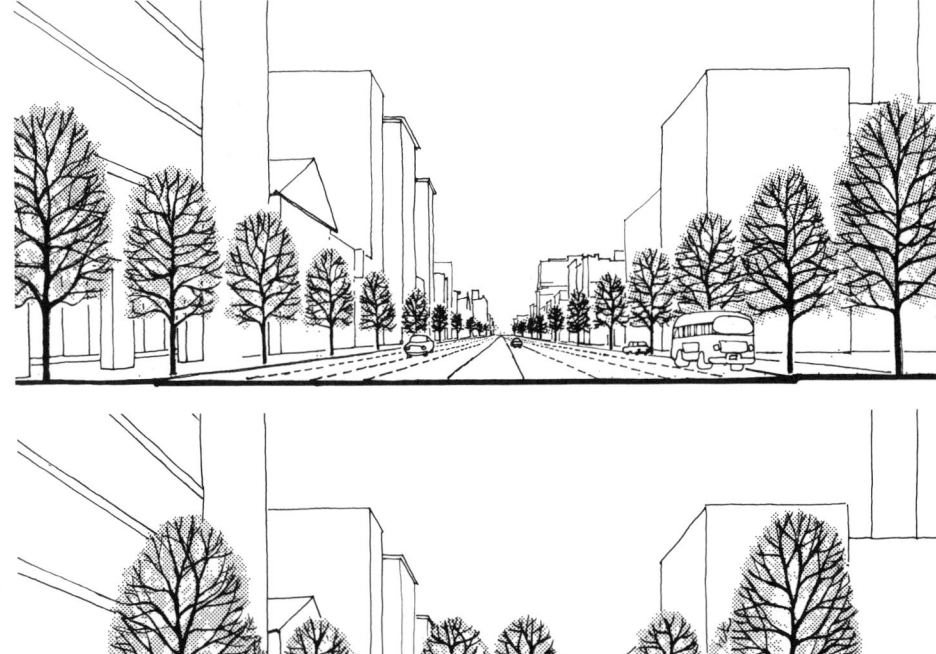

4-11 Single row of trees planted on each side of 8 lane (90 feet wide) street showing the scale weakness. Trees are of peripheral interest.

4-12 Two additional rows of trees planted within 8 lane (90 feet wide) street showing how the trees become an appropriately dominant element in the space.

4-13 Parkway with 12 traffic lanes planted with six rows of trees.

A further benefit of street trees located near the curb is the separation they afford both visually and psychologically between vehicles and pedestrians. The value of summer shade without loss of winter sunlight is usually taken for granted. Again, trees near the curb are more effective for the entire right-of-way in shading the street and sidewalk and reducing the glare of the intense summer sun.

53

Closely observed geometry

The architecture of the city creates an interlocking pattern of rhythms experienced by the pedestrian as he moves along the street. By locating trees so that they extend, reflect, or magnify these patterns, the street gains in coherence. By recognizing column spacings and duplicating their rhythms with trees, a living arcade is formed that extends the internal spaces beyond the building walls. Where the tree patterns were planned as part of the building design, this pleasing sense of spatial unity is amplified. Occasionally we come upon a street such as the one in Cleveland, where the trees echo a building colonnade to create a sense of continuity along the street.

4-15

4-14   Trees planted as an extension of a building arcade.

4-15   Building colonnade and trees seen in perspective.

4-16   The same trees echoing building colonnade of previous block.

Circulation. By planting close to the street curb in a continuous row at proper intervals, trees form a space frame of branches that establish a pedestrian scale between street and buildings. This is perceived as an extension of the building space—a kind of outdoor gallery. In perspective the trunks make a vertical screen along the street that reinforces the sidewalk space. If the trees were planted in a single row on the opposite side of the walk, they would visually give more space to the motorist creating a less hospitable place to walk.

Traffic sight distance at intersections will not be impeded by tree trunks arranged to allow the driver of a vehicle a 75 foot view in both directions. At driveway exits, trees along the street should be located far enough from the driveway to allow a driver to see at least 50 feet in both directions before entering the street.

Obstructions. Below grade utilities or structures may eliminate choice tree locations if street trees are not part of the planning criteria. Where utility lines are less than four feet deep, it is usually desirable to keep trees away from the space directly over the lines for future accessibility. Tree roots do not damage properly installed utility lines that are more than three feet below the surface. Where utilities are in vaults, there should be a provision for a four foot soil depth and at least 100 square feet of soil area per tree. Dwarf trees, including shade trees in pots, are not the answer to above or below ground utilities because they do not fit the scale requirements for public urban spaces. Nor are small trees appropriate for narrow streets. Small trees interrupt and fragment the street space, while large trees cover and contain the space. Large deciduous trees adapt to a narrow space by producing a higher-branched, less dense crown that reinforces rather than interrupts the space.

Overhead lighting, particularly in streets and parking areas must be coordinated with tree planting to achieve a beneficial integration of the two. The basic

4-17   The trees seen as a colonnade.

4-18 Definition of the pedestrian's space by trees planted 30 inches from the curb in a 6 foot wide planting strip.

principles concern locating the light standards in relation to the trees so that they reinforce rather than distort the visual rhythm and pattern. In selecting a pole height, take advantage of the tree branch structure to shield the lighting element without interfering with the ground lighting pattern. The best results in making these design judgments cannot be attained by installing one and then repositioning the other. As a functional concern, the tree shade is probably of greater importance than the night light pattern because of the longer daylight use hours. However, planning the tree spacing in relation to the light spacing is likely to produce the best solution. This method may also bring to mind an alternate tree form or light fixture distribution pattern and may produce a better design. From both aesthetic and functional viewpoints, lighting of paved tree areas is best accomplished from fixtures that shine down from pole mounts or from a building. Low fixtures, mounted a few feet away from the ground, are less efficient and more obtrusive visually. Lighting the undersides of tree

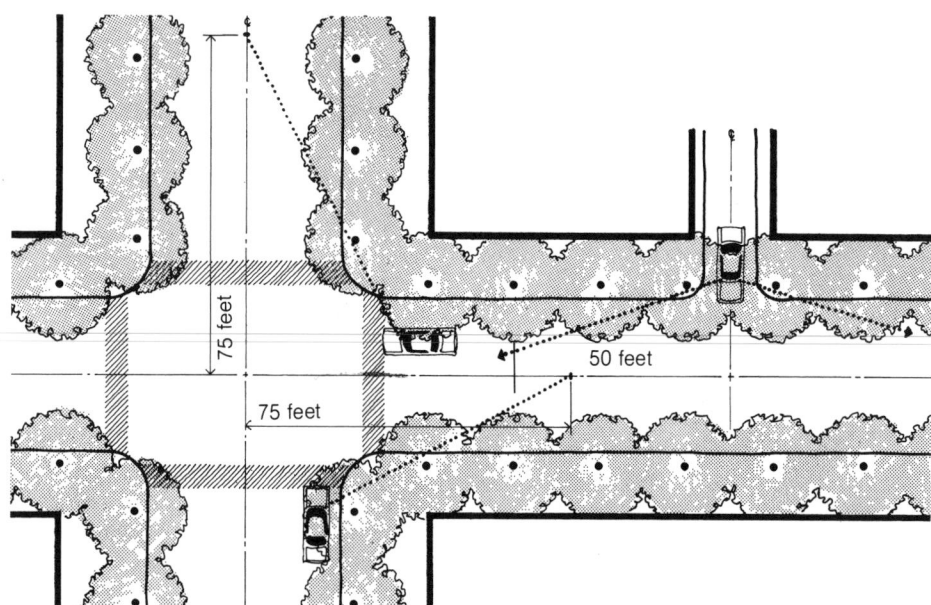

4-19 Horizontal sight distance for safety. Plan diagram showing how sight lines from cars and trucks effect street tree locations.

crowns from ground level fixtures creates a funereal effect, produces very little illumination, and is the most susceptible to interference from obstructions, snowfall, and vandalism.

Arrangement of trees

The thoroughness with which the principles of Euclidean geometry have been disavowed in our time for arranging trees is illustrated by a recurring attitude about straight lines, or any clearly geometric arrangement of trees. The admonition to avoid "rigid" lines of trees has become a cliche. Proponents of naturalistic landscapes speak of free flowing lines in nature as if the wilderness were an English garden composed more of sinuous curves than jagged edges. Even if regularly spaced trees in straight lines extended on an exact rectangular grid throughout an entire city and we could suspend the dynamic visual effects of observer movement and continual change in natural light, the effect would be no more "rigid" than the sky or forest or ocean. Every tree has a different form and pattern, making every segment in every line different, just as every croissant from a bakery is different and no two chorus lines look the same. If you have seen one line of trees, you haven't seen them all.

4-20 Section: Street trees: Comparison of the spatial effects of large and small trees showing the visual and functional superiority of large tree types.

4-21 Trees in a straight line demonstrating the implausibility of the term "rigid" in referring to trees arranged regularly.

Closely observed geometry

Though we are accustomed to making an arbitrary association between randomness and curves in two dimensional plan drawings, it is clear from looking at trees in perspective that we do not see them in this way. No matter how trees are arranged, we see straight lines and can construct only rows of trees in our memory-vision. The two perspective views of twenty trees in regular and irregular arrangements demonstrate this. The principal difference between the two views is the regularity in intervals between trees seen down the rows. When we move through the two arrangements, the difference is more dramatic. In the one with randomly spaced trees, regular movement produces an erratic and completely nonrhythmic visual impression. In the regular tree arrangement, the tree rows come to life creating a continuous and gradually changing view with rhythmic intervals. The latter can be compared to the effect of looking through a kaleidoscope. A striking analogy is seen in the large modular cube sculptures of Sol Le Witt. Moving past these three dimensional grids produces a dynamic visual effect that is like moving through a modular plantation of trees. A living example of this phenomenon is seen in Grant Park, where Elm trees planted on a rectilinear grid can be viewed from two different positions.

4-22 Comparison between two perspective views of 20 trees, one arranged in random pattern uniformly dispersed, the other arranged symmetrically in an orthogonal grid.

4-23
4-24

4-23 Trees in a park aligned at right angles in both directions viewed on axis. The classical way of depicting trees in lines.

4-24 The same grid pattern of trees viewed from another direction demonstrating how the natural distortions in individual tree form change the visual symmetry to create a fascinating occult order.

It is this rhythmic order, expressed everywhere in art, that is lacking in random arrangement. Urban design depends on many of the same organizing principles as poetry, painting, and music. The intervals between the trees can be used as a metrical device reflecting the speed of movement through urban spaces. In this way, purposeful tree spacing gives scale and rhythm. In urban situations, we need strong organizing devices such as these to surmount the prevailing confusion. Small subtle design ideas can easily be swallowed up in the urban visual turmoil. Arranging trees in random patterns in the city creates disorder that is neither expressive of the intrinsic urban geometry nor like undisturbed nature. Deliberate randomization reflects a profound misunderstanding of nature.

Spatial composition

Spatial opportunities. The possibilities for spatial composition with trees remain almost unexplored. The experience of moving through geometric groves of trees makes the forest seem dull because the natural organization of trees is so much more subtle. Trees provide an opportunity to create exciting urban compositions combining the art of sculpture and architecture at the scale of the city.

4-25 An urban park. Trees in ordered patterns complement and link the variety of architectural rhythms of the city. Seeing filtered views of buildings through a gauze of tree trunks can produce moire patterns in three dimensions.

4-26 Spatial organization. Trees define space both vertically and horizontally.

Closely observed geometry

Trees organize spaces in two distinctly different ways—horizontally and vertically. Horizontally they do it by visually enclosing, completing or defining an area of open space. Vertically they define space by creating an airy ceiling of branches. Filling a space with trees actually means covering the area with a canopy of branches and leaves, rather than annihilating the void.

Horizontal enclosure. Creating an horizontal enclosure with trees is different from using architectural building materials. Unlike the solid enclosure of a building, it depends on visual suggestion and illusion. When viewing a space from the ground, there is a feeling of enclosure when the surroundings are tall enough to intercept our entire cone of vision. A convenient rule of thumb is that the observer should not be further away from the defining edge than three times the enclosure height. To create a complete sense of enclosure with 50 foot tall trees, an observer in the space should not be more than 150 feet away from the defining tree line.

Vertical enclosure. The vertical definition of space with trees is important to a high density urban situation where tall buildings can create an intimidating scale for pedestrians. Street trees, colonnades of trees, and tree covered squares each contribute in this way. The ever-changing translucent canopy of leaves and branches allows for a simultaneous experience of the smaller space within the larger volume. In this sense, trees are more valuable than a building arcade for reducing the overwhelming scale of large structures. They function as an arcade with skylights, provide filtered light at seasonally appropriate intensity, lend a sense of protection, and give rich detail to the space.

Patterns. The employment of trees is of course not limited to creating these simple forms of enclosure. However, in most urban contexts, trees in straight lines, circles, and rectangles are appropriate because they echo the city and fit comfortably within the man-made geometry of circulation and structure. Some

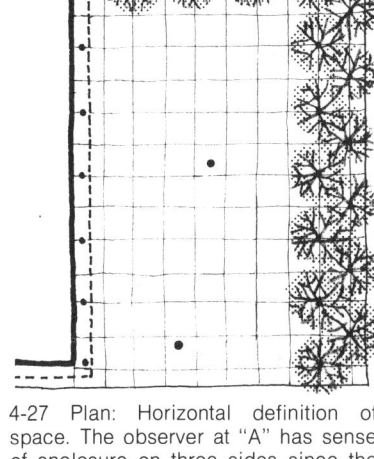

4-27 Plan: Horizontal definition of space. The observer at "A" has sense of enclosure on three sides since the distance from observer to wall (trees) is less than 3 times the tree height. The observer at "B" begins to lose sense of spatial definition at far end of plaza because distance is greater than 3 times tree height.

4-28 Horizontal definition of space. Perspective view from edge of plaza.

4-29 Vertical definition of space. Trees as a canopy.

4-30 Vertical definition of space. Trees as a canopy.

of the many possible layouts to modify a small urban space are suggested in the plan diagrams. In every instance, the locations of the trees should be as purposeful as the location of the buildings. Where it is logical to do so, the tree pattern can grow out of some established pattern in the surroundings, such as building fenestration or column spacing. In general, the less arbitrary the pattern the more we will feel comfortable with the space. In each of these patterns, the tree trunks are conceived as columns supporting a diffuse leaf canopy beginning 15 feet above the ground. The space under the trees would be perceived as an enclosure modulated by the columns. No dimensions are indicated for the space because the same tree configurations could be used for a wide

4-31

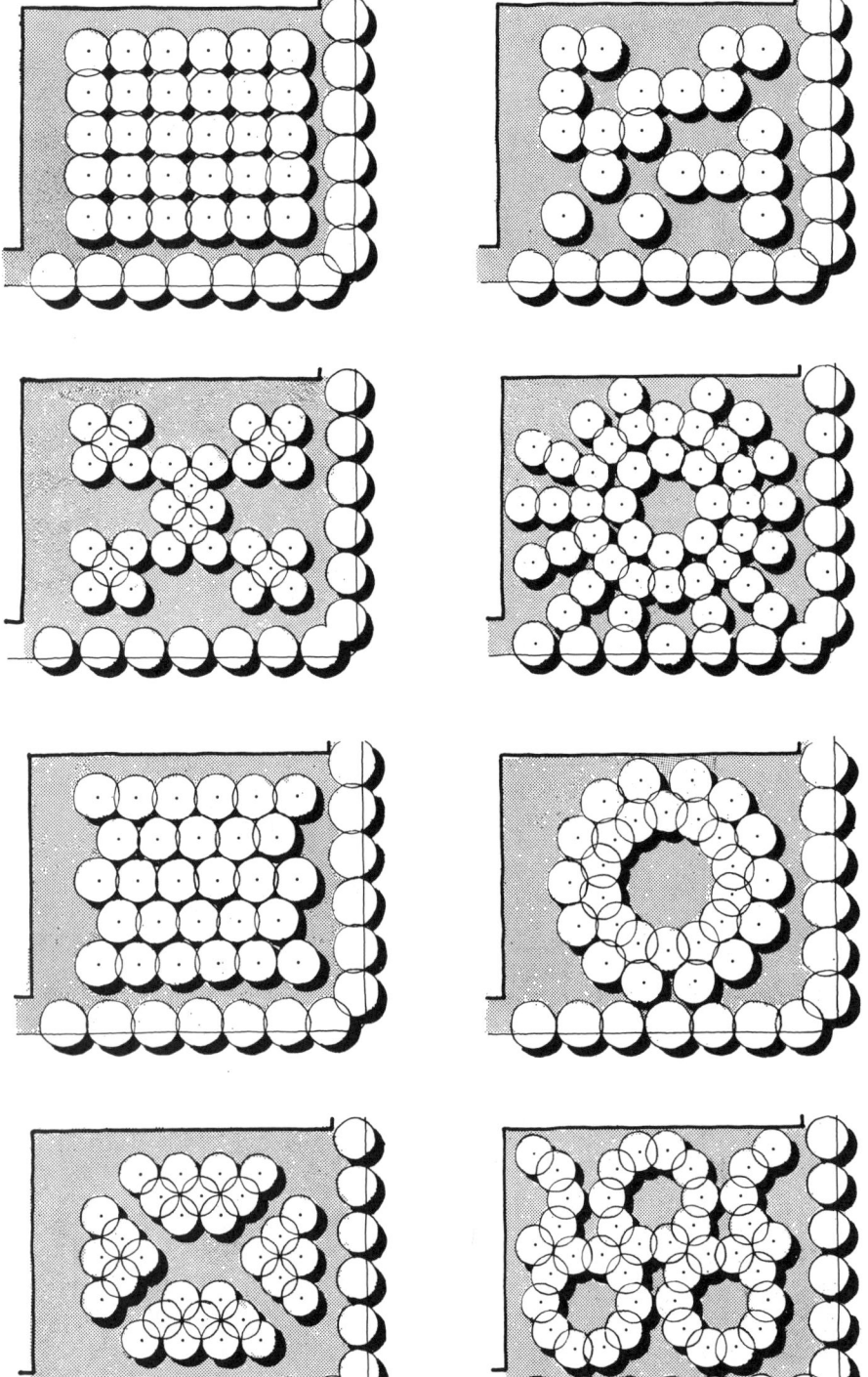

4-31 Square grid. Simple flexible coherent pattern, rhythmic, uniform, directionally uncommitted tree arrangement.

4-32 Square grid incomplete. A randomized variation of the square grid in which fewer trees are used. All trees are on grid intersection points.

4-33 Quincunx. Trees used in groups of five to create a more complicated pattern less spatially coherent than grid.

4-34 Radial circular. Trees aligned radially to form concentric circles. Centripetal focus, strongly coherent pattern for close tree spacings and increasing density toward center.

4-35 Staggered rows. Greater density than square grid with a shift in trunk spacing. Decreasing the distance between rows gives the most compact uniform pattern when trunks are all equidistant, i.e. on an equilateral triangular lattice.

4-36 Concentric circular. A useful pattern to give spatial definition with open center. Close circumferential trunk spacing necessary for articulation of circular form.

4-37 Triangular. Diagonal circulation emphasis with open center.

4-38 Multiple circles. Many possible variations allowing definition of smaller spaces within the larger volume. Least coherent for use in a small well defined space.

range of different size spaces. The trees would always provide a transition to a comfortable human scale. It is, of course possible to arrange trees in patterns that satisfy predetermined mathematical criteria. If a designer were asked to arrange 16 trees in 15 rows, for example, the pattern shown in Figure 4-39 is one solution to fit a predetermined set of conditions. Both this arrangement and the one shown in Figure 4-40 are solutions to this type of mathematical problem. (Gardner) A practical application of these problems based on geometric criteria would be in the layout of a building courtyard where the architecture and planting are designed together, and the building structure suggests the tree locations.

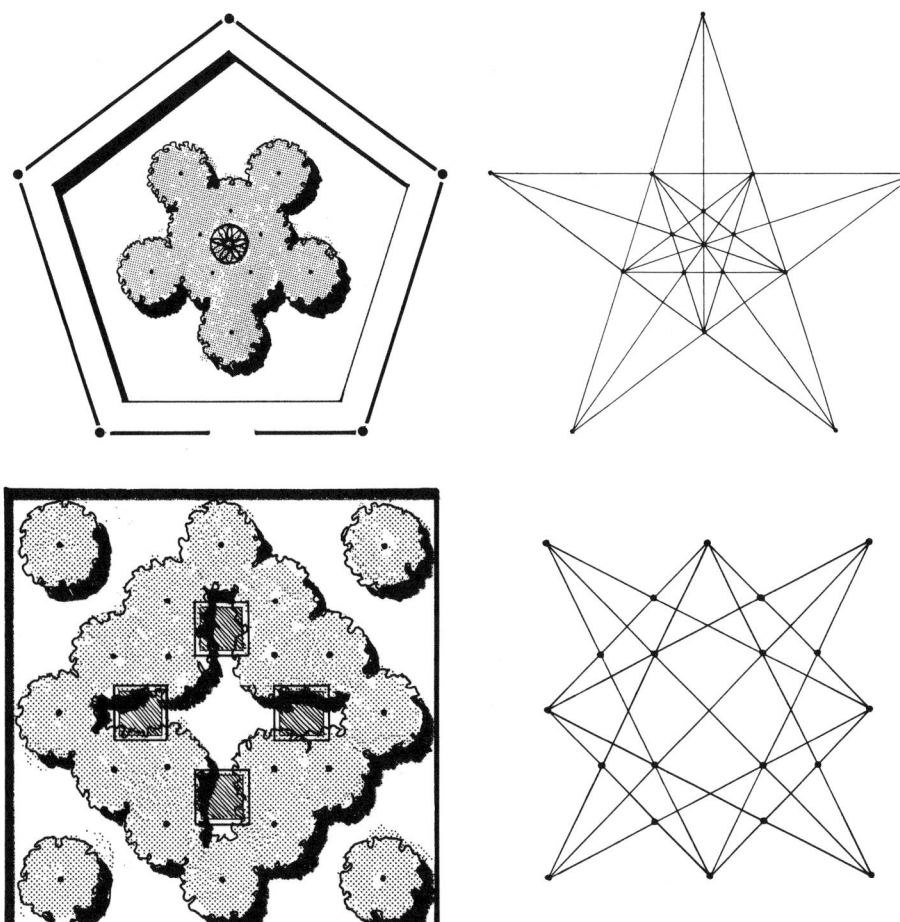

4-39 Diagram on right shows how 16 trees can be arranged to make 15 rows of 4 trees. Plan on left shows arrangement adapted to courtyard where outer vertices are building columns and center point is a fountain.

4-40 Diagram on right shows how 20 trees are set in 14 rows of 4 trees. Plan on left shows how this arrangement is adapted to a square courtyard with fountains or pools.

Tree spacing. Arrangements of trees in a city space, as shown in Figure 4-31 to 4-38 are possible within a 160 by 200 foot area with trees placed no closer together than 18 feet. If this minimum distance is increased, fewer arrangements are possible. The distance between trees is critical in design, primarily because of the limitations that wide spacing imposes. Urban designs that depend on trees for their unity are weakened by spreading trees too far apart. Figure 4-41 shows the increase in aesthetic possibilities for arranging trees with one of the simplest solutions, a circular pattern. Plan possibilities are increased sevenfold by allowing a minimum spacing between trees of 15 feet instead of 50 feet. There are many places where an arbitrary 50 foot spacing is actually recommended or even required. The result is to diminish not only the design flexibility but the number of trees that can be planted, as Figure 4-41 shows for an 80 foot square space.

4-41

The distances between trees must be established on an aesthetic basis giving considerations to scale relationships, surrounding geometry, paving pattern, height of canopy, rhythm of movement through the space, light quality, and desired tree form. Valid cultural limitations include the spread of the branches and roots when planted, soil type and conditions, and circulation in the space. Trees gain rather than suffer from propinquity. In most urban situations, spacing trees between 10 and 25 feet is reasonable and permits effective design and healthy growth. This does not mean that closer or wider spacings are never appropriate.

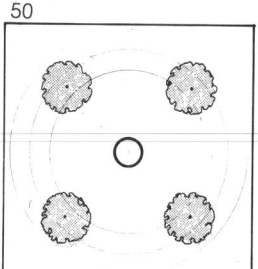 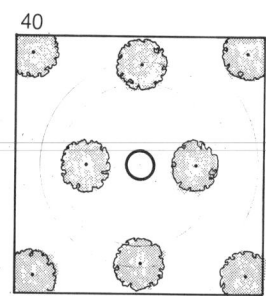 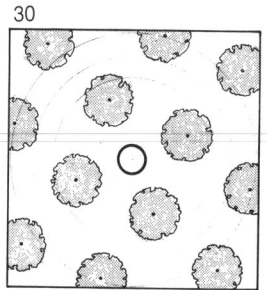 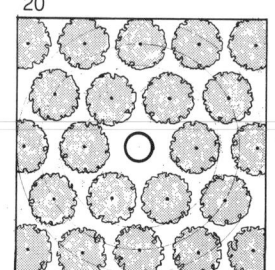 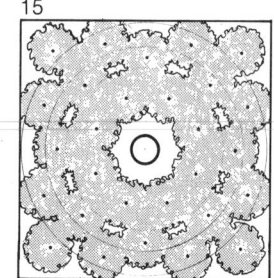

In observing street tree spacings, it is apparent that they lose their visual effectiveness when planted more than 30 feet apart, at least until they become large trees. Since this usually takes a long time in a city, it is more desirable to space street trees no more than 20 feet apart center to center. Where economy does not dictate otherwise, closer spacings may be used, especially when utility posts, signs, and other obstructions cause gaps in the row.

The habit of growth, that is the branch structure of the tree, also helps determine spacing. The Pin Oak has a denser branch pattern than the Plane Tree or the Sugar Maple, and does not seem to adapt gracefully to very close spacing. The Honeylocust, Ginkgo, and Plane Tree, because of their structure and their less dense foliage, are more adaptable to different planting densities. Every tree species has a unique response to spacing. The stately form of the American Elm tree in great allee's illustrates the structural adaptation of the species to the spacing. The Elm trees on the Federal Mall in Washington are spread 50 feet apart and have developed into nearly open grown form. If planted closer together, they would be taller with more ascending branches like the Elm trees in Grant Park, Chicago. Closely spaced trees become more spectacular as they grow to maturity.

4-41 Diagrammatic plans. The sequence depicts a square area with trees in five different configurations. Where the minimum spacing between trees is set at 50 feet, only 4 trees can be arranged around the center in a concentric pattern. With each successive decrease in the space between trees, more trees can be accommodated. The trees do not begin to define a circle until the spacing between trees is reduced to 15 feet.

4-42 Street trees. Close tree spacing benefits most urban streets like this one in Philadelphia because it compensates for the wider gaps in the treeline caused by inevitable obstructions. The benefits of close spacing apply to narrow streets as well as more expansive sites.

4-43 Pin Oak Trees 18 inches in diameter are growing 18 feet apart showing less graceful branch structure for close spacing than is characteristic of the Red or White Oak.

Growth rate and planting size

There is a critical relationship between tree spacing at planting, the size of the tree, and the rate of growth. The old guiding rule that we are planting trees for posterity and can therefore wait for 50 to 100 years for the tree to mature is hardly relevant in the contemporary city. We need the beneficial psychological impact caused by a dramatic transformation of the urban environment. For trees to change the character of cities, they must be large enough and numerous enough to create a bold form. Trees used in this way could become living signs that American cities are indeed centers of civilization.

The best measure of the visual impact of trees is the crown volume. We see the mass of the tree tops as both the silhouette of the branch spread and the depth of the crown mass, because of the transparency of the branch structure even when in leaf. There is a vast difference between the volume of a tree at economical planting size and the volume of a mature tree. A Red Maple four inches in caliper with a ten foot branch spread would have a crown volume of roughly 400 cubic feet. The same tree when mature in a grove could easily have a crown volume of over 24,000 cubic feet. This emphasizes one of the major difficulties in dealing with trees initially—attaining a large enough scale to suit the urban landscape.

There are two approaches to the problem of meeting the scale requirements initially when installing trees: larger trees or more trees. It can be shown that there is an optimum size of tree to transplant based on the cost per inch of diameter. Therefore the least expensive way to provide maximum initial volume, and hence maximum visual impact, is to plant the optimum size at an appropri-

4-44 Thornless Honeylocust Trees in the third block of Independence Mall, Philadelphia, are planted on a 12 foot by 18 foot grid. The branch structure of this species is well adapted to close spacing. Wider spacing would weaken the design.

4-45 Ginkgo Trees in Fort Green Park, Brooklyn growing in a triple row with trees spaced seven feet apart in both directions. The average diameter is 11 inches. An example of branch form adapted to close spacing.

4-46 Plane Trees in Princeton, New Jersey in two rows 40 feet apart with trees spaced 20 feet apart within rows. A visually successful spacing for a 30 foot wide street.

4-47 American Elm Trees in Washington D.C. planted 50 feet apart on the Federal Mall. Trees at this spacing develop with an open grown crown form.

4-49

4-50

4-48 European Beech Trees showing how trees planted less than 10 feet apart modify their shape in adapting to the space. (Photo by A. E. Bye)

ate spacing. Thus to some extent and under some circumstances, a larger quantity of trees can be substituted for larger trees.

It is technically possible, though not always economically practical to transplant any size tree. Economic constraints and availability preclude moving large numbers of trees greater than 25 to 30 feet tall in the city. The simplest way to compare aesthetic value with cost is to assess the cost per inch of trunk diameter for different size trees. In cases where this has been done, trees of four to five inch caliper (18 to 22 feet tall) usually prove most economical because they provide more branch coverage per unit cost of the planted tree. This will vary somewhat among species, locations, and site conditions. Trees over six inches in caliper (25 to 30 feet tall), even though expensive, are often planted because of the need for large size to satisfy the scale requirements and actually cost less per volume of crown than smaller trees, though they do not cover as great an area.

Since we are usually limited by availability and cost to a tree of about 20 feet tall with a branch spread of eight to ten feet when planting a grove of trees in the city, they cannot be spaced much further than 25 feet and still give the appearance of a grove during the first ten years after planting. For an average spreading crown type of tree, a spacing around 20 feet in both directions would be reasonable if planted on a uniform square grid pattern. If the trees are staggered in rows, the spacing might be reduced to about 15 feet. This density of planting would be a good one to use with Plane Trees, for instance, where a high-branched canopy effect is desired in an area that requires shade during midday in summer. In this way, an immediate visual scale is achieved. The best arrangement and spacing must, of course, be determined individually for each different set of site conditions.

The rate of growth for the trees after planting is important because of the significant differences among city tolerant species. The Ginkgo tree grows so slowly that unless a very large tree is used, it may still be visually ineffective ten years after it is planted. The London Plane Tree, on the other hand, will make impressive growth in the first five years after planting on most urban sites. It is not uncommon for them to triple their crown volume in that time. Maple and Oak trees fall somewhere in between the slow and fast growing species, making extensive growth within ten years after planting, but usually growing very slowly during the first five years after planting. See Figure 5-2 in Chapter 5 for some comparative growth rates by species.

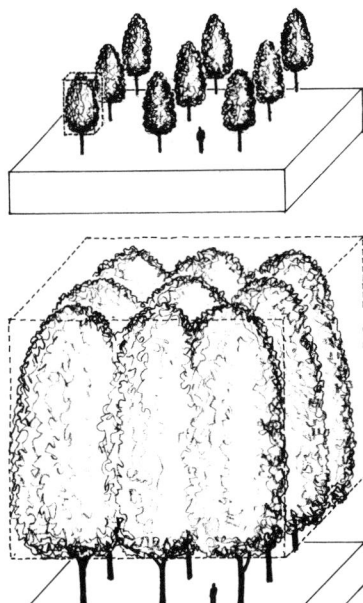

4-49 Diagram illustrating the volumetric difference between trees when they are planted and forty years later. The visual impact of trees is largely dependent on the mass or volume of the crowns.

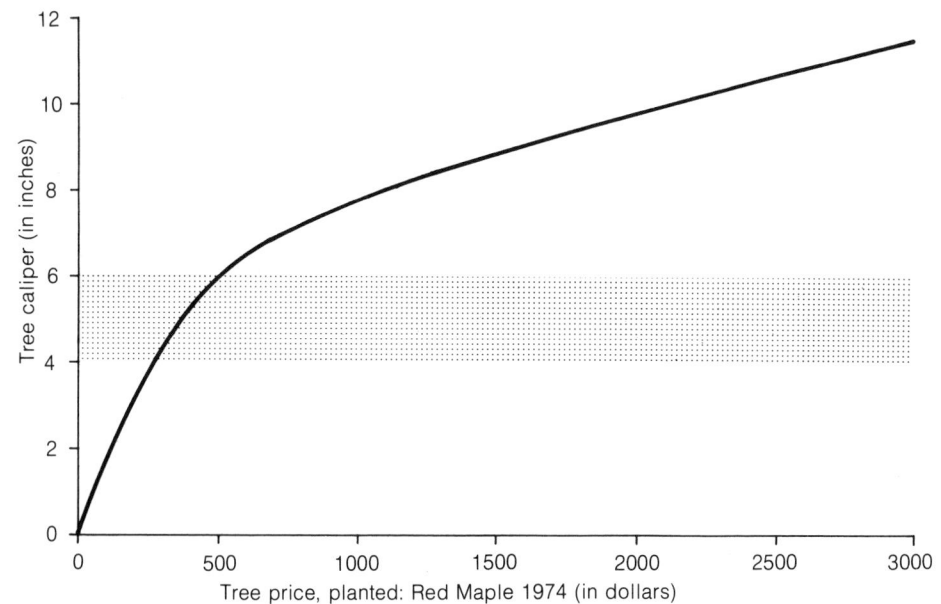

4-50 Graph showing how the cost of planted shade trees varies with tree trunk caliper (diameter 12″ high). Trees less than 6 inch caliper represent an economical size for transplanting where the budget is small, because larger trees cost more per inch caliper. Trees larger than 6 inch caliper however, produce more crown volume per inch of caliper and may be the most economical to use where the budget does not critically limit the number of trees necessary to implement the design. Optimum size trees on most projects are 4 to 6 inches in caliper. These provide the widest area of coverage for a restricted budget. Source: Landscape Architects Cost Files, Arnold Associates.

Organizing trees in large parks

Size and character. The large urban park incorporates many of the same organizing principles that we see in a small urban park, but introduces a broader scope of opportunity. It is possible to grow a wider range of species. Conditions of soil and air are more like the uncivilized forest, and the visual context is less emphatically urban. We are not concerned here with parks that are regional preserves in size and function, i.e. with over two square miles of relatively undisturbed natural landscape. The concern here is with large parks, completely surrounded by urban development, less than 1000 acres in size, and designed to accommodate a large population. Most American city parks, in this category average between 100 and 500 acres. Some examples giving an impression of scale are the Inland Regional Parks in Chicago, 150 to 300 acres; Central Park in New York, 840 acres; and Franklin Park in Boston, 500 acres. Despite their diverse character, they are similar in scale and proximity to intense urban development. A major difference is the density of residential population surrounding parks in cities of the United States. Central Park probably needs to accommodate the highest density of people living adjacent to the park. Franklin Park is in an area of lower population density for a large city park. The corresponding differences in pressure for use of the park will make a difference in the detail design; however, the population should not alter the fundamental purpose and character of large city parks.

Design approach. The primary mission of a large urban park in a large city is to provide a sense of release from the pressures of daily life, outdoors, in contact with natural elements, in a social rather than isolated context. This definition transcends issues of style or detailed activities within the park. It does not mean, however, that questions of programming and design are irrelevant in satisfying this fundamental purpose of a park. On the contrary, inappropriate design forms or activities could seriously compromise this primary mission.

In one serious respect, we have failed to satisfy the first purpose of the large city park by the design of these open spaces. We have confused the functions and therefore the furnishings of the public park and the private garden. The functional and material differences of the two can be separated by scale and social purpose. The following comparison suggests appropriate design features of each:

Public Park	*Private Garden*
Wide uncluttered space	Small enclosed space
Contact with many people	Intimacy and privacy
Large trees in organized patterns	Single trees, smaller plants, flowers
Freedom of circulation	Restricted circulation
Sweeping flat or undulating ground	Flat or abrupt level changes
Broad uncomplicated ground materials	Varied intricate ground texture

Even though, a clear line does not always exist to differentiate these discrete categories, and there can be some overlapping, the generalization is useful. Scale and social purpose are meaningful in the design of public spaces and help decide what functions are appropriate in the park.

To what extent is the park an escape from the city and to what extent is the park an extension of the city? The issues are complicated. If one takes the view that a park is designed for those who actively use it as well as those who look into it from the surrounding streets, the park cannot be a complete escape from urban experience. Attempting to create a patch of unstructured nature within a dense urban area is inappropriate for several reasons. Both the theoretical nature of the city as explored by Doxiadis, and the experienced nature of the city as described by Jacobs argue against the desirability of under utilized land within a large city. (Doxiadis, Jacobs) A large park that is not designed for intensive activity fits this category. The kinds of uses required to make such a land area appropriate are not compatible with a wild or agrarian landscape. Even without such desirable, more intensive human use, the urban environment does not provide a suitable habitat for imitating forest-based plant growth. A large scale park can provide relief from the turmoil of the urban environment without obliterating or ignoring the city.

It is impractical to recreate forest plant communities in an urban context. Over 100 years of undisturbed human activity are required for plant succession to reach a climax of dominant forest trees. We have not yet acquired the knowledge to closely approximate and maintain a forest condition in any stage of succession by artificially transplanting trees and understory vegetation. Even if we could learn to do this effectively, the multilayered growth of a natural plant association is not compatible with urban park use. Maintenance of natural areas in the city is difficult. There are additional philosophical and technical arguments to demonstrate the impracticality of "natural" planting in the city. Unfortunately there is not space in this book to review them all.*

The example of Central Park. Central Park, New York, is a good example to analyze because it is the forerunner and prototype for large parks in American cities. It exemplifies a lingering style that has become obsolete as cities grow and change socially. The original design by Calvert Vaux and Frederick Law Olmsted was appropriate and probably inevitable for its time. The plan was conservative enough to preserve the site's natural features, and forward-looking enough to resolve the problem of vehicular/pedestrian circulation and conflict. Even if the needs of New York's future population could have been accurately predicted, it is unlikely that a more sophisticated park development could have been financed at the time. Furthermore, the nation was in the midst of a period of romantic revival making this design especially appealing.

The strength of Vaux and Olmsted's plan lay in its resolution of circulation, exploitation of natural features, and unity of scale. There is a consistency in the overall design that is lacking in details. The irregular walks, roads, plantings, and terrain give the park a unified texture as seen from the air and certainly achieved Olmsted's expressed desire to make the park a "single work of art." (Olmstead)

Without speculating on what might have been, the shortcomings in today's Central Park demonstrate its poor adaption to modern social conditions and needs. A picturesque park layout designed primarily for strolling, carriage riding, and observing nature was appropriate to genteel nineteenth century notions of what people needed. In contemporary New York, dense population, economic hardship, ethnic diversity, and more egalitarian views exert different demands on the park from those envisioned by Vaux and Olmsted. This does not mean that the basic nature of a park has changed, that is, its function of providing informal social contact and a sense of release from the pressure of the city within the city. It does imply that the means of satisfying these age old needs has changed. We still need the contrast of a big space and the intimate contact with plants, water and rock that a large park can provide. As much as we would like to experience pastoral nature right in the city, the impracticality of doing so in Central Park has been adequately demonstrated. The failure of the park to absorb contemporary pressure for more users is apparent where the grass is completely worn out, and on weekends, where the more accessible areas of the park are overcrowded.

The overall layout of Central Park still provides a physically adequate and historically vital framework for fulfilling today's needs. Within the original structure, changes can be made to ground surfaces to accommodate appropriate activities without destroying what is irreplaceable and historically unique. Grass should only be used in areas where it can be maintained, either because of lower intensity of use or specially adopted replacement programs. Well designed hard and soft paving materials need to replace the grassless, muddy and bald areas. These changes in detail would also involve removing enough sections of the park boundary wall and shrub plantings to permit free flowing access and egress. New trees are needed in areas of the park where facilities were added without proper tree plantings. It is also necessary to clarify the best aspects of the original design by improving areas where the spatial intent is not clearly expressed. Many of the low plantings need to be removed because they interrupt important views, increase maintenance difficulty, and make the park both less attractive and less safe. After more than 100 years of experience with the original trees, we can simplify the plantings by removing species that have grown poorly and adding those that are best adapted to prevailing urban conditions. None of these measures is inconsistent with the historically important parts of the original design concept.

4-51
4-52

4-53
4-54
4-55
4-56

* One of the most interesting is a theory developed by Robert McArthur that demonstrates a numerical correlation between various species that nature will sustain in an area and the size of the natural area. If this theory is correct and could be extended to a city park, which is essentially an island of planting isolated by development, then there are probably very few species that would grow naturally in an area the size of Central Park even without the impinging urban influences. (McArthur)

4-51 Central Park existing condition. Edges of the park present barriers both visual and physical that deter access and make the park forbidding as viewed from the outside. The park is cut off from the city at pedestrian level, and can conceal crime behind the wall.

4-53 Central Park existing condition. Recreation facilities have been set down within the park without regard for their proper integration with the site. Surprisingly, new tree plantings have not been considered an essential part of added facilities, such as the Wollman ice skating rink.

4-55 Central Park existing condition. A typical view along the park's path system. Low shrubbery and flowering trees interrupt views of city and park, make the park less attractive and provide concealed spaces. Such garden-like clutter is inappropriate in a public space with heavy use. The short annual blossoming period of these plants does not justify their negative aesthetic impact during the rest of the year.

4-52 Central Park improved. Removal or relocation of large segments of the surrounding wall and all of the dense peripheral shrub planting would open the park to the sidewalk and greatly enhance passive and casual use. One important purpose of a large city park is to provide a contrasting sense of openness adjacent to continuous, often scaleless facades.

4-54 Central Park improved. New trees are an essential linking device to make a harmonious transition between structure and park. Shown here, trees are used to reduce the scale of the skating rink, suffuse the conspicuous ungainly light poles, and visually connect the rink with the park.

4-56 Central Park improved. The same typical pathway with low plantings removed, showing the advantage of being able to see through the trees into the park, and equally important, being able to see the contrasting urban backdrop.

Just as buildings undergo changes in their interiors to serve changing functions, so a park must occasionally be renovated. As with historically important buildings, the success depends on the sensitivity of the designer. Where it is handled skillfully, the result is often superior both aesthetically and functionally to a completely new building that may not be as appropriate in its surroundings. Such adaptive reuse is an eminently sensible way to make the city richer and more interesting. Failure of an area the size of Central Park to adapt to modern conditions could eventually result in complete destruction of the original conceptual design. In fact this is slowly happening.

Beyond Central Park. Given this imperative need for change in our old parks, what specified weaknesses can be corrected? How can the use of new trees improve city parks? Here are seven specific conditions where trees would play an important part in redesign:

1.   Improvement in the transition from the linear geometry of the city to the flowing geometry of the park. Add more ordered arrangements of trees at the park edges and entrances to reinforce the intensively used areas and make a subtle transition between the regular geometry of edges and the less ordered arrangement of the interior spaces by graduated changes in tree spacing and alignment. A similar transitional device was proposed in the design for a new   4-57
park in Washington, D.C., where the tree spacing and arrangement reflect a change from organized to casual geometry.   4-58

2.   Simplify the planting by removing underbrush and unhealthy trees. Add city adapted tree types to increase the spatial coherence by establishing one or two dominant unifying tree species that reoccur throughout the park.   4-59

3.   Add trees in areas where ground plane is redesigned to accommodate heavy use. Arrange trees to improve scale, rhythmic continuity, and integration of the new facility.   4-60

4.   Replace dense thicket plantings with flowering trees that provide a thin band of intermediate height foliage and blossoms threaded under the high-branched tree groves. Maintain only low groundcover or paving at ground level so that filtered views through the park are maintained and the undulating ground surface is visible through the tree trunks.   4-61

5.   Strengthen the overall compositional arrangement of tree groves in relation to open meadow by applying appropriate rules of proportion, scale, and visual definition. This kind of compositional unity applied to the west end of the Federal Mall is illustrated in plan view. The contrast between tree groves and   4-62
open lawn is a major theme.

6.   Arrange trees within groups and lines to create purposeful visual rhythms when moving through the park on foot. Tree spacing intervals can be uniform or varied to create subtle or dramatic changes that are reflected by the light and shade patterns magnified in the ground shadows. Straight lines of trees with uniform spacing become extraordinary expressions of ground form on undulating land. At the scale of the large city park, variations of tree form can be   4-63
usefully employed to heighten the spatial contrast. For example, narrow vertical trees are used in continuous bands to connect spaces together. This is a linking device that can be effective in a large park by threading lines of vertical trees throughout the landscape.   4-64

7.   Arrange tree types to maintain distinct layers of foilage and create spatial compression and contraction by consistency in use of high and low branched trees. Avoid interruption of ground plane with low plantings, allowing clear vertical expression of tree trunks growing out of the ground. The Honeylocust tree,   4-65
with its translucent crown of fern-like leaves, can be exploited to create two layers of foliage within the same ground area. Light shading tree types admit enough light to allow development of a lower layer of leaves. By underplanting smaller trees between the grid arrangement of the Honeylocust trunks, two separate leaf canopies occur at different levels in the space.   4-66

4-57 View of a large city park near the edge. The orderly arrangement of trees in lines is modified by variation in the terrain and irregularities in the view beyond. In the heart of the park, the trees become less uniformly ordered.

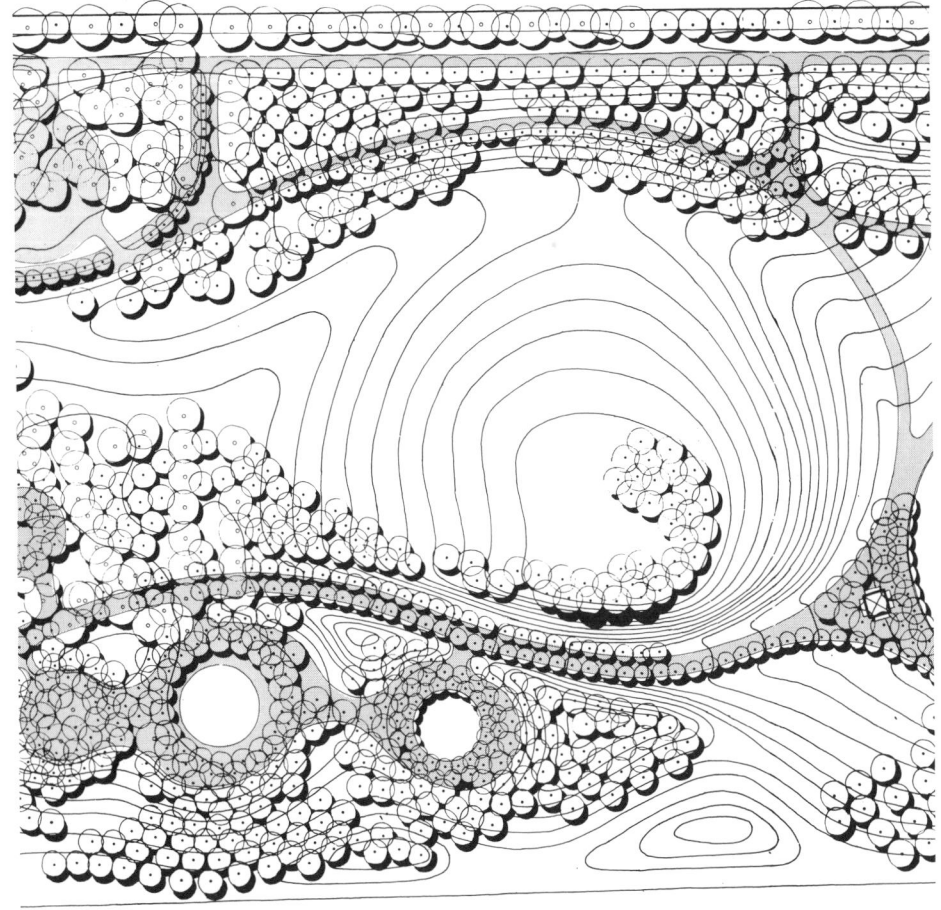

4-58 Planting plan. A segment of an early design for Constitution Gardens, a city park in Washington, D.C., showing how the tree spacing and arrangement are varied from regular and linear at the edges to less regular lines following the contours within. Topography, circulation and tree layout are closely interrelated.

4-59 Adding trees of a single species for continuity, and planting closely enough together to develop a high forest crown are measures that can improve the coherence of most large city parks. Removal of low plantings to improve visibility allows the tree pattern to better articulate the land form.

71

4-60 Trees used in a park to define an activity area. In most cities of the United States, the climate requires that trees provide shaded paths, and shaded paved areas for activities during the summer.

4-61 Understory trees are used sparingly under the large tree canopy as a lower level linking element strategically placed to preserve views and the open character of the park.

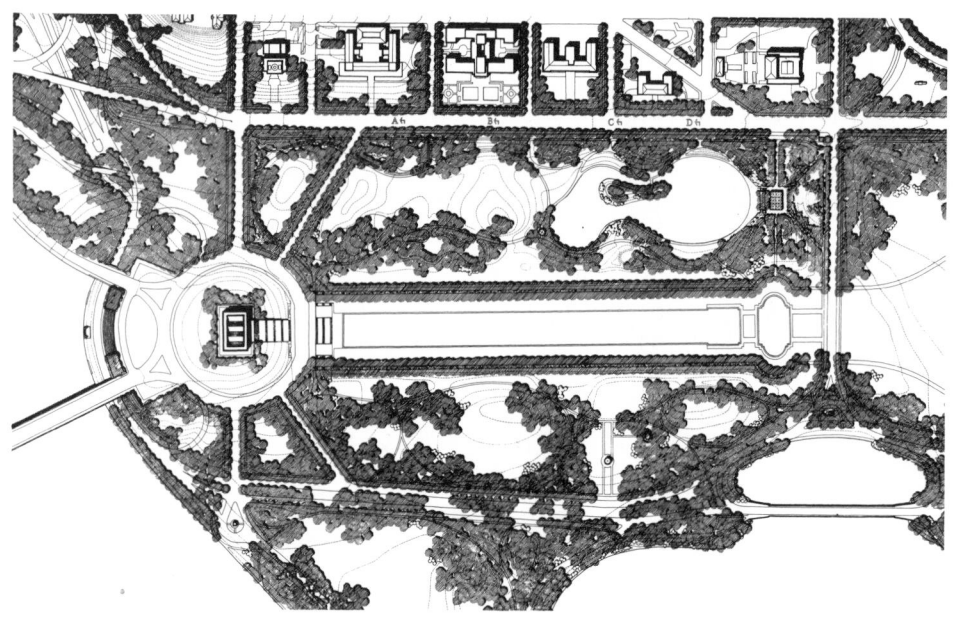

4-62 Plan: West end of the Federal Mall, Washington, D.C. Compositional unity is achieved by the way tree groves are arranged in relation to open meadow, observing principles of scale, proportion and spatial definition. (Drawing by Skidmore, Owings and Merrill, Washington, D.C.)

4-63 The juxtaposition of straight lines of trees on undulating ground produces a marvelous coincidence of natural form and human purpose.

4-64 Columnar trees provide orientation by following major circulation routes within park. In this way a special tree form is exploited to strengthen visual unity and add drama to the scene.

4-65 Clear articulation of vertical space is achieved by trees that are selected and arranged to create layers of foliage. Unity of species, age at planting and tree spacing are planned to achieve vertical clarity.

4-66 Small trees planted under a canopy of tall, light foliage trees. In temperate climates, the Honeylocust could be used as a tall canopy tree for this purpose.

Additional large shade trees arranged in and around areas of hard and soft paving are essential to increasing a park's capacity for heavier use. The key to the successful use of ground materials lies in the arrangement of trees, with grass always in full sunlight where it grows best and paving always shaded by deciduous trees that enrich the ground surface with shade in summer and shadow patterns in winter. This principle, found in Parisian parks, is almost unknown in this country. Opposition arises from the bucolic notion that we need more grass in cities, even though planting grass where it will not grow does not provide more grass. An acre of trees can provide 20 to 50 times the amount of chlorophyll that an acre of grass produces, and more conspicuously. What is lacking most in Central Park is the serenity of great groves of ordered tree trunks with their cathedral-like spaces that create a moving visual poetry. Symmetrical organization of trees can provide the aesthetic link between humanized geometry and ordered irregularity—a tension that is found in modern art. Such compositions of symmetry contrasted with extreme diversity express the quintessential meaning of park—man as part of nature. The scarcity of this expression in most American city parks reflects a national obsession with a late Victorian style. In park design, as in most contemporary architecture, simply copying a style has produced sterility.

* A compilation of plan drawing techniques by Theodore Walker illustrates the type of conventions typically used in drawing trees. (Walker)

Conveying the design

It seems curious that the essential tools used by the landscape architect and urban designer to convey design information to clients and contractors have perpetuated and reinforced erroneous ideas about trees and their use. In some instances, the drawings actually gave rise to faulty design because of their ineffectiveness in conveying a three dimensional character. A look at the typical drawing used professionally to show trees in design demonstrates this paradox.* Design and planting plans nearly always give the impression that trees are visual barriers at eye level because of the way the tree crowns are shown superimposed solidly on the ground plane. The established drawing technique does not conform to the architectural convention of showing overhead forms with a dotted line. The problem is not easily avoidable, even if there were better ways to show trees in design, it means ignoring long established conventions of draftsmanship within the profession of landscape architecture.

Designers have difficulty with visual presentation techniques for showing trees for several reasons. Trees change in volume by a factor of 60 between the time that they are planted and the time they have reached what could be called a full mature size. Landscape architects are in the habit of showing trees in plans with circles that represent the full mature spread of an open grown tree under ideal growing conditions. It is misleading, not only because they do not grow that large in the city, but also because the trees will be much smaller than the represented size for many years after planting. Furthermore, the circle convention implies an open grown, symmetrically formed tree, not the shape of a tree as it adapts to its location in a grove or line. The use of this kind of tree symbol has reinforced the conventional notion of the open grown tree form by suggesting an unvarying symmetry and shape. The actual plan shape of a tree is never circular when trees are planted close enough together to interact visually as a unitary mass. For this reason, designers would serve their client's needs better by portraying tree groups in presentation plans as an undifferentiated canopy of leaves, rather than by showing circles that can be misinterpreted as an indication of the individual tree crown outline. See Figure 2-1.

On drawings, where it is not necessary to convey a suggestion of the future design intent, trees are better shown on plan at the actual planting size or slightly larger, as they adapt to the proximity of other trees and buildings. A more honest convention for showing trees in a plan that illustrates the ground

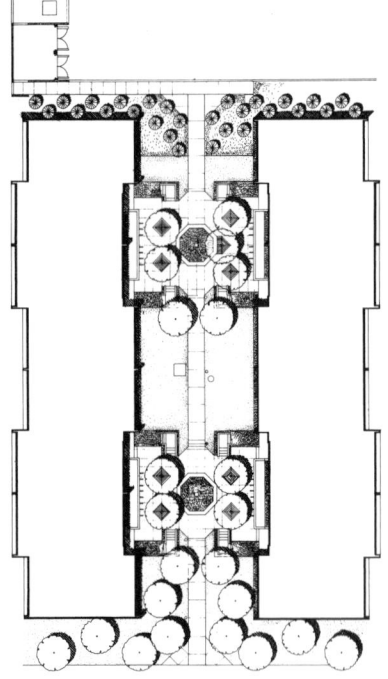

4-67 Planting plan. This type of representation is often used to show a design to the client. The shadows give a sense of the building and the tree heights. Here the size (branch spread) of trees is shown to represent the actual size at planting even though the intent of the design is to eventually cover the courtyard with a monolithic tree canopy. Showing the trees as they will appear 25 years after planting is misleading because most clients are concerned with the immediate effect.

plane is to show only the diameter of the trunk at something less than mature size. Showing the crown spread of a high-branched tree in plan view is often difficult to correctly interpret even for design professionals, who tend to read the trees as visual obstacles at eye level. Architects voice concern that trees shown this way are hiding their buildings even though they must know from experience how difficult it is to hide a building with deciduous shade trees. Showing the trees as columns (trunks) in plan also more clearly represents trees planted in groves or arcades at the pedestrian level. In the two illustrations, trees are shown in the conventional way, as blobs, and in a more revealing way as transparent circles with columns in the centers.

4-68

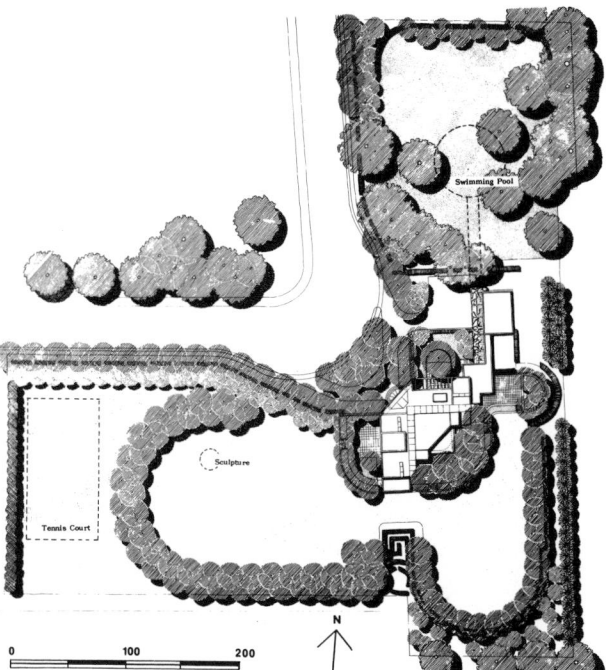

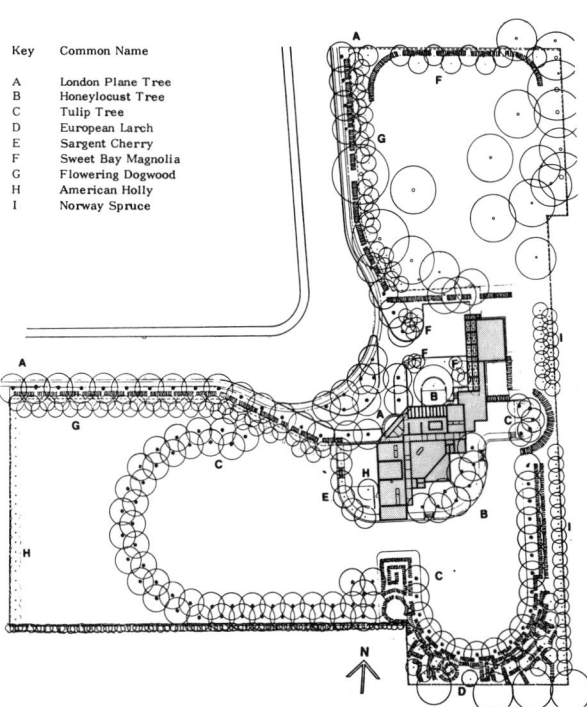

Key	Common Name
A	London Plane Tree
B	Honeylocust Tree
C	Tulip Tree
D	European Larch
E	Sargent Cherry
F	Sweet Bay Magnolia
G	Flowering Dogwood
H	American Holly
I	Norway Spruce

Showing trees in elevation or section has similar disadvantages, allowing accurate portrayal of only one plane. The distortion that occurs by not showing depth is deceiving because we tend to read a section as an actual view even though it cannot show distance. Sections and elevations can, however, be useful in illustrating the branch and crown heights that are often misinterpreted in plan. An eye level perspective can portray both the depth and height, and sometimes give a sense of the plan; however, its limitation of being accurate from only one viewpoint, makes it useful only for very specific visual information. It is useful in showing how trees frame rather than mask a view from an eye level vantage point. An aerial perspective is a useful compromise in giving both plan and three dimensional information in a single drawing. This kind of drawing, because of its persuasiveness, can often mislead. It shows more than the viewer would see from the ground at eye level and reinforces the misconception given by plan views that trees are opaque at ground level.

Axonometric and isometric drawings have the same merits and disadvantages as the aerial perspective except that they appear more distorted. The preference for them over the perspective view also adds to the remoteness of these drawings and their lack of connection to the ground and human viewers. The disadvantage of all forms of drawing for accurately depicting trees is that it requires a large expenditure of time for a single static view that is always somewhat misleading. A more expensive alternative is to make a scale model of the site showing the trees. This appears to be the best graphic tool for studying and illustrating a design in all of its dimensions. However, the model has a major limitation as a presentation technique because trees are almost impossible to duplicate ac-

4-68 Planting plan. These two drawings of the same site show two different ways of illustrating the tree layout. Plan A shows an aerial view with shadows. This best describes the massing of the tree canopies, but does not give a true picture of what happens at ground level. Plan B emphasizes the ground level by making the tree canopies transparent and showing the tree trunks as the dominant element—as they are at eye level on the ground. This technique does not depict the overall spatial impact of the trees.

curately to scale. The best models employ very crude surrogates for trees. The subtle qualities are completely lost in scale translation and even such critical qualities as light and shade patterns cannot be successfully duplicated. In one important sense, at least, the scale model is a misleading method of illustrating trees. Its convincing realism often fascinates the observer and diverts attention from important but incorrect details of deciduous trees. The inefficacy of full scale artificial plants is magnified ten times in scale reproductions of trees. If anything like the true quality of trees can ever be duplicated at a scale model size, drawing trees will become obsolete. Holography, if it becomes inexpensive, might eventually depict trees accurately in three dimensions. Until such an improved technique is perfected, the designer will need to employ the old conventional design forms of illustrations for showing trees, but with carefully stated qualifications.

To avoid expenditures, the process of planning and executing an urban design with trees is sometimes short circuited by simply eliminating the design stages and proceeding to construction without developing working drawings. Trees and other site elements are positioned in the field by a landscape architect who is presumed to have omniscience concerning aesthetic matters, even without the benefit of prior design studies. It should be unnecessary to cite the folly of such spurious economics; however, there are governmental agencies which routinely pursue this expedient approach to urban landscape design.

4-69 Site sections. These slices drawn through two areas of a park illustrate the vertical relationships of trees to the other elements of the site. They do not give a good indication of depth, a major limitation of this drawing device. Vertical elements in different planes appear at the same scale, unlike a perspective which more nearly approximates the actual view of an observer from a single fixed point.

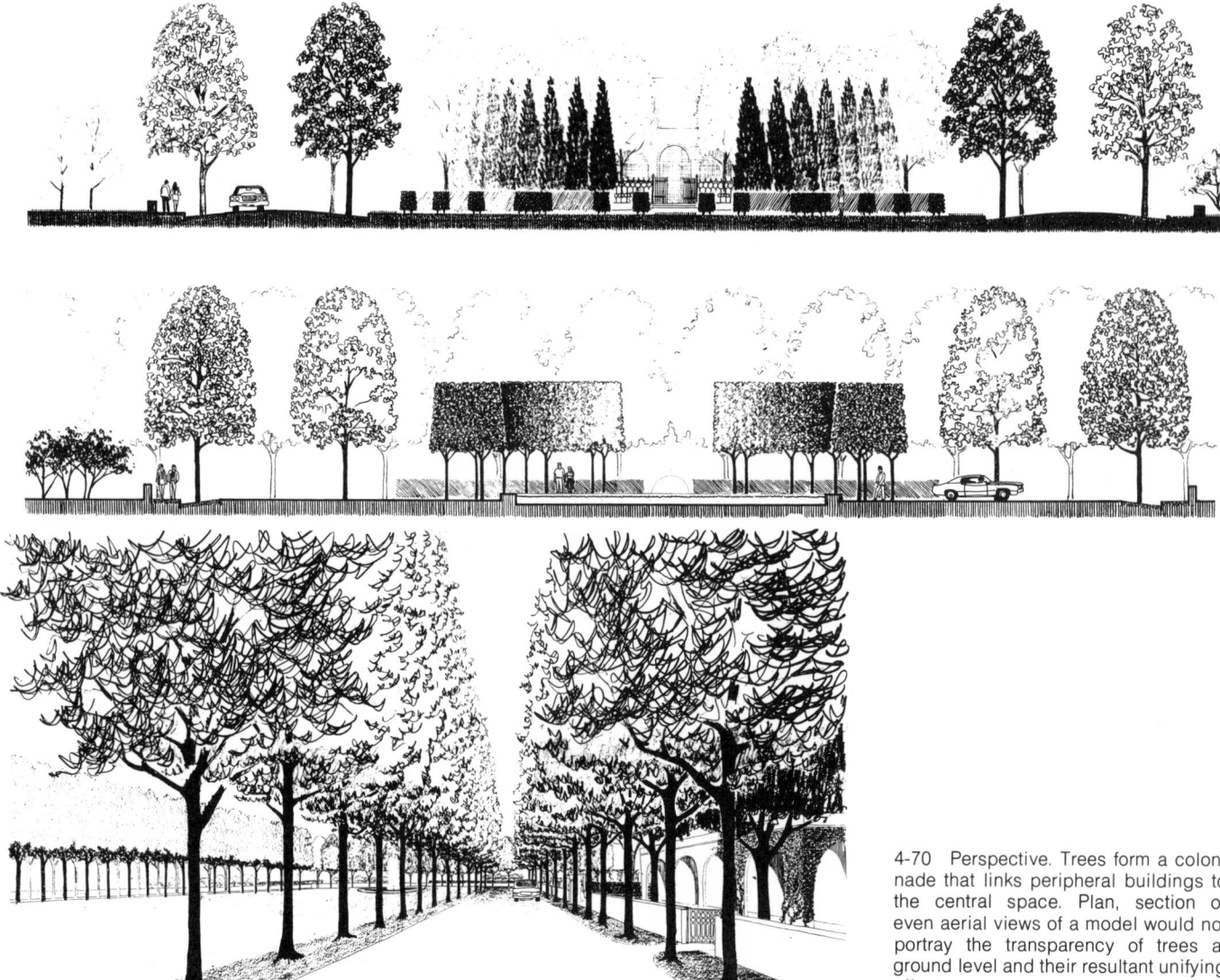

4-70 Perspective. Trees form a colonnade that links peripheral buildings to the central space. Plan, section or even aerial views of a model would not portray the transparency of trees at ground level and their resultant unifying effect.

The physical variables and subtleties of an urban space are not mastered in one brief encounter. Practical constraints must be resolved in harmony with aesthetic disciplines. Hundreds of hours of vigorous study are typically spent in producing a deceptively uncomplicated design. Whimsical arrangements, even by the most talented designers, are unlikely to produce an artistic achievement appropriate to our centers of culture.

References

Dobzhansky, Theodesius. *Genetics and the Origin of Species,* Third Ed. New York: Columbia University Press, 1951.

Stout, Benjamin R. *Studies of the Root Systems of Deciduous Trees,* Black Rock Forest, Bulletin #15. Mass: Harvard University Printing Office, 1956.

Gardner, Martin. Mathematical Games: The symmetrical arrangement of the stars on the American flag and related matters. *Scientific American* 235: 102–109 (1976).

Doxiadis, Constantinos. *Ekistics.* New York: Oxford University Press, 1968.

Jacobs, Jane. *The Death and Life of Great American Cities.* New York: Random House, 1961.

McArthur, Robert. *Geographical Ecology, Patterns in the Distribution of Species.* New York: Harper and Row, 1972.

Olmsted, Frederick Law, Sr. *Forty Years of Landscape Architecture: Central Park.* Edited by Frederick L. Olmsted, Jr., and Theodora Kimball. Mass: M.I.T. Press, 1973.

Walker, Theodore. *Plan Graphics.* Indiana: PDA Publishers, 1975.

5

Choice of type

Selecting trees for design

Evaluating trees. Selecting the most appropriate species and variety of tree for a particular location and function profoundly influences the quality of a design. Trees define spaces, regulate light, induce scale, and record the seasons. These aesthetic characteristics vary greatly among different species. The open space designer attempts to find the perfect compromise among the complex criteria like location, climate, and use. In an urban habitat, there may be only one variety of tree that is completely acceptable botanically. However, since the different natural science disciplines often provide conflicting views, the designer must weigh the data and choose. In urban situations, there are so few choices that often the design is based on the single type that will grow best in that locality. Often the designer compromises among several tree types for a specific habitat, and for the design requirements such as the tree's spatial qualities and regulation of light. There is rarely more than one species that fulfills the particular functions well at a particular urban site. An experienced designer does not usually go through the formal process of listing many tree types and comparing them with a list of criteria before making a selection. The design solution and the tree type selection converge. They are both usually governed by constraints that leave little room for arbitrary choice.

Names and examples. Plants are accurately identified according to their botanical classification by genus, species, and sometimes variety. Botanically, it is necessary to give the Latin genus and species name to identify a specific species of tree. Some species of tree have a distinct breed or breeds that are separately propagated and sold in the nursery trade. These "clones" are referred to as varieties or cultivars. They are named and usually patented by the original propagator. A plant variety is given a name and perpetuated when it is found to have some desirable characteristic that is not common to the species. There are a number of named varieties, for example Honeylocust without thorns and Red Maple trees with exceptional fall leaf color.

Common names are used here to avoid sounding technical. Often the word "type" is used in discussing kinds of trees where it is intended to include more than species. For example, "Norway Maple" will be used for the species and "Emerald Queen Maple," for that particular variety of Norway Maple. Norway Maples, including varieties, will be referred to as a "type" rather than a "species." A list of common and botanical names for the trees mentioned in this book are given in Appendix A.

Generalizing from specific examples requires some caution because the continent is divided into ten different climatic plant zones. Since the primary purpose here is to show the method and criteria used for selection, the design implications of most examples can be applied regardless of climate. Most of the examples used will be temperate climate types which grow in the widest distribution of latitudes.

Criteria for evaluation. There are many lists of trees for special purposes that are published for each region of the country.* Knowledge of the locality and a survey of all the trees that have been growing there for a long time is of great importance to the designer in dealing with tree types. The kinds of criteria that bear upon tree type selection and the names of tree species found growing in the same locality are shown in Figure 5-1 for a landscape design project in Philadelphia. Only tree "species" are shown in the table. In actual practice, the choice would be complicated by over 40 varieties with special characteristics. Some species have as many as six varieties that are propagated commercially and have significantly different characteristics. The matrix represents a crude rating system shown here to demonstrate the limitations of an objective process for evaluating trees. Since the relative values given to each criterion are subjective, variation will occur with different designers.

* Of the many publications about trees with lists of trees for city conditions, the most useful standard reference is Donald Wyman's *Trees for American Gardens*. (Wyman)

Rating for specific site	Species possibilities WEIGHTED VALUE	Sugar Maple	Red Maple	Norway Maple	Ginkgo	Honeylocust	Red Oak	Pin Oak	Tulip Tree	Sweet Gum	White Ash	Japanese Pagota Tree	Sycamore Maple	London Plane	Horsechestnut	American Linden	Willow Oak	Littleleaf Linden
AESTHETIC/ FUNCTIONAL CRITERIA																		
Scale at maturity	5	■	■	■	■	■	■	■	■	■	■	■	■	■		■	■	
Structure of crown	2	■	■	■		■	■			■		■	■	■		■		
Density of foliage	5		■		■	■								■				
Growth rate	3	■	■	■			■	■	■	■							■	
Seasonal attributes	1	■	■		■	■	■	■		■	■			■				■
Relation to surroundings	1																	
Texture	1		■		■	■				■		■					■	■
Special properties	1					■								■				
CULTURAL CRITERIA																		
City tolerance	5		■	■	■	■	■					■	■	■	■			■
Hardiness	5	■		■	■	■	■	■	■	■	■			■				■
Local habit characteristics	4			■	■	■	■	■						■				■
Resistance to pests	3					■												
Salt tolerance	2		■			■	■	■			■	■	■	■		■		
OPERATIONAL CRITERIA																		
Client requirements	5	■	■	■	■	■		■	■	■		■	■	■			■	■
Transplanting limitations	3	■	■	■	■	■		■		■		■	■	■	■	■		■
Maintenance requirements	2	■	■	■	■	■	■		■	■		■		■			■	■
Cost of transplanting (size)	1																	
Availability in suitable size	5	■	■	■	■			■	■	■		■	■			■		
Experience factor*	10		■	■	■			■						■				■
Rating		31	42	51	49	60	31	50	25	31	20	32	35	58	22	13	20	36
Ranking of acceptable species		10	6	3	5	1	10	4	11	10	13	9	8	2	12	14	13	7

*Based on observation of trees growing in the immediate area that are healthy and have been growing for at least 25 years.

5-1 Selection critera for shade trees for an urban square in Philadelphia

Aesthetic criteria

Dimensions. The height and spread of a tree are of more concern to the landscape architect than any other visual characteristics in choosing a tree type. This scale requirement is immutably linked to human dimensions and space perception rather than to the size of a particular space. Large size trees like the Oak or Plane tree fulfill the function of connecting the human psyche to the immensity of the city. Small trees, including most flowering varieties, cannot achieve this scale transition. This point is generally not well understood. From the viewpoint of scale in design, no tree can be too large for use in public urban spaces. The structure and details of trees assure that they will make an effective transition between human scale and spaces larger than human perception can apprehend. Large trees have an extraordinary flexibility in complementing a range of spaces from the size of a small back yard to a regional park. In this sense, they have the property of a richly detailed architecture to transmute the visual perception of size.

The popularized concept that small trees are better for city streets began with a concern about tree maintenance. (Pirone) The ensuing campaign to eliminate large shade trees has proceeded with almost evangelical fervor. The tangible evidence of the movement's success is visible in the pathetic decorative fringe of low foliage that now lines many avenues and boulevards in American cities—a self-conscious tribute to misplaced zeal. Small tree thinking has influenced governmental studies that could have profound consequences for the future form of urban spaces. One of these studies recommends that no more large trees be planted on the streets of the nation's Capital. (Bartlett) The fault lies more with public agencies who commission tree surgeons to make city planning recommendations than with consultants who are asked to perform such studies. Since the greatest single value of urban trees is their aesthetic impact, the conduct of a street tree study is a logical task for a landscape architect or other designer trained and experienced in the overlapping disciplines of urban planting, engineering, and aesthetics. A rational assessment needs to be made of a city's spatial quality as it is affected by coordinated functional, visual, and operational demands. Tree pruning and utility locations are only two of several dozen specialized disciplines that must be considered.

Appropriate sized shade trees reach 45 to 60 feet in height even under adverse growing conditions. Mature urban trees often grow larger; however, they seldom reach the proportions of forest trees. Also a slower growth rate is to be anticipated. The mature heights mentioned in reference books on trees refer to optimum growing conditions. Both height and conditions are subject to great variation. Approximations are shown in Figure 5-2 for comparison useful in urban design. Not many tree types are likely to exceed four stories in height, even after growing for a long time under city growting conditions.

5-2

A second important distinction between small and large size trees is their branch height above the ground and the ratio of branch height to overall height. In most places, a visually comfortable branch height for walking underneath will be required. This implies a branch height from 8 to 15 feet. For street trees where vehicular traffic clearance is necessary, a minimum of 15 feet is required. It can be seen from the diagram that aesthetic proportion suggests a ratio of at least one to two and one-half between the branch height and the overall height. We can conclude then, that trees at least 40 feet tall are required for pedestrian areas. This establishes a criterion for large trees—trees that can be expected to reach 40 feet within 15 years after planting. It also explains why most ornamental and flowering trees do not meet the scale requirements for shade trees in cities.

5-3

While small (18 feet to 35 feet) trees have a limited place in urban design, they fulfill certain functions such as screening, and are often suitable as understory trees in parks to add texture and seasonal color. Because of their lower branching, they take up more ground space than full sized shade trees, and can only be used where they do not impede circulation or block important vistas. Where ornamental trees are used along streets and in public spaces, they tend to fill the space rather than shade it. It is almost axiomatic that large trees should be used in small urban spaces and that small trees should be used only in large spaces which will not become crowded by the low branching. They are usually best suited to groves or bands to avoid fragmenting the space with isolated objects.

EXPECTED HEIGHT IN FEET

Tree Species	Average Constriction	Severe Constriction	Growth Rate
LARGE SHADE TREES			
Tulip Tree	80	60	Fast
Japanese Larch	75	65	Fast
Willow Oak	70	55	Medium
London Plane	70	50	Fast
Ginkgo	65	55	Slow
Honeylocust	60	45–50	Fast
Red Oak	60	45	Medium
Pin Oak	60	45	Medium
Sugar Maple	60	45	Medium
Live Oak	60	50	Medium
Sweet Gum	55	45	Medium
Red Maple	55	45	Medium
Japanese Pagoda Tree	55	45	Medium
Spanish Oak	55	45	Medium
Norway Maple	50	40	Medium
Zelkova	50	40	Medium
Sargent Cherry	50	40	Medium
Sycamore Maple	50	40	Medium
Littleleaf Linden	45	35	Slow
Silver Linden	45	35	Slow
Bradford Pear	45	35	Fast
Camphor Tree	45	35	Slow
SMALL TREES			
Amur Cork	40	35	Fast
Brazilian Pepper Tree	40	35	Fast
Yellow Wood	40	30	Slow
Jacaranda	40	30	Fast
American Holly	35	25	Slow
Golden Rain Tree	30	25	Slow
Japanese Tree Lilac	30	25	Medium
Strawberry Tree	30	20	Slow
Washington Hawthorn	25	20	Medium
Russian Olive	25	20	Fast
Saucer Magnolia	25	20	Slow
Crape Myrtle	20	18	Medium

5-2 Comparative mature tree heights.

This partial list of city tolerant tree types shows *comparative* average mature heights of trees growing under conditions of urban stress. These are estimated approximations to serve as a general guide. The table does not reflect the differences in response of each species to specific stress factors. Rates of growth are relative, since there is a wide variation in the rate of growth of any particular species for different habitat conditions.

Average Constrictions: trees planted 20 feet apart in urban park lawn, receive an average of six hours of sunlight daily during the growing season, and have adequate water in all seasons.

Severe Constrictions: trees planted 20 feet apart along city street in pavement with adequate soil for root growth, average four hours of daily sunlight during growing season, and are watered during drought periods only.

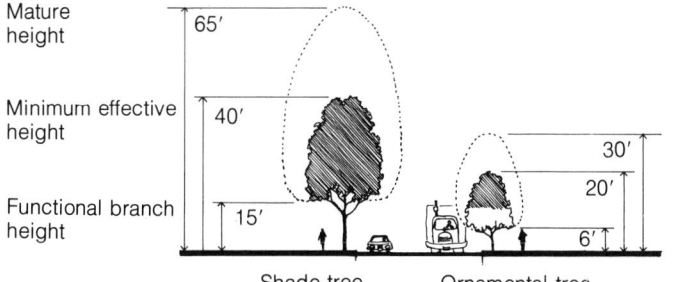

Mature height — 65'

Minimum effective height — 40'

Functional branch height — 15'

Mature height

Average height — 30' / 20'

Branch height at planting — 6'

Shade tree   Ornamental tree

5-3   Section: Branch extension of trees. Diagram shows why small ornamental tree types are functionally unsuitable for most urban uses. Low branches of flowering trees obstruct the visual space of the pedestrian.

5-4   Branch Structure: Ginkgo Tree. Philadelphia, Pennsylvania. 20 feet apart.

5-5   Branch Structure: Red Oak. Princeton, New Jersey. 15 feet apart.

Structure. Structural form of the species is next in importance for selecting the right tree type. In urban design, trees should be grown close enough together to form groves, arcades, and allées. For this reason, the branch structure of trees grown closer together is of critical aesthetic importance, not the open grown silhouette. These properties of trees can only be learned by on-site observation, since published illustrations have concentrated solely on the suburban or open grown tree form. However, observation of trees growing closely together reveals pronounced differences in branch structure among species. Even differences in local climate can effect the structural form of trees. Compare the branches of Plane trees growing in Deal, New Jersey (near the ocean) and in Princeton, 80 miles west.

5-4

5-5

5-6

The branch and twig structures of deciduous trees in winter are of concern to the designer.* In cool climates where the dormant form of the tree persists for five or six months of the year, it is as important visually as the tree in leaf. Close spacing is desirable because the visual mass of a tree is reduced in winter. In cool climates, close planting and structure are especially important because trees grow more slowly than they do in warm climates. Species selection will favor trees with a more emphatic branch structure and a more intricate twig structure.

* Photographs by Stephen V. Chelminski in *The Tree Identification Book* show the branch structure differences among tree types as mature individual specimens in winter. (Symonds)

5-7

One of the unheralded attributes of trees is their habit of projecting mosaics of light and shadow onto pavement. Unexpectedly, the cost difference between brick and asphalt paving can buy enough immediate tree cover to justify using the most disparaged material of urban civilization—asphalt paving—which, with trees, assumes the richness of a Spanish tile floor that changes with the seasons. Deciduous tree types having intricate twig structure lend themselves to this use and thereby cost nothing if installed to avoid expensive paving.

5-8

5-9

The Honeylocust, which is valued most in summer for its light shade, is least effective when not in leaf because of a naturally sparse branch structure. It is a tree that, when small, almost disappears in winter. The Horsechestnut, a tree used in many of the formal spaces in Paris, has one of the most effective winter forms, because of its thick twigs organized in a provocative symmetry. The Plane Tree in the north has a sculptural branch structure that is only rivaled by

5-10

5-11

Choice of type

5-6   Branch Structure: Plane Tree.
Deal, New Jersey. 20 feet apart.

5-7   Branch Structure: Horsechestnut.
Brooklyn, New York. 18 feet apart.

5-8   Shadow pattern on pavement in
winter.

5-9   Shadow pattern on pavement in
winter.

the southern Live Oak tree. Many trees do not develop an exceptional branch structure until they become older. The American Elm, the Sugar Maple, and the White Ash are examples of species that typically attain their extraordinary branching forms after they are 40 or 50 years old. On the other hand, tree types like the Pin Oak and the Sweet Gum attain their branch structure earlier, and enlarge more uniformly with age. The branch pattern of a species owes its form to the way that the twigs grow and divide. With Maple trees, the new buds arise on opposite sides of the twig, creating a tree whose symmetry reflects this uniformity. On Oaks and the majority of other species, except for Ash and Dogwood, the new leaf buds arise on alternate sides of the stem, resulting in a less uniform branching. This is just one of the infinite number of bold and subtle differences between trees of different species. Knowledge of these differences demonstrates why designers should prudently avoid the indiscriminate mixing of different species. The complexity of detail seen in the trees of one species provides adequate diversity for functional and aesthetic needs. Intermingling species on an urban site can lead to visual disharmony. Not all tree types are visually compatible.

The extraordinary differences in the way trees of various species branch is not conveyed by the work of most artists. Trees are stylized in drawings and paintings and tend to illustrate an idealized form that has more in common with the Plane Tree structure than, for instance, the Pin Oak, which by comparison has stiff, horizontal, crowded-looking branches. Some of the structural details and aesthetic differences in growth habit of common trees are discussed in *The Artistic Anatomy of Trees*. (Cole) To what extent this unconscious artistic bias has affected the work of designers is uncertain. Each designer has his own preference in tree species which is reflected in his work. Among urban designers probably the branch structure more than any other visual tree characteristic, except scale, influences preferences.

5-12
5-13
5-14
5-15
5-16
5-17

5-11 Branches and Twigs: Horsechestnut. Burlington, Vermont.

5-10 Branches and Twigs: Honeylocust. Philadelphia, Pennsylvania.

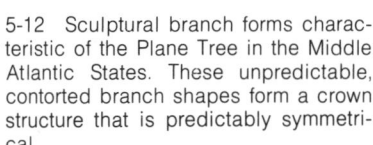

5-12 Sculptural branch forms characteristic of the Plane Tree in the Middle Atlantic States. These unpredictable, contorted branch shapes form a crown structure that is predictably symmetrical.

5-13 The Live Oak Tree growing in the south also exhibits remarkable sculptural branches that produce a uniform crown.

5-14 The American Elm is one of the tree types producing spindly, ratty saplings that many years later mature into handsome, well formed adult trees with arching branches.

5-17 The Sweet Gum begins as a symmetrical tree and maintains its symmetry and form to maturity, probably changing less than any other common temperate climate tree type.

5-15 The Sugar Maple Tree produces attractive young trees that develop exceptional branch forms after fifty years. (Photo by A. E. Bye)

5-16 The Pin Oak is a tree type that forms symmetrical young trees with branches that grow out almost at right angles to the trunk. As they mature the branches become pendulous, particularly among trees grown as individual specimens.

Density. The density or transparency of trees in leaf is the third critical factor for consideration in selecting tree type. The amount of light under the canopies of trees is a function of branch height, spacing, and, most importantly, tree type. The variations in shade densities among different species result from the arrangement of the leaves on the branches and leaf size. A study of forest tree geometry suggests two basic kinds of leaf arrangement, monolayer and multilayer. (Horn) In the former, most of the leaves in a single layer are distributed around the periphery of the crown, while in the latter the leaves are more uniformly distributed in layers throughout the crown. Trees with monolayered leaf arrangement tend to cast more dense shade.

Density and texture are often confused in discussing trees. The common observation that smaller leaved trees admit more light is not necessarily true. The Plane tree admits more light than the Japanese Pagoda Tree, even though the average leaflet size of the latter is 15 times smaller in surface area than that of the former. The Honeylocust tree, with leaves even smaller than the Japanese Pagoda tree, has the least dense crown of any shade tree grown in the temperate climate zones of the United States. Direct observation of trees growing under different conditions of spacing and habitat is the best way to learn about the differences in crown transparency and leaf shadow patterns among various species of trees. Figures 5-18 through 5-21 illustrate some of the many variations among trees in leaf.

5-19 Crown detail of trees in leaf. The Thornless Honeylocust has a fine texture and a very light crown density.

5-21 Crown detail of trees in leaf. The Olive Tree has a fine texture but a very dense crown.

In northern climates, there is very little choice in tree types with light crown densities. Most trees cast a dense shadow when in full leaf. The Honeylocust tree is unique to cooler climates of this country by producing a very open pattern of dappled shade and sunlight. The Larch and the Kentucky Coffee Tree are also very light shading, but have not been used extensively enough in the city to be sure of durability under severely constricting conditions. The Ginkgo and Plane Trees, when growing in city conditions, tend to be the next lightest shading of commonly used city trees in temperate climates. In the more tropical areas of the country, the Jacaranda and the California Pepper Tree match the Honeylocust in transparency. In the tropics, there are more species with foilage that produce light shade, such as the Madras Thorn tree and the Casuarina. The different species of Acacias, the Desert Willow, and the Palo Verde tree are among the many desert types of light shading trees that grow in the southwestern United States.

Because it is the only proven city tolerant, very light shading tree that grows well in northern climates, the Honeylocust is an indispensable and much-used species.* This poses a problem for the designer who is criticized for overplanting one species; however, there is simply no alternative in cities like New York and Philadelphia when an open crown type of tree is necessitated by the design configuration. Indeed, in most high density urban areas, natural light is so critical that a more dense shade can make trees a liability in tightly confined spaces.

5-20 Crown detail of trees in leaf. The Norway Maple has a medium texture and a dense crown.

5-18 Crown detail of trees in leaf. The London Plane has a medium texture and a moderate to light crown density.

5-19

* In recent years emasculated thornless varieties have almost replaced the species with its attractive but menacing two inch long triple branched thorns.

5-22 The Larch Tree shown here in a courtyard in Fredonia, New York is a deciduous conifer that casts light shade and has a very fine leaf texture.

5-24 The Madras Thorn growing in Singapore is one of many tropical species that casts light shade.

5-23 The Kentucky Coffee Tree shown here in a nursery casts moderately light shade and has a light texture.

5-25 The Casuarina which grows in southern Florida and in the tropics is fine textured and casts a moderate to light shade.

The Plane Tree is the second most useful tree type where dense shade needs to be avoided, but it does not resemble the Honeylocust in either texture or degree of transparency. Maples and Oaks tend to produce a more dense shade than our previous examples. The Norway Maple, in particular, which has been widely planted because of its city tolerance, casts a very dense shade that makes it difficult to grow grass or ground cover underneath. The Red Maple may be the least dense shading of the two genera, having a mature crown that is almost as open as the Plane Tree. Personal observation suggests that the Tulip Tree and the Sweet Gum tree are intermediate in shade density, while the Horsechestnut, Japanese Pagoda, Red Oak, and Willow Oak trees tend to produce very dense shade.

In an effort to make some comparison without establishing a strict classification, Figure 5-26 lists thirty species of city tolerant trees ranked in comparable order of shade density. This is only an approximate guide from personal observation, since trees vary greatly in density under differing site conditions. A multitude of variables such as pruning practices, tree spacing, daily duration of direct sunlight, and root growth conditions affect the foliage density of trees. Unfortunately for urban design, tree types that are more tolerant of shade tend also to cast more dense shade because of a leaf arrangement that intercepts more light. The shadiest site may be tolerated best by the most dense shading tree type.

Tree Species	Density	Tree Species	Density
Palo Verde	1	Tulip Tree	4
Horsetail Casuarina	1	Sweet Gum	4
Thornless Honeylocust	1	Dawn Redwood	4
Jacaranda	1	Pin Oak	4
Desert Willow	1	Modesto Ash	4
California Pepper Tree	1	Sugar Maple	4
		Red Oak	4
Larch	2		
Kentucky Coffee Tree	2	Japanese Pagoda Tree	5
Ginkgo	2	Littleleaf Linden	5
Amur Cork	2	Norway Maple	5
Yellowwood	2	Willow Oak	5
		Live Oak	5
Tree of Heaven	3	Chinese Elm	5
Bald Cypress	3	Sterile Mulberry	5
Camphor Tree	3	Indian Laurel	5
London Plane	3	American Holly	5
Red Maple	3	Southern Magnolia	5

5-26 Comparative crown density. Approximate comparative values of crown density listed in order from least dense to most dense crown, as estimated from personal observation of large trees in leaf, growing in urban areas.

Growth rate. Planting trees in cities now for their effect in 40 to 50 years is impractical because cities change so rapidly. It is even difficult to predict what a particular urban landscape will look like in ten years. Therefore the growth rate of different tree types is potentially an important design consideration. Most suitable northern climate types of city trees grow at about the same rate. Under city conditions, a growth rate between one and three feet per year is common for immature trees. There are important exceptions: the Honeylocust and Plane Trees are faster growers. The Ginkgo and the Japanese Pagoda Tree are significantly slower. All trees grow more slowly in urban habitats than in a suburban or rural environment. Trees generally grow faster in warmer climates because of the longer growing season. Pollutants, especially from dogs and from salt used in snow removal, retard the growth rate, even if the concentration is not great enough to kill the tree immediately. Some average comparative rates of growth are listed in Figure 5-2 for a number of species.

Before they are visually effective, trees planted 20 feet apart need to develop a branch spread of at least 16 feet. In the warmer climates, rapid growing species such as the Black Olive Tree in Florida and the Pepper Tree in California can be effective within five years after planting, even if they are less than 20 feet tall when planted. In northern cities a Red Maple might require ten years if planted when 18 feet tall, a London Plane Tree six years, and a Ginkgo 20 years to reach the same effective size.

These comparisons are based on estimated averages. Under urban conditions, there are so many variables that it is difficult to predict growth rates for different species. Usually, though, the relative growth rates of different tree types in identical habitats remain the same.

Other characteristics. Another aesthetic consideration in selecting tree type is the visual compatibility of different species. Observation of natural plant communities provides a helpful guide to aesthetically satisfactory tree combinations. There seems to be an unerring if inexplicable rightness about combinations of foliage that occur naturally in the forest. The difficulty in successfully combining tree types harmoniously is a strong reason to avoid indiscriminate mixing of different species. Different types of trees should be used together only where there is a clear aesthetic purpose. Nature's most striking examples of visual coherence are found in a pure stand of trees such as a whole forest of Aspens, a mountainside covered with only Beech trees, or a stand of Tulip Trees. The natu-

90

ral occurrences of pure stands of trees in North America are nearly as numerous as the mixed stands (i.e., associations of trees with more than one species).

There is great emphasis in horticultural literature on the importance of seasonal color and other plant details such as bark color. As a result, plant breeders place undue emphasis on detail. These attributes are important in selecting tree types for decorative effects in individual gardens. They rarely are relevant to the selection of trees for streets or public spaces. The criteria of scale, branch structure, and foliage density are nearly always decisive in selecting the most effective city tree. It is not that these more subtle characteristics are unimportant, but that they are necessarily subordinated to the larger spatial effects.

5-27 Tulip Tree: A pure stand. The occurrence of a single species of tree covering a large area is common in temperate climate forests. (Photo by A. E. Bye)

Cultural criteria

In evaluating trees, cultural constraints have been separated into two broad categories, namely regional and specific. The principal geographic determinants of plant distribution or range are climate and topography. Such factors are treated extensively in the literature on plants. They will be discussed here in relation to choosing a species for design.

Regional determinants. The *range* is the natural geographic area where a particular tree species grows. It is determined principally by climate. Plant ecologists have shown that for a given climate and geology, certain predictable species will dominate an undisturbed forest by a process referred to as plant succession. These discoveries demonstrate the importance of natural conditions in determining what trees grow best in a region. Even more interesting for the designer, they show how ordered and selective nature is in arranging and grouping species. Our inability to completely understand this complex natural order explains why we are unable to copy nature successfully with plants. Forests are not random arrangements.

Climate determines the range of a particular species, principally through temperature and rainfall. Temperature affects plant hardiness and limits the northern boundaries of a given tree species range by its ability to survive the cold weather. Rainfall separates trees adapted to wet or dry conditions. Together, they are the principal natural factors determining the climatic limits of natural growth for the species. The range limits for each species have been categorized in ten plant hardiness zones for the United States and Canada. These zones are shown on a map published by the U. S. Department of Agriculture which is reproduced in Figure 5-28.

5-28 Map: Plant hardiness zones. Source: U.S. Department of Agriculture. Approximate range of average annual minimum temperatures for each zone:

Zone 1 below   −50° F
Zone 2 −50° to −40°
Zone 3 −40° to −30°
Zone 4 −30° to −20°
Zone 5 −20° to −10°
Zone 6 −10° to   0°
Zone 7   0° to 10°
Zone 8   10° to 20°
Zone 9   20° to 30°
Zone 10 30° to 40°

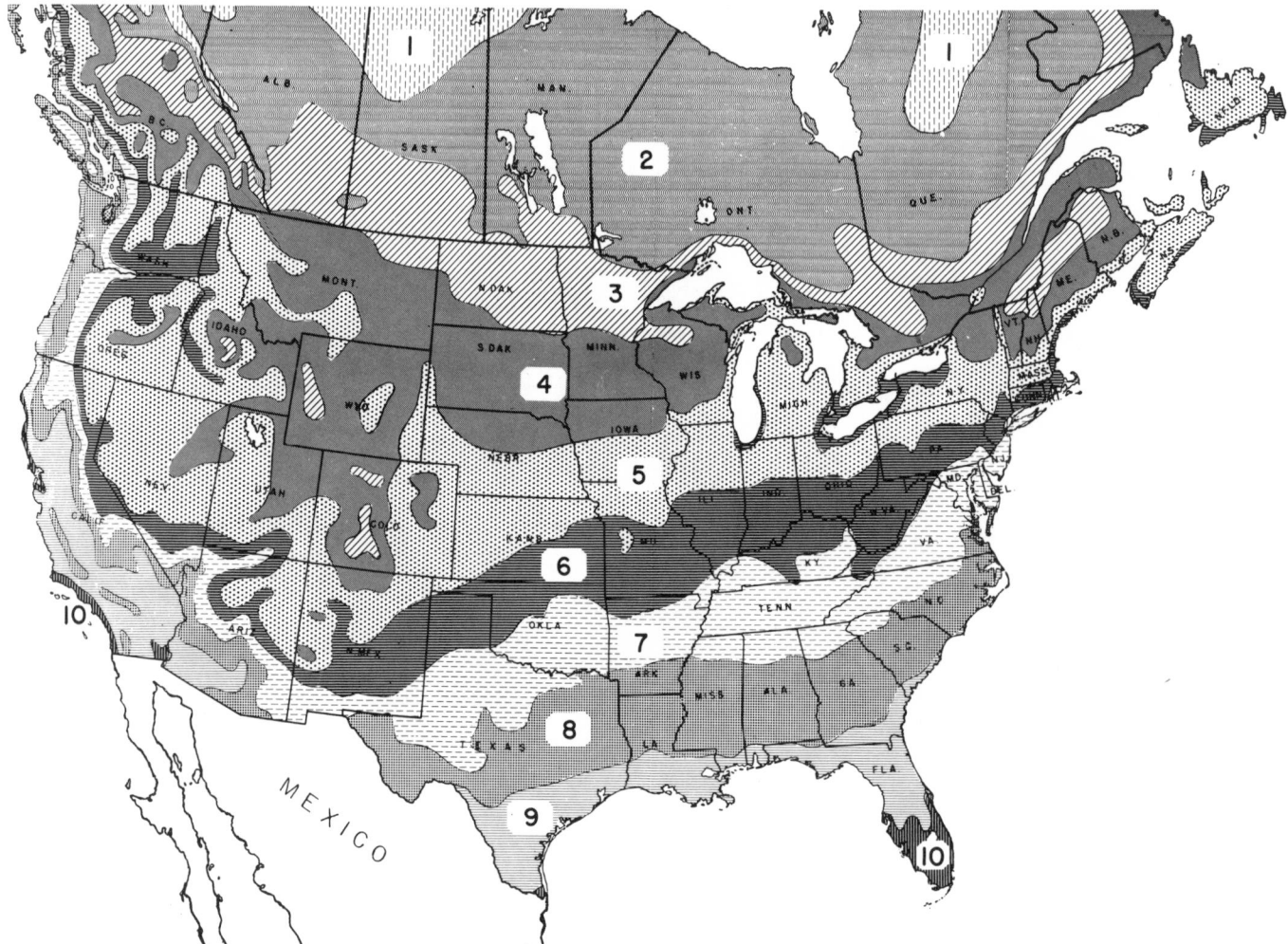

Topography affects range by its modification of climatic conditions and altitude. The elevation of ground above sea level affects what trees will grow on a particular site, generally restricting the number of species more severely as the altitude increases. Slope orientation affects the intensity of sunlight and wind, and in mountain regions influences the local climate. Distinct vegetation types are often found on the opposite sides of a mountain.

Soil type is the immediate natural factor affecting a tree's local distribution. In nature, plants are so selective about soil preference that agronomists can often identify the soil type of an area by observing what is growing there. On urban sites, we usually deal with artificial soils. In nature, a plant grows where the soil condition is right. In cities, soil can be formulated or adjusted to suit the tree type selected.

Plants that are indigenous to a particular area are regarded as "native" plants. They are purported to be better adapted to growing conditions of the region than introduced species. This notion is not supported by our knowledge of urban trees. There are many examples of introduced trees growing in our cities that have survived for well over a century and are among the healthiest trees growing there today. The native American Elm, planted extensively in cities, has been almost completely eliminated in the Northeast by disease. On the other hand, three of the best adapted city trees in the country are introduced species. The London Plane, the Norway Maple, and the Ginkgo are growing better than most indigenous species in urban areas of the northeastern United States. (Elias) From the evidence it appears that successfully introduced species of trees can do even better in some cases than native trees. However, it is best to use tree types that have been growing well under similar conditions in the same region for a significant number of years, regardless of their geographical origin.

Natural woodland diversity occurs on a broad scale and involves organisms that range in size from the submicroscopic to the largest forest tree. These living plants and animals form exceedingly intricate webs with many scales and textures that overlap and coexist. Only very large areas of undisturbed land can support this total diversity. For example, a regional park of 1000 acres may contain only a minor fraction of the possible organisms that inhabit a region. Very large size is an absolute prerequisite for a land area to approach optimum species diversity. Furthermore, there is a direct proportional relationship between size of the area of land and number of species of plants and animals that the land will support. (McArthur) To artificially increase the number of species of plants on a small land area would only temporarily increase the species diversity without increasing the natural stability. In time, if there is no further intervention, the land would revert to a smaller number of plant species. Observation of land that has undergone even low density suburban development shows a pronounced decline in plant species diversity.

Just as plant monocultures are necessary in the rural landscape for modern agriculture, so, too, they play a necessary part in the city to sustain trees and flowers. Agricultural "monoculture" denotes the practice of using land to grow only one type of crop. It is a tenent of modern farming which trades certain older customs for modern economic and human benefits. In the case of agriculture, the benefit is increased productivity through mechanized farm methods, and the price is susceptibility to pestilence and epidemics. Invidious application of the term monoculture to urban planting ignores the distinction between agrarian and urban habitats. Sustaining plants in cities is a highly sophisticated, artificial practice that relies on technology to an even greater extent than modern farming. Urban designs do not conform to the principle of wild plant communities with their diveristy and symbiotic interdependence.

Local determinants. On Urban sites, specific local determinants are subject to some control or modification. We can improve the soil, sometimes the air, and less frequently the amount of natural light. Growing requirements for trees commonly planted are documented in horticultural literature. The designer needs to try to understand the biological requirements as they are applied to city habitats.

Air provides one of the primary building materials for the process of photosynthesis: carbon, in the form of carbon dioxide. Though the atmosphere contains only .04 percent carbon dioxide, plants use this source of carbon to capture the sun's energy. Trees play a role in preserving an atmospheric balance of carbon dioxide. The loss of large areas of the earth's forests is a critical cause of the continuing increase in the carbon dioxide content of the atmosphere. (Woodwell) Though *urban* trees have a questionable role in maintaining this biospheric stability, there is general agreement about their local benefits in improving the air. (Grey) Moreover, the crucial question here is one of level of air quality. What level must be sustained to keep trees healthy? Studies have shown that trees are damaged by atmospheric pollutants common in cities. The most harmful of these appear to be ozone, sulfur dioxide, and hydrogen fluoride. Automobile exhausts account for a high percentage of the first two air pollutants. It is significant that the deleterious effects of automobile exhausts on human beings have been widely documented. One implication for trees is that we will have to rely on the most tolerant species for center city planting until the use of automobiles is curtailed. Local research should be consulted in addition to national and more generalized publications for lists of tolerant tree types. (Davis U.S. Department of Agriculture, Grey)

Water is one of the most critical requirements in growing trees in cities, even though it may be one of the easiest needs to satisfy from a purely technical standpoint. Ideally, the ground around the roots should be continuously moist but not saturated to a depth of about three feet. Tree roots also need air. Therefore, excess water should be able to drain away fast enough to prevent standing water from accumulating. Proper drainage is even more important than irrigation. Most trees have the natural ability to survive drought longer than they can tolerate saturated soil. Failure to deal effectively with this requirement when transplanting trees can often be attributed to the fallacy that tree types which grow naturally in wet areas, such as the Red Maple and Pin Oak, will grow when transplanted to poorly drained sites. The adaptability of certain tree species to wet sites results from their ability to develop a very shallow root system when grown from seedlings in wet soil. Trees with this type of root system are difficult to transplant. Nurseries do not grow trees on swampy sites and the trees that are grown on drier sites are not adapted to wet conditions. Therefore Red Maple or other swamp species are just as susceptible to drowning as any other species of tree when transplanted from a nursery to a poorly drained area.

Though less serious than over-watering, prolonged drought can kill trees, particularly within the first two years after transplanting. Trees in paved areas where little rain water can seep into the ground are especially susceptible unless provisions are made for irrigation. Since trees constantly transpire water when not dormant, principally through the leaf pores, the soil around the roots must retain enough capillary water to replace the transpiration loss. A large tree may use more than a barrel of water per day. Drought tolerance varies among species and is an important characteristic in determining a tree's ability to adapt to city conditions. Nursery catalogues sometimes list the trees that are drought tolerant and standard references on trees, like Wyman, contain information on susceptibility to and tolerance of drought. (Wyman, Kozlowski)

Soil for city tree planting should consist of a specially formulated mixture filling as large a root zone as is feasible. The soil quality requirements for different tree species in the same climatic zone do not differ appreciably for urban trees. The quantity of soil suitable for tree growth is usually more critical. For large trees, a four foot depth of prepared soil mixture is adequate, as most feeder roots are found in the upper soil layers. Raised planters less than ten feet square are too small to support large shade tree growth regardless of species. In smaller raised planters, temperature and moisture fluctuations seriously impair a tree's health. Therefore, the volume of soil suitable for tree growth is a critical determinant of tree type for a specific site. The soil quantity required is directly proportional to the mature size of the tree crown. In situations where smaller tree types like the Hawthorn or Flowering Cherry can be used, insulated raised planters with three feet of soil depth and at least 25 square feet of surface area per tree will suffice.

Soil drainage must be good to support any tree type that is transplanted from a dry site. Soil compaction is harmful to all trees because of the reduction of essential soil pore space that it entails; however, certain trees are especially sensitive. The Tulip Tree, Sugar Maple, and American Beech are particularly susceptible to harm from soil that becomes too dense. (Patterson) More detailed technical and visual constraints imposed by growing media and planter limitations are discussed and illustrated in Chapter 6.

Light, ever changing in intensity, is the sole source of energy for photosynthesis. From our experience, we know that trees grow fastest when they are fully exposed to direct sunlight all day. Yet a tree utilizes a maximum of 25 percent of the direct sunlight that falls on a leaf surface for full photosynthesis. In fact a leaf needs only two to three percent of full sunlight for its photosynthesis to balance its respiration. This explains why trees can grow in less than full sun. As light declines from optimum intensity, branching becomes more sparse and often the tree shape is distorted as the tree grows toward the light. This property of phototrophism is one of the adaptive responses that allows trees to survive and to adjust to adverse city conditions. The natural leaf arrangement of trees is an adaptation to light, reflecting the evolving forest position of different tree types. Tree species with leaves arranged in multiple layers throughout the crown such as the Aspen and the Silver Maple, tend to grow fastest in full sunlight because they expose more leaf surface to the sun. These trees tend to admit more light at ground level, have smaller leaves, and are less tolerant of shade. The single layer species, trees such as Sugar Maple and American Beech, tend to have greater shade tolerance in the forest and can grow up under the more open canopies of multilayer trees. These eventually become the climax species of the mature forest. (Horn)

The implications of leaf arrangements for city tolerance are not clear. The theory suggests favoring multilayer trees because of their less dense shade and their resistance to drought; however, monolayer trees might be more tolerant of urban shade conditions. Clearly trees adapt to different conditions of light, and certain species have natural adaptive advantages over other species in specific situations.

In evaluating different types of trees for shade tolerance, most references allude to natural understory tree types such as Dogwood. These are small trees, not suitable for shade tree use in cities. Research has not yet identified significant low light tolerances among large tree types. Experience suggests that monolayer types, such as the Norway Maple, grow better in shade; however, they have the disadvantage of creating the densest shade where it is least desired. For these reasons, there are no simple rules for selecting species for shaded sites. Furthermore, there are no desirable shade tree types which will dependably grow in locations that receive less than three hours of direct sunlight daily during the growing season.

Physical damage to city trees is common from salt, dog emissions, bark wounds, branches broken by vehicles, and wind. Certain species are more resistant to salt. These are generally the tree types that grow in seashore locations and have developed salt tolerance naturally. A number of references classify trees according to salt tolerance. (Wyman, Dirr, Grey) Where salt is used excessively, even the more tolerant species will be stunted or killed. Cheap and harmless alternative chemicals for snow removal have not been found.

Some tree types such as the American Linden and Silver Maples have brittle branches, even though they are otherwise adapted to urban growth conditions. Most literature on trees makes some mention of these species, which have fallen into disrepute and are infrequently planted because of their susceptibility to storm damage. (Wyman)

The cumulative effect of injurious conditions for plant growth in large modern cities is such that only a small number of desirable shade tree species will survive in temperate climate inner city areas. (Elias and Irwin) Cities in the northeastern United States will support fewer than six different types of large shade trees from over 40 species native to the region. There are perhaps ten other species normally classified as suitable city trees for this region that must be excluded because of aesthetic limitations. These nominally acceptable trees are limited in their design use by such characteristics as slow growth (e.g., Ginkgo) or poorly adaptable form (e.g., Boxelder Maple). There are, in addition to the basic species and older varieties, a number of promising new cultivars. These have not yet withstood the test of long term durability. For now, it is best to rely on the few dependable city tree types when making major investments in urban trees.

Operations and tree type

Transplanting and availability. White Oaks and Sassafras might make good city trees but they are not available in large sizes and quantities in nurseries because of their limited tolerance for transplanting. For species not difficult to transplant, availability and planting season are our principal concerns. Cost and size relationships are discussed in Chapter 4. The commercial supply of a large quantity of one tree species declines sharply when the size is greater than four to five inches in caliper. It is usually possible to find ten trees of any common species up to ten inches in caliper. However, to find 50 or 100 trees of the same kind in a six to eight inch caliper range in commercial nurseries is often difficult or impossible. Figure 5-29 describes this supply problem for Red Maple trees in 1975. Most other tree types are even less numerous. On large planting projects it may be necessary to transport trees from distant nurseries because the species is not available locally in the required quantity and size. When trees can be ordered a year or more in advance for a specific project, there is an increased chance of availability in larger sizes.

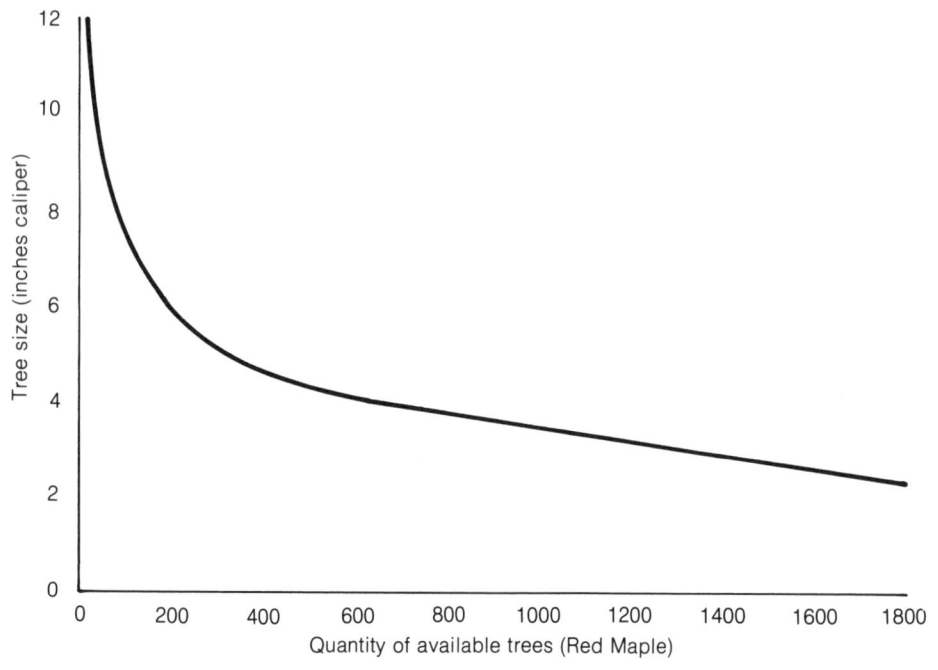

5-29 Graph of availability by size category of Red Maple. 1975. The nursery supply of any tree type normally declines with increased size as shown here for a common but perennially scarce species, Red Maple. The relatively small size of trees of any type over 4 inches in caliper reflects the high annual cost of raising trees and an undependable market for larger caliper trees. Source: Survey of 50 large nurseries in the eastern United States by Arnold Associates.

The most inflexible of all operational constraints is the availability of large quantities of a single tree type. Many good urban tree types are not produced by nurseries in large enough quantity and size to fill the needs of a large project. The pressure to grow diverse forms and varieties of trees has not helped this situation. The productive capacity of suppliers is being spread over a wide range of types rather than being concentrated among the tree types that are in greatest demand.

In the northeast some species such as the Red Oak and Tulip Tree are difficult to move successfully in the fall. When fall planting is mandatory, it could eliminate these harder to transplant species from consideration. In northern climates, early spring is the best time to plant shade trees; however, Plane Trees, Honeylocusts, Lindens, and Maples can safely be moved in the fall. Information about many practical constraints in transplanting can be obtained from local sources, especially contracting firms, nurseries, colleges, and arboretums. The local County Agent, the State or District Forester, and local shade tree commissions are good sources of information on transplanting trees. See *Trees, The Yearbook of Agriculture,* 1949, for the names and locations of state forest agencies. (U.S. Department of Agriculture)

Site use. Use of the site, particularly future access requirements, might effect species selection. Wherever trees are planted along streets, drives, or emergency and service access lanes, they must be high enough branched when planted to permit trucks to pass underneath. For trash compactor trucks, this can require 15 feet of vertical clearance at the center of the truck lane. Large and high-branched trees may be difficult to obtain and thus will limit the choice of species to one that is available with these characteristics.

Intensively used paved areas under trees may preclude the planting of tree types such as the Horsechestnut or Sweet Gum that drop large seed pods. There is however no justification for simply eliminating such species of trees from city planting. There are places where their special characteristics far outweigh the inconvenience of removing the organic litter. Referring to these trees as *dirty trees* is a curious attitude in a society that tolerates garbage and animal wastes strewn over public streets and parks.

The additional benefits of our maligned tree types—those that drop seed pods and fruits—have been discovered by children while playing. The red and black seeds of the Saga tree in Singapore are collected and treasured by children who

5-30

5-30 Horsechestnut as a street tree. This species bears large nuts that are attractive and provide a unique organic toy. Unusual games can be played with these shiny hemispheres.

string them to make necklaces and bracelets. The seeds of the Horsechestnut and Kentucky Coffee Trees are collected by children in this country to use in games. Catalpa Tree seed pods and Beech nuts are among the numerous tree types that provide a wealth of useful organic litter. The benefits of utilizing these tree types in playgrounds has been largely overlooked, perhaps as a result of their undeserved bad reputation. In this energy-conscious age, we would benefit from an examination of games played with natural materials and avoid those made of petroleum-based plastics.

Management. Tree *management* implies a more extensive nuturing program than tree "maintenance." In addition to the usual remedial operations (like removing dead limbs), it would also include the replacement of dead trees, regular inspection of trees for infestations and damage, and practices such as selective removal of trees planted at very close spacing to produce an immediate effect. These operations are discussed in Chapter 6. Available local care and training programs might affect species selection. If, for instance, there will be no provision for watering after the tree is initially established, drought tolerant species should be given preference. (Kozlowski)

If tree management includes formally clipped trees in special areas, that choice would affect species selection. Many maintenance guidelines cited in the literature on species selection are not cogent. They have been popularized by the spurious notion of "maintenance free" trees. All trees require maintenance for optimum appearance. There is relatively little predictable difference in maintenance needs among different desirable shade tree types under most normal city growing conditions. The American Elm tree is the one notable exception, requiring frequent sprayings for protection from a number of predators. Trees prone to insect pests requiring regular spraying are often expensive to maintain. However, all city shade trees have predators, and the few that are rarely damaged by insects, such as the Ginkgo, do not fill most design needs. Among the aesthetically desirable large shade tree species there is no way to predict pest infestation because it varies from year to year, and place to place, among trees of the same species. For several years in parts of the northeastern United States mimosa web-worm infestations of Honeylocust trees were wide spread and severe. In most places, probably as a result of control measures and an unusually cold winter, they are not a problem now. When the infestation was wide-spread, there was a strong sentiment against planting Honeylocust trees. There have been similar experiences with most species of useful shade tree and it is possible that we will see these problems arise again. The usual recommendation is to plant a mixture of species in case an epidemic develops. This is a poor solution because it merely scatters potential host trees, making pest control more costly.

Trees growing in cities today survive virtually without maintenance. They would be healthier and more attractive if better maintained. Maintenance needs are often exaggerated when discussing new tree planting in most cities because of an inflated notion of maintenance cost, even though actual expenditures for tree maintenance are almost nil.

These are the principal criteria that bear upon selecting a tree type for a particular design use. It should be apparent that the process is not arbitrary. There is need for informed judgment, but often not much latitude for artistic license in choosing a species. The relatively few types of trees that are growing in most cities reflect these practical cultural constraints. Trees that have been successful historically are still usually the best choice for any extensive new planting. As a practical matter experimentation with other species and new varieties will be limited to smaller, pilot projects. Experimentation and scientific inquiry are necessary and together they temper expensive risks with experience gained over long periods. There are a number of organizations carrying on government-sponsored projects involving research on new varieties of trees. (Santamour, Elias, Chapin)

Examples of trees and sites

The plane tree. Ancient tree species, like the Ginkgo and Dawn Redwood, which have been growing for millions of years still inhabit the modern world. Other species, known from fossil remains, have become extinct. In our century the American Chestnut has disappeared as a result of disease. The extraordinary differences in longevity of these tree types demonstrate that species resist pestilence with varying success. The Plane Tree has a lengthy history as a successful city tree. There are three very similar members of the same genus, *Platanus*, that grow in the United States and several smaller species that are native in the west. The two most commonly planted are the London Plane and the American Plane (Sycamore). The London Plane, a hybrid, is favored because of greater disease resistance. Because the trees are so similar in appearance and usefulness, the generic term, Plane Tree, will be used in discussing the two principally planted species without making a distinction. It is worth noting that the Sycamore is hardy further north than the London Plane and is therefore safer to plant in most parts of plant zone 5 (see Plant Hardiness Zone Map, Fig. 5-28). The London Plane (*Platanus acerifolia*) is propagated and planted in urban areas in greater quantity than any other species in the United States, and with good cause. Within the extensive range of this species, in the eastern part of the United States from New York City southward (excluding southern Florida), there is no large scale shade tree that grows as well under as wide a range of city conditions.

5-28

The Plane Tree, like every other city tree including the Ginkgo, has some predators. The most common of these is a fungus that causes the leaves to drop off prematurely. Referred to as Anthracnose or Blight, this disease attacks the Sycamore tree. Anthracnose does not kill the tree but can impair its vigor. The London Plane tree is less susceptible. The widely propagated Bloodgood strain of the London Plane is a highly resistant variant. A more threatening disease called Canker Stain has caused many London Plane trees to die. (Pirone) Sycamore trees seem to be resistant or only mildly susceptible. Since the disease is transmitted most often by pruning tools and requires an injury to gain access to the tree trunk, it is subject to preventative control measures. The Canker Stain disease has not reached epidemic proportions, although Philadelphia suffered serious losses at one time and Washington, D.C. is experiencing losses of London Plane trees in the southwest part of the city.

Concern about over-planting the Plane Tree results from our experience with Dutch Elm disease and the danger that some new predator will appear and wipe out all of the Planes. The American Elm tree, which appears to be on its way to extinction because of disease, was planted in cities for less than 200 years before the Dutch Elm disease became a problem.* It was always a less vigorous city tree than the Plane Tree, with a much shorter natural life span. While the Elm seldom exceeded 150 years in age, Plane Trees (Sycamores) grow to be 500 to 600 years old. (Johnson) Further, they have been planted in cities since ancient times. Historically, the Plane Tree has a better record than any other urban tree including Oak trees, which often live longer than 1000 years in forest conditions but do not equal the Plane Tree for city longevity and vigorous growth.

The Plane Tree is an ecological anomaly. Based on its natural occurrence in flood plains, it could be expected to grow very poorly on droughty urban sites. Yet it is more tolerant of these adverse conditions than almost every upland species. One cannot always predict how a tree will grow in the city on the basis of its natural ecological occurrence. Botanists do not seem able to offer a plausible explanation for the Plane Tree's drought tolerance.

* The extinction of the American Elm tree may be averted if a variety resistant to the Dutch Elm disease is found. Thus far most substitute trees, such as the Groenveldt Elm and the Zelkova, do not match the American Elm in habit and stature. The most promising development in recent years is a strain of American Elm discoverd and propagated by Princeton Nurseries named the Dedfree Elm. The parent tree exhibits the typical graceful form and stature of the much admired species. Even if a successful resistant cultivar is confirmed, it would be safe to avoid extensive planting under intensive urban conditions until the tree has had a longer test period. Elms are subject to leaf beetles and other predators that make them more expensive to maintain than other city trees.

In addition to its resilience and durability, the Plane Tree has admirable aesthetic properties for use as a city shade tree. The most important of these are:

Choice of type

1. The strong, symmetrical branch structure is consistently varied in details, yet forms a regular crown. The open branching habit is adaptable to any spacing, becoming horizontal and spreading when the trees are far apart, and vertical and ascending when the trees are planted close together. 5-31, 5-32

2. The Plane Tree grows more rapidly than other suitable city shade trees in northern climates except the Honeylocust, and reaches majestic proportions needed to complement the scale of most urban places. Unlike many other species, even the young tree has admirable proportions. It attains a decent mature size even under difficult city growing conditions. 5-33, 5-34

3. In leaf, under partially shaded conditions, the crown is open enough to admit light. This is important where buildings block light and dense shade is undesirable. 5-35

4. The changes of color and texture occurring throughout the year are unrivaled in diversity by any other species. The seasonal drama and textural interest of this tree are often overlooked because it is less blatant in fall color than many other species which lack the Plane Tree's more subtle variety. The mottled bark of the trunk and branches, the foliage texture, and the twig pattern add aesthetic dimensions to this unique tree. 5-36

5-31 London Plane with wide spacing between trees develops a more horizontal branch configuration than closely spaced trees.

5-33 London Plane Trees develop a symmetrical crown shape even though the branches are irregular and at times erratic. Unlike some species, the young trees are well formed.

5-32 London Plane growing in closely spaced rows develops ascending branches. Under any condition of spacing these trees exhibit sculptural and sometimes weirdly contorted branch shapes.

5-34 London Plane. The tenacity of this tree for growing in difficult city surroundings is unmatched except by the Tree of Heaven.

5-35 London Plane. A crown structure and leaf arrangement that diffuse sunlight are characteristic of this tree type particularly when grown closely enough together to develop a high branched open centered crown as shown here where trees are 18 to 20 feet apart.

5-36 London Plane. Even in winter the tree form is strong enough to provide a sense of enclosure.

An assessment of the risks attendant on planting any city tree suggests the use of the Plane Tree should not be drastically curtailed as some arborists have advised. In view of the tree's overwhelming attributes as a city tree, its known longevity and history in cities, it ranks as one of the most durable of all the urban trees known to man. There is little logic in planting only less vigorous, alternate species as assurance against pestilence. Certainly other trees should be planted, but in a coherent way that does not rob the city of unity and continuity. In an insurance conscious society, it is very easy to compromise away a primary aesthetic gain for some promise of perpetuity. This is being done in modern cities where the dramatic unity of a single species planted in an allée or grove is forfeited by mixing diverse tree types that destroy visual harmony. The use of one species for each visually or functionally discrete site condition is a cardinal principle of effective design. The species that are referred to generically as Plane Trees are ideally suited to such homogeneous planting.

Odd tree types. There are columnar or dwarf varieties of many tree species that will grow in city conditions. These special diminutive forms have been adequately emphasized in books and trade publications. Occasionally these odd tree forms are useful in meeting design requirements in special circumstances. Most urban circumstances require large spreading crown trees that will create the needed volume of foliage. They adjust to a space as they grow. Many of the smaller trees propagated by grafting are slower growing, and cost more per tree, in addition to requiring closer spacing and hence, a greater number of trees.

Where narrow trees are required for design effect, the Lombardy Poplar is an exceptional tree type. It has been used in multiple rows to create striking displays of spatial geometry. The Fredonia campus of New York State University has a circular entry road one mile in circumference defined by a double row of Lombardy Poplar trees planted in 1967 following a landscape plan by Dan Kiley. The trees are planted eight feet apart in each row and are reinforced by a third row of Columnar Maple trees, that may in 40 years, grow as tall as the Lombardy Poplars did in eight years. In southern climates, this species is subject to disease, however, the Theves strain of Lombardy Poplar survives and grows well from Philadelphia northward in the eastern United States. Though the Lombardy Poplar is unrivaled for rate of growth and compact narrow form, the tree is disliked by some because of its vigorous root system to which the tree owes its astonishing growth rate. Alternatives to the Lombardy Poplar may be found among a number of Columnar varieties of Maple. Because of the disparity in growth rates, however, a Columnar Maple tree costing three times as much as the Poplar will not be as tall five years after planting. The Poplars are among the trees more tolerant of city conditions, except where air pollution levels are high.

5-37

5-37 Lombardy Poplar. Fredonia, New York. A double row of columnar trees that are planted in a circle with a one-mile circumference. These 40-foot trees were 12 feet tall when planted 8 years earlier. (Photo by Joe Karr)

102

During this century, many new varieties and clones of trees have been developed and propagated. At present, considerable research is directed toward selection of new cultivars. Some of these efforts are specifically aimed at producing more city tolerant tree varieties. From the hundreds of new tree types developed to date, two have made a pronounced positive impact on urban public spaces, namely the Thornless Honeylocust varieties and the Bloodgood strain of the London Plane Tree.* Extensive planting of this Plane Tree strain and the numerous Honeylocust cultivars in northeastern cities of the United States have greatly enhanced many urban areas. However, the widespread use of clones poses another environmental danger, the loss of genetic diversity that is characteristic of sexually propagated species. (Santamour) If a clone becomes susceptible to a pest or disease, there is a greater likelihood of an epidemic because all of the clones will be equally susceptible. The subtle differences among members of the same species grown from seed offer the chance that some of the trees will be less susceptible to any particular disease. In many urban circumstances, the minor changes in aesthetic characteristics of seedling grown trees is more desirable than the greater visual uniformity of an army of clones.

Appropriate use: examples. The following examples of urban tree plantings illustrate the successful use of different tree species: they are models of correct choice of tree type.

In New York City, two small parks exemplify the value of using a single kind of shade tree and the importance of this choice to the quality of the space. Paley Park in Manhattan, designed by the firm of Zion and Breen, is only 100 by 40 feet in size and contains 12 Thornless Honeylocust trees. Five more of the same species are in the sidewalk adjacent to the park. This exquisite little park is a model of restraint in its selection of materials, including the trees. The pattern of dappled sunlight that is mirrored in the sparkling waterfall backdrop could only have been achieved with Honeylocust in New York's climate. Here the designer resisted the temptation to use a different species of trees along the street, a circumstance that adds unity and breadth to the design.

* There are at least six good green-leaved varieties of Thornless Honeylocust that are patented and propagated by nurseries. The Bloodgood strain of the London Plane Tree is resistant to Anthracnose, a leaf disease common to all of the Plane Tree species. The introduction of this strain has removed a frequent objection to urban planting of Plane Trees.

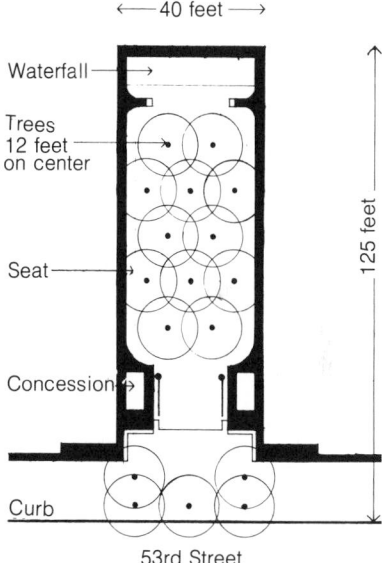

5-38 Plan: Paley Park. New York. An extraordinary small urban space providing shade, filtered light and canopy with Honeylocust Trees. Any other city tolerant species would make too much shade when in leaf. The quality of the space depends on the light patterns that cascade between falling water and lacy foliage. Trees are spaced on a 12 foot staggered grid.

5-39 Paley Park. New York. Thornless Honeylocust.

5-40

Cadman Plaza Park, in Brooklyn, designed by Clarke and Rapuano in 1950 consists of about 12 acres with four rows of Plane Trees bordering both sides of the park parallel with the main axis. There were 336 London Plane trees, three to three and one-half inches in caliper when planted. About 80 existing Plane Trees, ranging from 8 to 12 inches in caliper were transplanted north of the War

Memorial Building at the same time. The eight rows south of the W   Memorial Building are spaced 20 feet apart in both directions. An additional row of Plane Trees not shown in the plan has been planted near the curb along Washington Street at 30 foot intervals. This example of classical restraint in the arrangement of trees is reinforced by the use of one very appropriate species, the London Plane tree. Not only is it a superb complement to the space in texture and scale, but the form of the branch structure is strong enough to define a space within a larger space. Making the correct choice of species in a cultural sense is substantiated by a group of Pin Oak trees surviving at one end of the park, but growing poorly despite their known city tolerance. The smaller Plane Trees in Cadman Plaza Park, planted about 25 years ago, have grown from a three inch caliper to their present eleven inch average diameter.

5-40 Plan: Cadman Plaza Park. Brooklyn. This 12 acre park demonstrates a rhythmically organized grove of trees that defines space with clarity and elegance. It is a park that is designed as part of the city rather than as an escape from the city, and as such, makes the city richer.

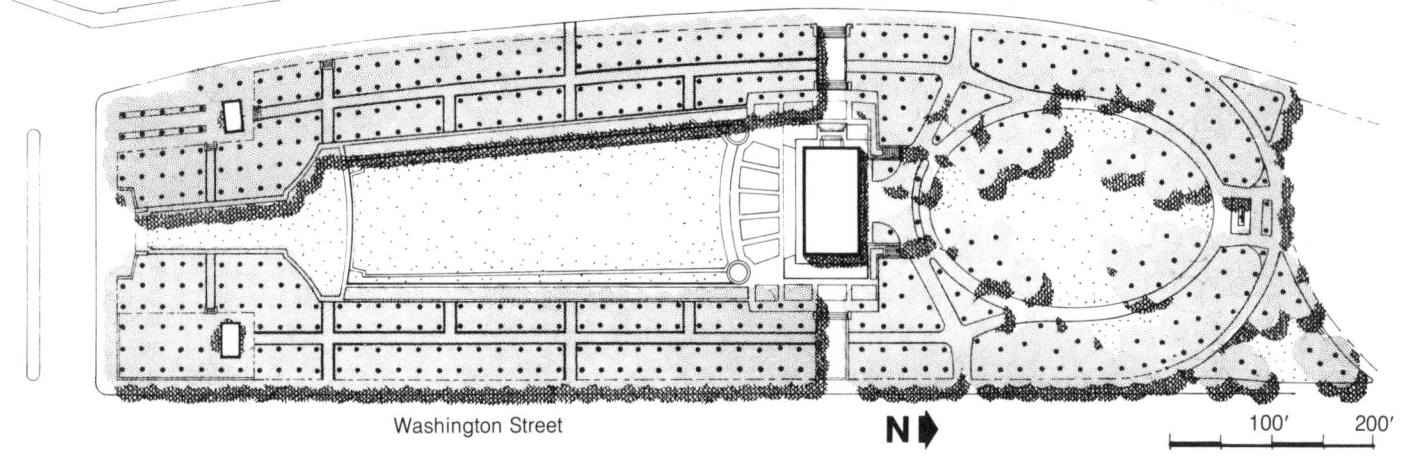

Washington Street

100'   200'

5-41 Cadman Plaza Park. Brooklyn. West edge. London Plane Trees are planted on a 20 foot square grid and averaged 11 inches in diameter in 1977.

5-42 Cadman Plaza Park. Brooklyn. East Edge. London Plane.

5-43 Cadman Plaza Park. Brooklyn. View of the central area looking south shows how trees define space horizontally in the center and vertically with a canopy of branches at the edges. Low wart-like plantings mar the internal open space providing the only flaw in an elegant design.

Near Chicago in the Oak Park Center Mall, Pin Oak trees are used very successfully to create one of the few handsome pedestrian mall spaces in the country. The landscape design is by Joe Karr. Pin Oak trees are usually thought of as specimen trees, used individually. In this example the choice of species reinforces a uniquely attractive pedestrian urban space. The aggregated use of trees and design clarity makes a virtue of the Pin Oak's horizontal branch habit. Trees are used in a manner that gives unity and strength to the entire space.

5-44

Along the Chicago River, a pedestrian promenade, also designed by Joe Karr, makes appropriate use of a tree type, Redmond Linden, that is not often well exploited in urban planning. While these are dense shading trees when in leaf, the strong form of the crown is a visual requirement in this location where there is only room to plant one row of trees. Because the site is very exposed, the

5-45

5-44 Oak Park Center Mall. Oak Park, Illinois. One of the few commercial mall spaces in the United States where trees dominate the fancy outdoor furniture. These trees have been in place for only 2 years. Ten years from now this superb space will be a showplace of urban design since trees have been planted with adequate soil for proper growth. (Photo by Joe Karr)

105

dense shade is welcome in summer and the branches make a pleasing pattern in winter.

In Houston, Texas, the Live Oak trees around the President's House at Rice University, and in double rows along the adjoining Main Street are welcome in this climate for their dense shade. They create a delightful arcade vaulted with sculptural branches. The Live Oak's ability to withstand Houston's heavy volume of automobile traffic is evidence of the cultural suitability of this tree type in this location.

5-46

5-47
5-48

5-45 Oak Park Center Mall. Oak Park, Illinois. Pin Oak. (Photo by Joe Karr)

5-47 Live Oak. Houston, Texas. Rice University.

5-48 Live Oak. Houston, Texas. Main Street.

5-49 Red Oak. Boston, Massachusetts. The Arbor Way.

5-46 Chicago River Park. Chicago, Il-linois. Redmond Linden. (Photo by Joe Karr)

The Arbor Way in Boston represents a good example of Red Oak tree use. These trees, though spaced 50 feet apart, are visually effective because they are nearly 100 years old and there are six rows of trees within the right-of-way. While the Plane Tree (Sycamore) used along Memorial Drive in Cambridge might have been as suitable a species, once the Oak trees reached effective size, they had the advantage of uniqueness over the Plane Tree, which has been used in many other places.

In Cleveland, the Public Mall utilizes Plane Trees (Sycamores) as the domi-nant tree type and Honeylocust trees (thornless variety) in small groups at each entry. The regular symmetrical design over a parking structure has a partially raised section for tree planting on each side. The Plane Tree is an appropriate

5-49

107

choice both for its scale and for its ability to grow here in limited soil depth. The unfortunate location of broad garage vent structures detracts visually from their placement and interrupts the ground plane. The clarity of trees growing directly out of the ground plane is lost in perspective.

Small symmetrical groves of Honeylocusts are located at gateways at each end of the mall. Because this is a distinctly different function—entry as opposed to major space definition—the use of a different species such as the Honeylocust is reasonable. These entry plantings are a weak aspect of the design, not because of the kind of trees that were used but because they are too small in height and breadth to make a visually convincing entry to such a grand space. The double row of Plane Trees in front of the office building across the street improves the context for the park. The success of the overall design would be compromised by the incorporation of any additional species and there is no sound "ecological" argument for using more species in an area of this size and shape. The Plane Trees make a rich, coherent statement that justifies the scale of the space.

Fairmont Park in Philadelphia, one of the longest city parks in the world, has a consistent unity that owes more to the Plane Trees than any other feature. The East River Drive through Fairmont Park is one of the few highways ever built that, owing to sensitive siting is an enjoyable experience from an au-

5-50

5-50 Sycamore. Cleveland, Ohio. The Public Mall on a rainy day.
5-51 Sycamore. Cleveland, Ohio. The Public Mall. An unfortunate visual intrusion of garage exhaust vents weakens the green arcade.

5-52 Sycamore. Cleveland, Ohio. Trees opposite the Public Mall.

tomobile. While the quality of this experience is threatened by over-planting along the river with small scale flowering trees, the structural frame of Plane Trees is still impressive. There is no better choice of tree type for tying together the man-made parts of this impressive park system. Indeed it is one of the best examples of the Plane's aesthetic contribution in this country. The regular lines of Plane Trees beginning at Penn Center, on through the Parkway to the Art Museum where they join the curving lines along the Schuylkill River make a perfect transition between the formality of center city and the meandering river-side park.

5-53
5-54

5-54 East River Drive. Philadelphia, Pennsylvania. Plane Tree. (Photo by A. E. Bye)

   The examples of smaller city parks owe their unique quality to the restrained selection of a single species of large shade tree. The coherence that such uncomplicated use of trees lends to discrete precincts of the city can easily be overlooked. If, however, we are dealing with larger areas of the city, some deference can be made to the principle of regional diversity, even though visual unity still demands consistency and restraint in the number of different tree types employed. It is satisfying to be in a city where repetitive use of a single species gives a sense of place, especially since architecture no longer does this. When contemporary notions about applying woodland diversity to the city give way to

109

deeper understanding, we may enjoy cities with an aesthetic integrity created by a single tree type linking the major street network.

Clarity can also be achieved on a city-wide basis through a pattern of different tree types that recognizes differences in geometry, orientation, light, and function. For example, there could be a city-wide system that employed several particular species in discrete ways. East-west streets might have Red Oak trees on the north side where the sun is more intense and Ginkgo trees along the more shaded south side. Small, open spaces could use Honeylocust trees to avoid over-shading. North-south streets would use Plane Trees on both sides reflecting the symmetrical light conditions. Columnar trees would line narrow pedestrian links, forecourts to public buildings might use Red Maple trees, and so forth. In this way a limited number of species would express different urban functions the way building facades can express the function of a building and thereby lend coherence and meaning to a city.

5-53 Benjamin Franklin Parkway. Philadelphia, Pennsylvania. Plane Tree.

Central Park trees. Within a large city park, function can dictate different tree and plant types. Central Park's scale can accommodate diversity in trees, not for ecological reasons, but as a visual response to variations in the urban habitat. In a park perhaps more than in any other *work of art,* the parts must merge into an expression of harmony. The design of a large city park represents a rare historic opportunity to compose a landscape that can inspire and delight millions of people. It is a challenge with greater potential for influencing human lives than the creation of a masterpiece on canvas or the achievement of a skyscraper. Central Park, despite considerable engineering innovations, never achieved this artistic potential.

It is improbable that a pastoral landscape could satisfy the symbolic or functional needs of a modern city. However, even within the romantic style a harmony could have been achieved in the choice and disposition of tree types. Central Park is a pervasive, uneven composition that speaks neither as nature nor as art. The trees in all of their splendor do not fit together either as forest or bosque. There appears to be no theme, subtle order, or restraint in the way that tree types are mixed together and spread out on the landscape.

When Central Park was designed, there was less understanding than exists now of the complexity of natural plant communities and their relation to their habitat. The combinations of tree species that Olmsted used do not reflect an attempt at duplicating native American plant associations. There does not seem to

110

be either an aesthetic theory or a design principle that explains why so many diverse and aesthetically divergent species were used. The earliest plantings included a mixture of native and introduced species such as Hemlock, Black Spruce, Norway Spruce, European Larch, American Arborvitae, and Scotch Pine. Mountain Ash, Sweet Gum, Dogwood, Weeping Willow, Oaks, Horsechestnut, Silver Poplar, Beech, Elms, and Lombardy Poplar were among the many deciduous species that were initially specified and planted. (Olmstead) To compose a serene landscape with this mixture of diverse tree types poses a design problem that is difficult—perhaps impossible—to resolve.

A look at the forest cover types identified by the Society of American Foresters shows little resemblance between Central Park tree plantings and native *forest types* for the region. (Society of American Foresters) If these were to be "native American" plantings, one would expect a composition similar to these forest types even though the proportions might vary. Conspicuously absent in Central Park are the "pure stands"* of trees which make up such a visually important part of our forest scenery.

Descriptions of the trees that were initially planted include many more tree types than mentioned here and a vast assortment of shrubs. (Olmsted) In 1900, Louis Peet identified over 180 different species and varieties of trees in Central Park. (Peet) Even with this number of different tree types, it might be possible to limit certain areas of the park, to vary diverse plantings and to link the entire park thematically with a small number of dominant tree types. This was not done, as anyone who walks through the entire park can perceive. In a 45 acre section of the park at the southeast corner, 57 different types of trees and over 70 smaller plant types were recorded growing there in 1900. For the same section of the Park there are 35 types of trees shown in a plant list for Central Park prepared by the City Parks Department in 1873, that is keyed to a plan of the Park. (Demcker) This area today reflects the confusion of plant diversity initiated when the park was built. A similar profusion of diverse plant types extends throughout the park. There is no precedent in nature for such a heterogeneous composition of unorganized plant species.

Olmsted's writings do reveal some incipient planting design principles, such as planting evergreen trees in the rocky areas of the park for their picturesque effects and distinguishing between normal wet habitat and dry habitat plant types. For a naturalist such as Olmsted, these were standard techniques. Indeed it would have been inexcusable for any plantsman to have ignored these cultural requirements.

Historically, the least credible aspect of Central Park as "a single work of art" was the manner of executing the design. There were apparently no detail drawings made to show where and what species of tree to plant beyond the small scale competition drawing, later revised. There was no planting plan with plant names. If Olmsted cared about important details of species placement and distribution, accurate large scale drawings would have been essential in addition to continuous on-site supervision. Considering Olmsted's administrative duties and the magnitude of the construction force, it would not have been possible for this one man to personally supervise the installation of from 10,000 to 50,000 trees and shrubs each year. Drawing the detailed plans for this work would have required many months of Olmsted's undivided time.

From historical records and the appearance of the park today, it seems that the placement and species arrangement of trees in Central Park was not guided by any well conceived design concept. If not by intent, then by accident, the initial plantings (over 234,000 trees and shrubs were installed between 1859 and 1869) were random compositions and arrangements.* This is apparent today in the restless mixture of tree types that characterizes the park's pastoral landscape. Ironically, the profuse variety becomes monotonous.

In a single limited foreground view along the east side of the park one sees English Oak, Sycamore, Elm, Norway Maple, Littleleaf Linden, Sugar Maple,

* "Pure Stand" is a forestry term denoting a natural area of trees containing a single native species or predominate species, as opposed to a "Mixed Stand" where two or more species predominate.

5-55

5-56

* A complete list of plants found in Central Park in 1873, prepared by Robert Demcker has been keyed to the Park Plan by the Department of Parks. This document clearly establishes the heterogeneity of the initial plantings and gives no indication of any unifying system of arranging species. (Demcker)

5-55 Plan: Central Park, 1873. A 45 acre section of the Park at the southeast corner in which over 35 different tree species were planted when the park was built. This area contained over 50 species of trees in 1900 and has at least as many different types growing there now. (From plan by New York City Department of Parks, Recreation and Cultural Affairs)

5-56 New York: Central Park. A riot of diversity in plant types. This man-made jungle in the southeast corner of the park is a sample of one 45 acre section of the park containing 57 varieties of trees mingled with a thicket of more than 70 smaller species. Nature's diversity is subtle and more pleasing.

American Holly, American Linden, Horsechestnut, Red Oak, and Pin Oak in addition to several understory tree types and shrubs. There is no apparent visual consistency in the way different tree types are mixed together: native and exotics, coarse textured and fine, large and small, evergreen and deciduous. In winter, Central Park is a tangle of brush. In the summertime, it is a giant tossed salad.

A view of a sloping meadow south of the Metropolitan Museum of Art is framed by a Sycamore (a native bottomland species), a Red Oak (a native upland species), and a Horsechestnut (an exotic tree introduced from Europe). Trees in the middle ground, Weeping Willow and Ginkgo, were planted in more recent times, but follow the Olmsted pattern of mixing many disparate tree types. Only two of the five types mentioned here, Sycamore and Willow, would be found growing together in a natural woodland.

There are areas within Central Park where native trees were preserved when the park was built, as shown on the rock outcrop near the northwest corner.

5-57 New York: Central Park. Where the underbrush is thinned out the heterogeneity of tree types is more conspicuous. This visually discordant collection of tree species is typical of plantings throughout the Park. Even an arboretum would gain by a more ordered arrangement of the dozen or more tree types that can be identified in the foreground. It is neither "nature" nor "art".

5-58 New York: Central Park. Another example of the peculiar mixture of tree types that comingle throughout the park. For those who insist upon the distinction between "native" and "introduced" tree types, there is fertile ground here for criticism. Where in the park is there evidence of a natural "plant community"?

5-59 New York: Central Park. A natural rock outcrop at the northwestern corner of the park illustrating a transitional tree stand containing native and exotic species. If the benign neglect that is advocated by some historic preservationists continues this section of woodland will evolve into an urban "plant community" probably containing mostly species like Tree of Heaven and Black Locust. Whatever the ensuing composition may be, it will resemble the original native stand of trees even less than the present miscellaneous collection.

Young White and Red Oaks and Hickory trees have propagated themselves from the original stand along with the exotic types, Norway Maple and Ginkgo, and a volunteer (self-seeded) Elm which now obscure the intended *natural* planting effect.

Black Locust trees have invaded some of the *natural areas* throughout the park, and are shown here at the northwest corner mingled with European Linden, Black Cherry, Ginkgo, and Ailanthus (Tree of Heaven). Black Locust and Cherry, along with the ubiquitous Ailanthus, have taken over a disproportionate amount of space compared to the aesthetically more desirable trees now found in the park. This is an urban forest management problem that requires a definitive policy regarding which major tree types to favor. An active silviculture program of selective thinning is also needed. Without this important policy and program, the wooded areas of city parks will continually decline in appearance and usefulness, as Central Park sadly demonstrates.

5-60

5-60 New York: Central Park. Along the upper west side of the park Black Locust, Wild Cherry and Tree-of-Heaven have begun to dominate an area that was once part of a more stable forest type growing here when the park was built. None of these volunteer species were planted by Olmsted and they are not ranked among the aesthetically more desirable tree types. This represents an extensive erosion of the Park's visual resources.

A natural forest succession (ecological) approach to park management in the city will usually result in the proliferation of the least desirable tree and understory plant types to the detriment of the most useful city trees. The conglomeration of plant species shown on the thicket-covered slope in the park at 102nd Street on the East side typifies a poor condition that will become worse if left to *nature* in the City. This tangle includes Hawthorn, Black Cherry, River Birch, Viburnum, Forsythia, Deutzia, and Regal Privet, under English Oak, Sycamore Maple, Elm, Silver Maple, and European Linden trees. When these woody plants are all in leaf, the visual dissonance is amplified. In addition, these plants obliterate the view into and from the park.

5-61

Olmsted recognized the management requirements of park trees, and in 1889 coauthored a long report entitled "Observations on the Treatment of Public Plantations, More Especially Relating to the Use of the Axe." Most of this paper was directed toward the need for planting trees close together and later thinning the plantation by selectively cutting out trees. The removal of volunteer trees is a similar maintenance concern that has become more critical than the original need to thin out planted trees. It is a crucial requirement for survival of a "city forest" that "hands-off" historic preservationists do not understand.

Design lessons. Trees are universally regarded as beautiful. Planting many trees in a large urban space will inevitably improve the human enjoyment of a place. Organizing the trees into a deliberate design that forms spaces with groves of trees will make a large urban space more attractive and more useful.

This is as far as the design concept for Central Park goes toward creating beauty—a showplace for trees in meadows.

When trees in a large urban space are not only organized for overall mass effect, but are also skillfully organized geometrically to produce patterns and rhythms, then the work aspires to art. When, in addition, subtle nuances are effected in the design through the modulation of species composition to produce a harmony of color, texture, light, and shade, the result can be a masterpiece of human achievement capable of moving the soul. This is what Central Park might have been.

Central Park is an arboretum with over 180 deciduous tree types and a much larger number of evergreens, shrubs, and smaller plant species and varieties. As such, it is a valuable educational display in the center of a large population with many people who might not otherwise have access to so many different specimens of nature. For the New Yorkers who have an interest in natural science this is a fortunate bounty. Even those who do not have a specific interest in botany could gain in knowledge and enjoyment from propinquity with so many different tree types.

An arboretum, a zoological garden, a nature preserve, or any other specialized function cannot be the first purpose of the central open space of any large city. These functions might be accommodated by proper design if they do not interfere with the primary mission of the urban park. Although Central Park is a defacto arboretum, it is not less valuable as a result of this function. However, both the park and the arboretum style suffer by the irresolute disposition of plant types that neither explain native plant associations nor compose a monumental tribute to man's sensitivity as an artist.

The principles of unity and continuity are not always clearly evident in a work of art. In Central Park there is large spatial integrity used as the main ordering device. At the gross scale the park is a success. Even as we walk through the space, there is a perceivable though sporadic repetition of species; for example, Elms, Pin Oaks, and Plane Trees occur throughout the park. However, the attempt was too weak both in magnitude and in consistency. It is an interrupted staccato experience rather than the repetition or variation on a theme.

Trees growing together in natural communities tend to look compatible when planted together. Selecting one or several species from a plant community on each soil condition encountered might be the initial step in evolving a set of appropriate tree types for discrete site conditions. For example, there might be separate species selected for flat high ground, sloping high ground, flat low

5-61 New York: Central Park. This profusion of plant types is a scrofulous example of misbegotten plant life. A trap for garbage, it is loathsome to the staunchest naturalist and untenable as a maintenance task. There is no visual or functional justification for wasting valuable urban park land for such worthless accumulation of derelict plants.

ground, and sloping low ground. Certain species might be suggested for use in paved areas, others in partially shaded areas. Monolayered tree types might be planted beneath multilayered taller trees to set up a kind of plant succession on certain parts of the site. Whatever the principles involved, they should reflect both the aesthetic opportunities and the cultural constraints of the site.

Observation of plants which grow together naturally is a good starting point. However, because city conditions are a special case, it is not always possible to utilize the same combinations. In fact the most tolerant urban trees often occupy a unique niche in the forest community. The Plane Tree, for example, occurs naturally as a sporadic tree or in small clusters in flood plains. Its associates are bottomland species that often do not grow well on urban sites because of the lack of water. The Ginkgo, an introduced tree, does not occur naturally with any native American species. The design problem then is to set in place the most visually complementary species of trees in a statement of complete harmony. Repetition, progression, and variations on a theme have their visual equivalent in landscape design. Usually a dominant species with one or several subordinate species can be used to create a thematic link.

An extensive discussion of Central Park would be incomplete without at least a mention of Prospect Park in Brooklyn, which was also designed by Olmsted less than a decade later. Like Central Park, the design significance of Prospect Park is most apparent in a plan view that shows the large scale spatial arrangement of tree masses and open meadows. Trees were widely spaced to create a pastoral setting. There is a somewhat greater consistency in the use of different tree types than in Central Park, but there is no dramatic improvement in the pedestrian scale unity. The designer's attention was focused on creating a series of picturesque scenes on the undulating landscape. Trees were not employed to create a subtle pervasive order using a few dominant tree types.

References

Wyman, Donald. *Trees for American Gardens.* New York: Macmillan Company, 1970.

Pirone, P. O. *Tree Maintenance,* Fourth Ed. New York: Oxford University Press, Inc., 1976.

Bartlett, F. A. Tree Expert Company. *Street Tree Study for the District of Columbia.* Washington, D.C.: U.S. Government Printing Office, 1968.

Symonds, George W. D. *The Tree Identification Book.* Photography by Steven V. Chelminski. New York: William Morrow & Co., Inc., 1958.

Cole, Rex Vicat. *The Artistic Anatomy of Trees.* Philadelphia: J. B. Lippincott Co., 1925.

Horn, Henry S. *The Adaptive Geometry of Trees.* New Jersey: Princeton University Press, 1976.

Elias, Thomas S., and Irwin, Howard S. Urban trees. *Scientific American.* 235: 110–118 (1976).

McArthur, Robert. *Geographical Ecology, Patterns in the Distribution of Species.* New York: Harper and Row, 1972.

Woodwell, George. The carbon dioxide question. *Scientific American,* 238: 34–43 (1978).

Grey, Gene W., and Deneke, Frederick J. *Urban Forestry*. New York: John Wiley and Sons, Inc., 1978.

Davis, Donald, and Gerhold, Henry. "Selection of Trees for Tolerance of Air Pollutants", *Better Trees for Metropolitan Landscapes,* Symposium Proceedings, USDA Forest Service General Technical Report NE-22, pp. 61–66. Washington, D.C.: U.S. Government Printing Office, 1976.

U.S. Department of Agriculture, Forest Service. *Our Air*. Washington, D.C.: USDA.

Kozlowski, T. T. "Drought and Transplantability of Trees", *Better Trees for Metropolitan Landscapes,* Symposium Proceedings. (pp. 77–89)

Patterson, James. "Soil Compaction and its Effects Upon Urban Vegetation", *Better Trees for Metropolitan Landscapes,* Symposium Proceedings. (pp. 91–100)

Dirr, Michael. "Salts and Woody-Plant Interactions in the Urban Environment", *Better Trees for Metropolitan Landscapes,* Symposium Proceedings. (pp. 103–110)

U.S. Department of Agriculture. *Trees, the Yearbook of Agriculture*. Washington, D.C.: U.S. Government Printing Office, 1949.

Santamour, Frank, Jr., Gerhold, Henry, and Little, Silas, eds. *Better Trees for Metropolitan Landscapes,* Symposium Proceedings. (p. 2)

Elias, Thomas S. and Irwin, Howard S. Urban trees. *Scientific American.*

Elias, Thomas S. *Trees and the Community*. New York: The Cary Arboretum of New York BotanicalGarden, 1976.

Chapin Raymond and Kozel, Philip. *Shade Tree Evaluation Studies,* Research Bulletin 1074. Ohio: Ohio Agricultural Research and Development Center, March 1975.

Johnson, Hugh. *The International Book of Trees*. New York: Simon and Schuster, 1973.

Santamour, Frank, Jr. "Breeding and Selecting Better Trees for Metropolitan Landscapes", *Better Trees for Metropolitan Landscapes,* Symposium Proceedings. (p. 2)

Olmsted, Frederick Law, Sr. *Forty Years of Landscape Architecture: Central Park,* Edited by Frederick Law Olmsted, Jr. and Theodora Kimball. Mass: M.I.T. Press, 1973.

Society of American Foresters. *Forest Cover Types of North America*. Washington, D.C.: Society of American Foresters, 1962.

Peet, Louis Harman. *Trees and Shrubs in Central Park*. New York: American Printing House, 1902.

Central Park. The Plant List of 1873. Prepared by Robert Demcker, Landscape Architect. Arranged by location by Arturo Parrilla, Department of Parks, 1966.

6

Latent opportunities

Concerns

What sometimes appear to be intractable hurdles, thwarting dreams of progress are, on more careful reflection, hidden opportunities. The vision of cities filled with trees is clouded with practical constraints that, on close scrutiny, become sources of hope. Trees not only become allies in the fight for cleaner air, but they are sensitive pollution detectors that warn us of poisonous air. Ordinances that restrict tree planting must be reshaped to require more tree planting. Maintenance departments that remove dead trees can become urban forest managers who replant the city. Major progress toward renewing our cities and towns will be made when there is a clearer understanding of the practical possibilities that trees offer. The purpose of this chapter is to eradicate the public concerns that too often become barriers which block the correct design use of trees. Misconceptions about technical tree growth requirements, costs, and design imperatives hamper more effective and extensive tree planting. Here we examine both the broad and narrow obstacles to rejuvenating urban places using trees, and attempt to show why often cited limitations need to be reexamined and redirected.

The economics of trees

Trees provide more benefits to more people per dollar cost than any material used in the construction industries. Costs of general building construction rose by more than 100 percent in the decade between 1968 and 1978. In this same ten year period, the installation cost of a tree in a city increased between 25 and 30 percent. Not only has the price of trees risen at less than one-third the rate of cost rise for the building construction industry, but the value of the same tree continues to increase after installation, when all other materials depreciate. Has this gone unnoticed in our tree starved cities?

The first difficulty in appreciating the intrinsic value of trees is the preconception that their presence is essentially for decoration rather than for function and structure. Another obstacle is the lack of criteria for assessing their value. It is therefore not surprising that municipal budgets for new trees are inadequate. When trees are planted, they are too small to give little more than an unfulfillable promise of future benefit. Thus inadequate city expenditures are counterproductive. Trees that are too small are funny-looking because of their scale—they tend to clutter our already chaotic streets and have the cartoonlike effect of a child's drawing. Further, they rarely survive the assault of city conditions because of their frailty and lack of public appreciation. They provide one more example of projects that fail because of inadequate scope and quality. Political opponents of urban projects have learned this lesson well. The best way to sabotage a large public expenditure for a specific project is to appropriate too small an amount of money, thereby assuring that the job is begun poorly.

Latent opportunities

To arrive at a correct appreciation of cost, one must understand three requisites for successful city tree planting. The trees must be *large enough* to give immediate shade, they must be *spaced closely* together, and there must be *enough trees* to create visual continuity. There is a positive correlation between the size of a tree at planting and the plant's ability to survive a hostile environment. The larger the tree, assuming proper transplanting methods, the greater the chance for survival. There is a widespread misconception, referred to in Chapter 4, that small trees are more successfully transplanted than larger trees of the same type. It is true that the transplanting cost for trees with an adequate ball of earth increases with size. However, if properly handled, there is no greater mortality rate from moving a six inch caliper tree than from moving a two inch caliper tree. Street trees of less than four inches caliper are a poor risk in most urban locations unless specially protected. To satisfy both immediate aesthetic demand and durability, the new city street trees should be at least five inches in caliper or larger when they are planted.

The implications of these standards for city policy can be seen by examining the relative costs of traditional and minimum recommended practice. When a municipality spends less than $1000 per block on street trees, it can expect two inch caliper trees spaced about 50 feet apart. To be effective it should plant trees that are five inches in caliper 20 feet apart, or six inches in caliper 30 feet apart, at a cost of $10,000.* Planting one block adequately is a decisively better choice than planting ten blocks with smaller and fewer trees at the same cost. This is illustrated by scattered examples in cities where trees planted five or more years ago have grown to become visually effective in public spaces. Along Hawcreek Boulevard in Columbus, Indiana, the Plane Trees were four inch caliper when planted, at Lincoln Center they were six inch caliper, and in southwest Washington, D.C., the trees were five inch caliper. In these examples, the trees were all less than 30 feet apart. In other municipalities where planting programs were undertaken using trees of two to three inch caliper spaced 40 to 50 feet apart, the results are barely visible nearly five years after planting.

The principal causes of tree losses are abuse and vandalism. In one instance in the Melrose section of the Bronx, New York, three inch caliper London Plane Trees were planted. Fewer than one half of the 37 trees planted lasted beyond the first planting season.

* The prices used are hypothetical, but are based on actual relative planting prices in northeastern U.S. cities during 1978 for trees on both sides of the street in blocks 250 feet long.

6-1
6-2
6-3

6-1 Plane Trees planted in 1962 along Hawcreek Boulevard in Columbus, Indiana were 4 inch caliper. Ten years later the trees were over 35 feet tall with 98 percent of the trees surviving.

6-2   Plane Trees planted at Lincoln Center, New York in 1965 were 6 inches in caliper when planted in a busy public space. Despite limited soil depth and other restrictive urban growing conditions all of the trees were growing and healthy when this photograph was taken in 1976.

6-3   Plane Trees planted in southwest Washington, D.C. have grown to 40 feet in height from 5 inch caliper trees when transplanted to this site in 1963.

Policy obstacles

Though many urban municipalities do not plant street trees, they usually maintain trees that are planted by adjacent property owners in the public right-of-way, and they often regulate the planting of new trees. The laws of New Jersey provide a legal basis for shade tree commissions in municipalities. (N.J. Federation of Shade Tree Commissions) In California, there are often city tree ordinances but, more rarely, master plans for street trees. (Beatty) One survey shows that ordinances regulating tree planting are now wide-spread in the United States, particularly in the northeastern states. (Gutman) Such regulations normally limit species, spacing, and the like, but do not specify a definite aesthetic treatment for each particular street. As a consequence, a recently planted urban street generally lacks unity. This is true of new plantings even in cities with examples of fine older streets and avenues. The regulations preventing owners from planting new trees within the public right-of-way are commonly based on maintenance concerns.

Planning for trees should be a design responsibility of the agency that prepares master plans for the city. This would give trees a place in the intense competition for public space now occupied by fire hydrants, litter cans, utility lines, manholes, directional devices, war memorials, pretzel vendors, subway entrances, and newspaper stands. Some day our social priorities may actually favor trees in such a competition. Until that time they need to be perceived as an urban requirement and not as a decorative afterthought.

Prohibitory regulations by government agencies concerning tree planting pose a major threat to urban design. The *Tree Planting Standards* of the Bureau of Forestry, Parkways, and Beautification, which is under the direction of the Commissioner of the Department of Streets and Sanitation of the City of Chicago, illustrates a common approach to city tree regulation. These standards require wide spacing between trees (30 feet minimum), enumerate the locations where trees cannot be planted, and give discretionary authority to other city agencies in deciding if trees can be planted in a particular location. Clearly, these regulations do not encourage tree planting. There are further requirements that would discourage tree planting even in desirable locations. Chicago's trees are regulated by agencies that view them as a maintenance problem. However, even where the tree ordinances and standards have been prepared by agencies that are primarily concerned with trees, they are over-restrictive. *A Sample City Tree Ordinance* for Kansas, and *Arboricultural Specifications and Standards of Practice for the Atlanta, Georgia Area,* are two other examples that are too restrictive. (Grey) They impose arbitrary design standards for conditions such as tree spacing. This type of provision reflects the interest of the tree specialist without due consideration for aesthetics. Such ostensibly beneficial tree ordinances can inadvertantly undermine government tree planting activity. Ordinances are needed to carry out a tree planting program based on a *master plan for trees*. The master plan should determine the design standards expressly related to actual city conditions.

The idea of preparing a master tree planting plan is not new and has considerable merit. Tree planting on all the broad avenues of Washington, D.C., was part of L'Enfant's original plan for the city, though not executed until after the Civil War when Alexander Robey Shepherd planted 60,000 trees. Less extensive tree planting plans were executed in New York City in the Fieldston and Riverdale areas of the Bronx around the turn of the century. Also sections of Philadelphia, and Vancouver, British Columbia, were planted in an organized way in the early part of this century. In a number of American cities, Dayton and Minneapolis for example, planning agencies have prepared plans for signs and graphics. Given the great visual impact and functional benefit of trees, a well conceived city-wide design for street tree planting should be made a high priority planning task. A whole city given coherence with a deliberate pattern of tree covered streets and open spaces could become the great humanistic contribution to civic design of this century. When tree plans become as common as zonning plans and transportation plans, we will have made a major change for more humane and liveable cities.

Physical constraints

Tree space. Cities restrict and inhibit the growth of trees spatially with overhead utilities, building form, and street width. Each remedy has social benefits, and in each the problem is connected with the insensitive applications of technology, often by designers.

If we regard the primary function of streets as the movement of people, utilities should be placed where they do not interfere with people or traffic. Expedient handling of wires has placed them where they clutter views and impinge on trees. Where this has happened, a visually acceptable compromise in tree planting still requires the use of large trees as close as possible to the street curb. Figures 6-4 and 6-5 show both wires and trees accommodated in a way that preserves the visual quality of the street. The additional pruning cost is a modest price to pay for an arching canopy over the street. The use of small trees is an unacceptable compromise that does more harm than good to the streetscape.

6-5 Trees and Wires. Norway Maple trees coexisting with poles and wires. Seen in perspective poles and wires merge into a pattern that subsumes the utilities.

6-4 Trees and Wires. Plane Trees mingle with telephone and electric lines in visual harmony. A better compromise than small self-conscious looking trees standing under the utility lines.

The interrelationship of tree form to building configuration in the city has remained almost unexplored because planting design is regarded as a decorative adjunct to building design. Rarely, if ever, are both treated as a single design discipline. In the Museum of Modern Art garden in New York, trees are used decoratively, as sculpture, interrupting the flow of the space which is created by building walls. Two blocks away in Paley Park, trees are used to reinforce the space defined by buildings by creating a roof of airy foliage, thereby enhancing the space. In both examples the trees were added to existing architectural spaces and bear no strong integral relationship to the structural form of adjacent buildings. In the example of the Museum garden, trees could have been used to reflect and intensify the architecture, because the garden was designed at the same time as the building.

5-38

Changing shape and adaptability of trees are closely related to their architectural use. An understanding of the flexibility possible in tree spacing and the light requirements for growth is essential in designing urban spaces where trees and buildings mingle.

The minimum spacing between tree trunks is limited by the size of the tree root ball and therefore by the size of the tree at transplanting, not by the mature spread of an open grown crown as is commonly supposed. A Maple tree that is four inches in caliper will require a root ball of 42 inches in diameter to be safely transplanted, therefore the minimum spacing between four inch caliper trees cannot be less than three and one half feet center to center.

Since trees will grow at such close spacings, the distance between trees is governed only by aesthetic and physical site considerations. When trees are planted very closely together, the branch spread at the time of planting may exceed the spacing, in which case branches will intertwine and may require pruning if the crown is dense.

The requirement of trees for direct sunlight can tell us something about building design. Where buildings are less than four stories tall, tree locations in relation to buildings are governed by the solar angle, as described and illustrated in Chapter 4. On the south side of a building, where light is not restricted by other buildings, trees can be grown as close to the south wall of the building as desired. In most situations, the trees in a grove or line will be kept at least 12 feet from a south-facing building wall and sometimes further away where the trees interfere with desired summer sunlight into the windows. The campus of Rockefeller University in Manhattan has large Plane Trees growing ten feet away from west building walls. The cross streets in Manhattan, with trees planted in 13 foot sidewalks, also illustrate this close building/tree relationship with buildings under four stories tall.

When buildings are taller than four stories, the building form must reflect the light requirements for photosynthesis if trees are to be grown along the south side of east-west running streets. These buildings setback requirements are illustrated in Figures 4-8 and 4-9. A shadow diagram for spaces next to tall buildings can be plotted for critical hours and seasons to design plaza configurations that will support tree growth. At the latitude of New York City, trees will grow very close to the south side of tall buildings, as illustrated at Stuyvesant Town, where the buildings are 12 stories high and trees are planted less than ten feet from them. With buildings this tall, trees planted at the same distance from a north wall would grow poorly, if at all.

6-6

6-6   Plane Trees in New York growing near the south wall of a tall building.

Many of the most admired small spaces in cities of the eastern United States are narrow streets with large trees. Georgetown, Charleston, Boston, and Philadelphia, to a large degree owe their character to the feeling of intimate scale that results from narrow tree-canopied streets and alleys. Ironically, the first caution given in tree publications is to avoid planting large tree types on narrow streets. The visual effects of this advice can be seen in the increasing number of narrow urban streets that are being cluttered with flowering trees. Every city in the country has its examples. Nowhere in the literature of advice is there any reasoned explanation of why we should not plant Plane Trees on streets like Cypress or Delancy in Philadelphia. There are statements deploring the extra cost of maintenance that can be attributed to planting large trees on small streets, but no estimates of what this extra cost might be and how it occurs.

The relationship of mature tree size to the size of an urban space is a critical design issue. In Chapter 4, we examined the spatial qualities that are produced by large and small trees on a narrow street, and how large trees better adapt their form to narrow city streets than do small tree types. If constricted space for crown growth damaged trees, then all forest trees would be unhealthy. As we

124

Latent opportunities

know from observation, both forest trees and city trees adapt very well to space that is much narrower than the full open grown crown spread. There are hundreds of thousands of trees in cities throughout the world that have adjusted their branch structure and leaf surface to grow in very narrow spaces. These city trees do not require nor receive extra maintenance attention. It is highly probable that trees growing in constricted urban spaces require less pruning and care than open grown trees that are less protected from wind and direct sunlight in winter. There are a number of illustrations in this book showing trees on narrow streets. To substitute small (or medium) size trees on any of these streets would effectively cancel the spatial quality that makes these spaces delightful.

1-20 2-24 2-25
4-42
6-7 6-8

6-7   Plane Trees and Norway Maples in Philadelphia where the street is 15 feet wide showing the value of large trees on small streets.

6-8   Plane Trees in Philadelphia on a street that is 18 feet wide. Here the trees are at least as important as the buildings in defining a pedestrian scale space.

In cities planned for pedestrians, walks should be wide enough to accommodate numerous rows of trees on all important streets. It is desirable to have at least 13 feet between the curb line and the building wall to accommodate a single row of trees. There are examples in many cities where large trees are growing well in narrower sidewalks. A ten foot wide increase in a walk is desirable for each additional row of trees. More than one row of trees on a sidewalk over 20 feet wide is a matter of scale and shade. There are, as yet, no notable precedents for this. However, many cities have some widened sidewalks with multiple rows of trees. An example partially built is Pennsylvania Avenue in Washington, D.C., near the new F.B.I. Building. There, three rows of shade trees have been placed on the north side of the Avenue for one block. The original plan by the President's Council on Pennsylvania Avenue, in 1964, called for three rows of Littleleaf Lindens on the north side and two rows on the south side for the entire distance between the Capitol terminus and 14th Street. (Report of the President's Council on Pennsylvania Avenue) If this plan is finally built as designed, Pennsylvania Avenue will become a world famous example of how trees can transform a city.*

The height of the leaf canopy, particularly the lowest branches, should allow comfortable circulation and a sense of overhead spaciousness. A ceiling height of less than ten feet in large outdoor spaces usually feels constricting. This is especially difficult to achieve at the time of planting because of limited tree sizes. When trees 20 to 25 feet tall are planted, the initial lowest branch height will not be more than seven or eight feet above the ground. Usually the lower branches are removed over a period of three to five years as the tree grows, until the clearance reaches ten feet.

6-9

6-10
6-11

*   The more recently formed Pennsylvania Avenue Development Corporation has modified the original plan, changing the tree species to Willow Oak instead of Littleleaf Linden. The Willow Oak trees will be manicured but not trimmed to the geometric form originally called for.

6-12

Latent opportunities

6-9   Pennsylvania Avenue, Washington, D.C. One block recently planted with Littleleaf Lindens as a small first stage of a design that would encompass the entire mile long stretch from the Capitol to the White House. The current plan calls for Willow Oak Trees instead of the Lindens.

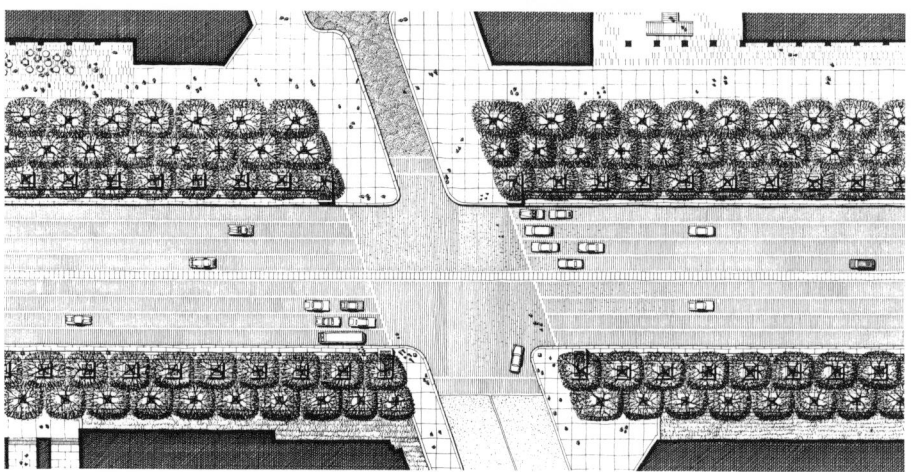

6-10   Plan: Pennsylvania Avenue Proposal. Washington, D.C. 1964. This typical segment of the Avenue at an intersection shows how trees were to be spaced on both sides of the cartway. Along the north side, where there are three rows of trees, there would eventually be a continuous building arcade complementing and extending the canopy effect of the trees. This design combines symbolic monumentality with human scale that could make Pennsylvania Avenue one of the outstanding civic designs of the twentieth century. (Illustrations from the Report of the President's Council on Pennsylvania Avenue. April 1964.)

6-11 Typical section: Pennsylvania Avenue, Washington, D.C. 1964. The original proposal calls for clipping trees to retain the uniform height and form illustrated. The splendid effect of an avenue of clipped trees has never been experienced in an American city. A mile long avenue of trees handled this way might have created an impressive order for our capitol parade route. (Illustration from the Report of the President's Council on Pennsylvania Avenue. April 1964.)

6-12 An arcade of Norway Maple Trees. The branch height of 6 feet is too low for a comfortably scaled pedestrian walkway. Pruning lower branches to a height of eight feet at first, and several years later, ten feet, would improve the visual success of this well conceived tree planting.

Root growth requirements. A benevolent ruler could vastly improve our cities by covering them with four feet of earth. A less drastic measure would be to see that every city installed enough good soil to grow large trees along every street and in every open space. An adequate quantity of good growing medium is such a necessity for city trees that its absence, perhaps more than any other physical condition, explains our paucity of urban trees.

Lack of friable soil is one limitation that is common in most cities. Soil for trees can be specially compounded to form an ideal mixture for the roots to stabilize and nurture the trees. Agronomists know enough about native soils to improve often on natural conditions.

Restricted space for root development is the most severe soil limitation for tree growth. Subways, underground utilities, and building structures have sterilized much of the ground surface within public rights-of-way, making tree growth impossible. Growing trees where there is limited friable soil impairs the root functions of support and supply. The resulting deficiency of water and nutrients is visible in the reduced growth rate and stunting of the tree. Reducing root space compromises the vitality and survival ability of the tree.

Under forest conditions, trees develop roots that spread ten feet or more before they encounter serious competition from other trees. An open grown tree develops a much more extensive root system, particularly in a porous soil. (Stout) Contrary to folklore, most trees do not develop a deep carrot-like tap root. Many natural soils are quite shallow and cause the main roots to spread laterally, even among species that would develop a deep central root on an unrestricted site. Because a root system needs air, the normal depth for most feeder roots is less than four feet. Trees in cities are able to survive in somewhat less than ideal root space if conditions of drainage, soil, and watering are unusually good and can compensate. A general guide for the minimum root space required for a shade tree (under optimum conditions of soil quality) is four to five feet of depth and a 12 to 15 feet diameter spread per tree.

Soil for city tree planting should consist of a specially formulated mixture that will allow excess (gravitational) water to drain away quickly, but retain adequate moisture for plant growth. Since most available soil in cities is severely restricted in volume, installing trees is effectively like planting in containers. A good soil mixture formulated for trees in containers consists of equal parts of screened topsoil, coarse sand for drainage, and a soil conditioner containing peatmoss and perlite. (Flemer)

A four feet deep, 12 feet by 12 feet square area of prepared planting soil provides over 21 cubic yards of optimum root growth space. Less than this amount of good soil will restrict growth of large shade trees, slowing their later growth rate and limiting their ultimate size. When the root zone is reduced to eight feet by eight feet (only 9.5 cubic yards), the root system of a large shade tree becomes too restricted for normal growth. Under the best of these conditions, the tree may grow to a small size at maturity and may decline in health thereafter. Increasing the soil depth beyond five feet does not compensate for reduced horizontal root spread.

Now trees are not being planted in cities with this necessary volume of prepared soil mixture because we have been following suburban planting practices that are related to native soil.* In areas of natural soil, it is only necessary to provide a small pocket of good growing medium to assist in starting a newly transplanted tree, because the roots can penetrate into and grow in the surrounding soil. Therefore the standard practice for transplanting trees in nonurban soils relates the size of the planting pit and, hence the volume of added prepared soil mixture, to the size of the tree (root ball) at planting. Trees in suburban lawns have proved that this standard practice is adequate in that type of habitat.

Urban soils pose a completely different problem. Soil scientists, who are now performing some of the first systematic research on urban soil conditions, have classified them into four groups that reflect highly man-influenced conditions. These soil types are: Scalpic—cut land where rock is near the surface; Garbic—the product of "sanitary" landfills; Urbic—miscellaneous urban fill; Spolic—locally derived earthy spoil. Within each of these groups, there is a wide range of conditions influencing plant growth. They range from soils that can be modified to support plant growth to materials that are actually toxic to plants. Given such undependable and highly erratic conditions, existing urban soils cannot be depended upon to grow trees. Sound practice requires that trees be provided with enough prepared soil mixture to support mature growth, therefore in the city, the volume of prepared soil must be related to the *full grown tree* size, not to the size of the tree at planting.

Minimum prepared soil mixture volume requirements for urban trees are shown in Figure 6-13, assuming: (1) soil mixture depth measured from the top of a porous drainage layer within the planting area; (2) top of soil mixture level with surrounding grade (not in a raised planter).

* An exception is Constitution Gardens, a new 40-acre park in Washington, D.C., where 85,000 cubic yards of specially formulated soil mixture were used in planting 2000 shade trees.

Mature Tree Height (in feet)	Square Area (in feet)	Depth of Mixture (in feet)	Volume/Tree (in cubic yards)
Large tree 41–70	12 x 12	4	21.3
Medium tree 21–40	8 x 8	3.5	8.3
Small tree 15–20	6 x 6	3	4.0

6-13 Minimum prepared soil mixture quantities.

Under ideal conditions, the soil mixture would be distributed in a symmetrical uniform configuration around the center of the tree. Under urban conditions, the shape of the prepared soil mixture area can vary to accommodate underground structures, since tree roots can adjust to highly irregular configurations of soil. The volume of the growing medium, however, must be maintained within a depth no greater than five feet.

Raised planters are a different matter. The commercial answer to the urban "beautification" movement of the 1960's is the raised outdoor tree planter. A discussion of the technical aspects of this device for growing trees in cities cannot ignore the visual ramifications of its size and form. Growing a single tree in a raised planter in an urban public space poses an aesthetic contradiction that is intrinsic to the morphology of a tree. The ratio of the root system to the crown of a tree requires that the horizontal root spread be equivalent to at least one-half of the crown diameter. Under natural conditions the ratio is about one to one. So even if we restrict the roots to one-half of their normal spread (one quarter of the area), we are faced with a planter that is 12 by 12 feet square and growing only one large city tree. In the forest, the principal feeder roots are located in the top five feet of soil. If we restrict this depth to four feet in a raised planter, that is 12 by 12 feet square, the result is a rectangular lump four and one half feet tall (including planter) that fills a 600 cubic foot volume of scarce ground-level space to grow one tree that has a crown volume of about 300 cubic feet at planting. The conventional practice is to plant a small tree in a 4 x 4 feet square by four feet deep planter. The 12 foot tall Callery Pear tree in Figure 6-14, if it survives the winter, will perhaps grow to a height of 20 feet before it is stunted by inadequate soil. The value of the tree will never equal the cost of the granite planter.

Since the vital function of trees in urban spaces is to create or reinforce the space, a single tree in a planter has little visual consequence. Where structural necessity dictates raised planters, planting groups of trees is most effectively accomplished by creating one large planter, rather than a series of individual planters—one for each tree. Large planters with many trees have greater visual coherence and provide better protection for root and crown growth. Freezing and thawing, the major technical problem for trees in free-standing planters, is more easily controlled, drainage is achieved more satisfactorily, and tree guying is simplified.

6-14 Street trees in planters. The Callery Pear trees on Chestnust Street in Philadelphia have far too little soil for growth to an effective size in this setting. The inappropriate scale of these little trees will continue to be a visual annoyance until the trees run out of root space and expire. Though inadequate for trees, the bulky planters do nothing to improve the pleasant pedestrian scale of this 60 foot wide open space.

6-15 Planter with London Plane Trees. Planted over a garage in four feet of soil mixture in a residential courtyard in the Bronx, these trees can grow to make a broad 50 foot tall canopy that will shade the inexpensive paving materials. The soil volume is great enough in this 40 foot wide partially recessed planter to protect the roots from excessive freezing and thawing, the principle liability of planting trees in small raised planters.

Planting contractors have learned that the predominant cause of tree mortality after transplanting is insufficient drainage. A properly constructed subsurface drainage system usually adds between 15 and 30 percent to the cost of tree planting at an average urban site. In unusual cases where a storm drain line is not easily accessible, or the project is very small, the percentage increase in planting cost may be greater. Despite the additional cost, provision for positive subsurface drainage is essential for all urban tree planting.

Subsoil drainage details vary greatly on different sites. The essential principle is to provide for positive continuous removal of excess capillary water to a depth of four feet or greater. Use a typical subsoil drainage system design having a minimum four inch diameter pipe connected to an outlet or storm drain. (Seelye) Many publications on tree planting show drainage details that do not connect each plant pit to an outlet with a pipe or drain tile. Such generalized details do not work in many soil conditions, and are therefore, unreliable except on sites where the water will percolate below the root zone within 48 hours after a heavy rain, when the water table is at its highest level usually in early spring.

Most trees can be killed faster from poor drainage than from drought. Even species of trees that naturally adapt to wet sites will not grow when transplanted into conditions of poor drainage. Though many horticultural publications recommend using swamp species of trees on wet sites, there is a practical reason why this will not work in transplanting trees (Chapter 5, p. 94). Good drainage must be assured for all types of trees. The correlative of good drainage, adequate water, is a more obvious necessity for tree growth and is therefore less frequently overlooked. Because most city trees are planted in paved areas, they require supplemental watering and sometimes a special watering system. (Zion) Occasionally the drainage system is designed to serve as a watering and drainage system. Automatic sprinkler systems are not recommended for most tree installations because of the great danger of over-watering. Thirst can be detected and remedied more easily and quickly than over-watering. On an established tree, leaves will gradually begin to wilt long before the tree is killed by drought.

Frequent and more serious hidden physical damage occurs to the tree roots from soil compaction. The ideal tree growing soil should have 50 percent pore space of which 25 percent is filled with air and 25 percent with water. When compaction reduces the air space to less than 15 percent, root growth is seriously restricted. Some desirable city trees, such as the Sugar Maple and the Tulip Tree, are severely susceptible to soil compaction. (Patterson)

Regular vehicular traffic should always be excluded from the area above the root zone. Where pedestrian traffic is heavy, the best measure to protect the roots is to provide a tree grate at least six feet wide that is supported on the adjacent pavement. Correct detailing of the tree grates by filling the spaces under and within them with pebbles or crushed stone is essential. Where this is not done, debris accumulates in the tree pit, creating an ugly and unsanitary condition that defies easy maintenance.

Where pedestrian traffic is moderate, the conventional practice of laying paving stones or bricks in a sand bed on top of the tree root area is usually acceptable. The damage caused by soil compaction is often not recognized because it leads to gradual deterioration of trees and is not distinguishable from many other causes of decline. Also the critical root need for air is not well understood. Many design details for the areas around new trees do not take into account this potential problem.

The most common cause of soil compaction around existing trees on construction sites is careless use of heavy construction equipment. Prevention of tree root damage requires that all equipment, materials, and operations be excluded from at least the area under the branch spread of the trees. Specifications hardly ever cover this problem adequately, if at all; and if they do, they are difficult to enforce. This is an insidious cause of tree damage that probably accounts for a significant proportion of trees that grow poorly or die within three or four years of planting, and effects old existing trees, as well. Where heavy pedestrian traffic under new trees is anticipated, they should be planted with protective measures to assure a well aerated root zone. Planting details for this purpose involve using permanently porous soil mixture, incorporating porous layers in the tree pit, and installation of tile drain systems. These special measures need to be designed for the particular circumstances of each different site.

Atmospheric conditions. The unhealthy quality of air in cities might be one of the most valid reasons for abandoning urban centers and pursuing the pastoral escape route to the suburbs, if it were not for the fact that we need automobiles to make our getaway. Concentrated automobile circulation is as unhealthy for trees as it is for people. A primary source of cancer-producing air contaminants in center cities (and suburban shopping centers) is the internal combustion engine, which produces 60 percent of all general air pollutants. (Davis) Though the specific gases that injure trees, ozone and sulfur dioxide, are different from the airborne carcinogens that harm human beings, both originate from the same source—the automobile. (Smith)

There are at least ten common air polluting substances in cities that can harm trees, mostly by absoption through the leaves. (U.S. Department of Agriculture, Forest Service) Fortunately, hardwood trees are generally less susceptible to these contaminants than conifers, and they are also affected less by airborne dust. Since sulfur dioxide is most prevalent near coal burning industries and oil refineries, it is less extensive in its effect than ozone. With the exception of Maples, many of the choicest urban tree species are sensitive to ozone. Honeylocust, Sycamore, Sweet Gum, Scarlet and Pin Oak, and Littleleaf Linden are among the trees most sensitive to this pollutant. Lombardy Poplar and Larch do not fare well in environments with sulfur dioxide, ozone and hydrogen flouride, the third most prevalent contaminant that harms trees.

The complete effects of air pollutants on trees are not known. In addition to genetic factors, susceptibility depends on a combination of environmental conditions. There are a number of published research sources assessing different tree types and air pollution, including lists of trees and their degree of susceptibility. (Loomis) Despite the availability of some species that are less susceptible to air pollution, finding trees that are more tolerant of conditions inimical to human life promises no lasting solution to this urban *social* problem. Likewise, the known ability of trees to filter our air offers the most hope for cities where pedestrians can meander freely. This approach should become a precondition to our search for environmental solutions. Trees can provide an incentive to resolve the more mundane problems of rejuvenating cities.

Other physical limitations

Trees in cities have to survive high levels of physical abuse. Damage to the trunk and bark are common and will often heal in one or two growing seasons if further damage does not occur. Where damage to the trunk is extensive, affecting structure, it may seriously impair the tree's health because living tissue lies in a layer immediately below the surface. Where a tree is girdled (cut or damaged around its entire circumference), it will usually die. To prevent trunk or bark damage, iron tree guards five or six feet high are sometimes installed around the tree trunk. Tree wrappings, which are applied to most newly transplanted trees to prevent damage from intense sunlight, may also protect the bark during the first growing season. Susceptibility to serious harm by most forms of physical damage decreases with large trees. By observation, it is clear that trees less than four inches in diameter have a high mortality rate in urban places and rarely survive on intensively used urban streets. Trees over five inches in diameter can survive significant amounts of physical abuse by people, but not by machinery. The survival rates of trees larger than five inches in diameter is great enough to warrant planting only large trees in urban areas. Where automobiles park at right angles to a line of trees, a curb or tire stop should be located at least 40 inches away from the tree trunk.

The most extensive damage to trees less than six inches in dimeter is surreptitiously brought about by dogs. (Dodge) There is a mistaken notion that because barnyard manure is used for fertilizer, all animal excreta is beneficial to plants. There are a number of technical reasons why this is not true. Animal urine is toxic because of its concentration. Manures must be well rotted before they are used as fertilizer, otherwise they can damage plants with their chemical salt concentrations. Not all animal manures are used as fertilizer because of differences in chemical composition. Manures used for fertilizer are only safe and beneficial if they are well rotted and used at claculated low concentrations. The chemical concentration and sheer quantity of animal excreta along many city streets will severely damage most trees, even if it does not immediately kill them. The metal collar that is sometimes installed around the base of a tree trunk does not protect the tree from seepage, and is therefore of little value in protecting the tree from dog damage. As with damage from soil compaction or salt, the decline of the trees is gradual. The cause is seldom understood, therefore the damaging practices are never halted. The problem is a difficult one to deal with in most urban neighborhoods because people are not aware that animal wastes are slowly killing the trees. There is an observable and dramatic difference between trees growing in areas with high dog populations and in other areas of the same city where the same species of trees are protected from animals. In the unaffected areas, the trees have larger leaves, grow more vigorously, and have a lower mortality rate.

An increasing problem to trees in urban areas occurs from the use of salts to melt snow. (Dirr) This is an example of a chemical approach that is marketed as an improvement to reduce labor, but at an undisclosed cost to the environment. Since the replacement of concrete sidewalks every three or four years from salt damage has not discouraged its use, it is unlikely that the destruction of trees will limit its use. Trees damaged by salinity exhibit a gradual decline not likely to be noticed until the tree is seriously weakened.

Though certain species of trees are more tolerant of salt concentrations in the soil, no city trees grow well under such conditions. (Pirone) Further, the use of salts for snow melting is such an environmentally destructive practice, that to encourage it by planting salt tolerant trees is not recommendable. Salts include both sodium chloride and calcium chloride. Salts used to melt snow on urban pavements now exceed 12 million tons per year in the northeastern states. This quantity is increasing, and is concentrated in urban areas. The run-off from such areas inevitably changes the chemical composition of streams and groundwater, adding another pollutant at a time when some are gradually being reduced. There is no justification for claims that calcium chloride or other effective snow melting chemicals are significantly *less harmful* to trees and natural drainage systems than sodium chloride.

There are important physical limitations governing the transplanting and growth of urban trees. The particular need for installation of prepared soil mixtures, drainage systems, and measures to prevent soil compaction have been mentioned. Because of abnormal stresses on urban trees, only nursery grown trees (dug with ball, and burlapped) should be used. Trees transplanted from fields or native sites are not well acclimated and suffer shock in transplanting. Bare root trees, that is, trees transplanted without soil on the roots, are weak and prone to damage when transplanted to an urban site. The cost saving from bare root tree planting in cities is not worth the risk of loss and the delay in growth that results. Like container grown trees, they are susceptible to future damage from girdling roots. This phenomena caused by manipulation, crowding, or disturbance to the tree root system before or during transplanting has become more common in recent years as a result of more mechanized nursery production means, most notably growing trees in containers. Container grown or bare root trees can get their roots misdirected or tangled in the process of growing or moving. When this happens, the results show up many years later in the form of a root or roots that kill all or part of the tree by cutting off the other feeding roots. (Pirone)

Continuous lighting by the introduction of all-night lighting sources can weaken trees and make them more susceptible to air pollution and early frost. The London Plane, Norway Maple, and American Elm are particularly sensitive to damage from artificial light. (Cathey)

Tree care systems

Maintenance. In addition to the actual physical limitations of an urban site, there is another major consideration—the care and perpetuation of trees. Institutionally it is referred to as "maintenance." Most cities and towns provide limited maintenance, if any. The services most frequently performed include removing leaves and litter, removing dead trees, pruning off dead branches, spraying for serious insect or disease infestations, and repairing storm damage. Only the last three operations provide any benefit to growing trees. In many cases the pruning operation is directed solely to protecting power lines. One of the most critical operations for urban tree health and survival, watering, is rarely performed as a routine part of public tree maintenance. Given the normal physical restrictions of tree growth of an urban site and the low level of prevailing maintenance, the trees that survive in the city show remarkable adaptability.

The kind of maintenance that the trees should receive depends on the location, species, and age of the trees. The location is related to stress. Park trees growing in grass will need less care than a tree growing in a paved traffic island. Plane trees will survive under conditions of severe stress, while Sugar Maple trees might also live in the same environment if they were regularly watered and occasionally fertilized. A city with mostly mature or long established trees may have to do more pruning and less watering than a city where the majority of trees were recently planted. Therefore, the needs of different trees in different cities vary significantly.

Basic tree care. In general, ordered basic tree care includes the following six maintenance catagories listed in order of importance for average city conditions in temperate climates:

Watering. Under urban conditions all trees need to be watered during the first two years after transplanting. During dry summer conditions, new trees may need to be watered twice a week. At other times, watering might not be required for a month or longer. The soil surrounding the roots should never dry out. However, excessive watering (causing roots to be saturated for longer than one day at a time) must be avoided. Regular surveillance and experienced judgment are indispensible for this task. Automatic irrigation systems are not recommended for watering trees unless they are constantly watched, which undercuts their usefulness. In paved areas, most of the rain water does not reach tree roots, which in many cases is advantageous, since pollutants in runoff can be harmful to tree growth. Watering can be accomplished more effectively and expediently where watering holes are incorporated in the surrounding paving when the tree is installed. Some authorities recommend a design detail that directs water from the street or sidewalk into the area around the tree. This results in standing water after a rainfall. In several instances, this type of detail has had disasterous consequences, causing all or many of the trees to die as a result of prolonged saturated soil. Provisions for manual watering in a city are safer and more certain.

Control of Pestilence. The need to control insects and disease may vary from treating trees once every three or four years, to making several pesticide applications in one season. There are no totally pest free trees. In each locality we learn which species seem less susceptible to infestations of insects and disease. Short term periodic infestations sometimes occur, then may not appear for a long time. In unusual cases where severe defoliation or other serious damage is done to the tree by the predator, chemical controls are necessary in urban areas.

The debate over the use of pesticides should center upon when and how to use them. In urban areas where we have become dependent on various artificial practices to grow plants, the complete cessation of pesticides would be far too costly without an effective alternative. Ecologists concur on the need for intelligently applied pesticides to deal with an unpredictable appearance of insects whose natural history is one of sudden, prodigious multiplication that lasts very briefly. These predators will vanish just as suddenly. (May)

Instead of spraying, some pests can be controlled by systemic insecticides, introduced through the roots. These have the advantages of effectiveness, safety to the public, and convenience. Regular and continued surveillance is the most important part of an effective maintenance program to contain and eliminate pestilence. In urban locations, trees are often isolated enough from the natural breeding grounds of pests that, if they are treated early, insects and diseases can be kept from spreading. It is usually inadvisable to carry on a program of preventative spraying because of its adverse effects on other plants and animals. It is also unwise to treat all infestations because trees have a natural ability to recover from most maladies. Unless there is a particularly heavy infestation, it may be combatted by natural predators without interference from technology. There are bugs such as leaf aphids on Tulip Trees, and diseases such as Anthracnose on the Sycamore that are very common, but do not ordinarily do serious harm to trees. These are often treated in urban areas because their effects are considered by some to be a nuisance. Anthracnose, a leaf disease common on Sycamore trees and other species, causes leaves to drop prematurely. Though the disease occasionally defoliates the tree completely, it is not lethal, and only rarely requires spraying. The aphid which occurs commonly on the Tulip Tree secrete a sticky substance that falls on parked cars, and is therefore considered a nuisance. Little is understood about the complex interrelationships of plants and animals generally, and we do not know yet whether elimination of the aphids by chemical treatment might accelerate the growth of a scale insect that is more harmful to Tulip Trees. The treatment aimed at the harmless aphids could conceivably destroy some unknown natural predator of the harmful scale. Knowledgeable guidelines on this subject have yet to be written.

It is a sound practice to avoid using pesticides when severe damage to trees is not based on historic experience. The contemporary response to most abnormal conditions seen on trees is to immediately use whatever chemical therapy is at hand, not unlike the way we frequently reach for medicine. The side effects may be more harmful than the original disease. Restraint is an essential counterforce to over-eager proliferation of environmental toxins.

Protection from Encroachment. Encroachment protection is usually not treated as a regular maintenance procedure. We could save a significant number of trees by regular surveillance and alteration of harmful conditions. Common encroachments are: vehicles driving or parking within the tree root zone, tire stops without enough clearance to protect tree trunks from parked cars, polluted runoff water directed toward tree roots, uncontrolled salting to remove snow, truck access routes that damage overhead branches, and damaged tree grates or tree guards. Some of these conditions occur surreptitiously and gradually erode the vitality of trees. In many cases a simple barrier or diversion will save valuable trees, if installed in time.

Damage Repair. If not properly trimmed and dressed, broken limbs and damaged trunks are common tree injuries that will allow deleterious organisms to invade the heartwood. This is one of the maintenance services that is easily neglected unless there are annual inspections to detect and repair injuries. More frequent inspections are desirable.

Feeding. Trees growing in their natural habitat obtain their nutrients from the soil. To overfertilize in urban settings may harm trees by upsetting the balance that natural systems attain. Trees adapt in nature to a wide range of soil types with a vast range of nutrient levels. They respond to the available nutrients by adjusting their growth rate. They remain healthy despite conditions that agronomists would consider less than ideal for growth. The reason for fertilizing urban trees is to compensate for very low nutrients available to restricted roots, limited rain water infiltration, and lack of forest litter, an important source of organic nutrients. The immediate need for fertilizing can be offset to a degree by including a large volume of good soil mixture around the roots when the trees are planted. Moderate applications of balanced fertilizer injected into the root zone will benefit trees later. Overfertilizing and fertilizing too late in the year can be damaging to trees. Once they are well established and large, trees are better off with very little fertilizer.

However, one should fertilize in conditions where nutrients are extremely limited. The practice of using liquid fertilizers for a "quick shot" is among the more questionable procedures that is regularly marketed. Feeding a tree can hardly ever be regarded as an emergency that requires quick action. A weakened tree may be more susceptible to damage from too much inorganic fertilizer than from too little. Where trees show evidence of nutrient deficiency, a soil analysis and report by a testing agency will often identify the precise need and provide remedies.*

* The U. S. Department of Agriculture, through the Cooperative Extension Service, provides a useful soil testing service.

Maintenance Pruning and Removals. Trees are pruned to preserve their health and appearance, and to prevent damage from falling limbs. The removal of dead and diseased branches prevents decay producing fungi from entering into the trunk of the tree. The usefulness of such pruning is often compromised by the incorrect use of pruning compounds which do not stop decay and can interfere with healing when not applied properly. Though pruning can be done at any season, the best time to prune is late in the dormant period. The worst time is when the leaves are expanding or soon after the leaves begin to fall.

Pruning for aesthetic reasons is sometimes done to maintain a certain size, or form, and could be incorporated into a maintenance pruning schedule. Some maintenance authorities believe that pruning the tops of trees to reduce the crown size keeps the foliage in balance with a restricted root system. This method substitutes an artificial process for a natural one. It may on occasion have some aesthetic justification by creating a lower, more dense crown, but is of doubtful benefit to the tree in helping it adjust to urban conditions. It is also argued that trees pruned this way are more wind firm, to compensate for smaller supporting roots. This hypothesis is dubious, since a taller, more open grown crown and a flexible trunk of a naturally adapted tree are better able to withstand strong winds. Their flexibility allows more air to pass through.

Pruning to maintain consistent geometric masses of foliage is a sophisticated way of using trees in a wholly urban context. The practice is not common in this country, because of the romantic concepts that have controlled urban park design. There is a notion that man should not interfere with the shape of plants. This is inconsistent with the idea of growing trees in cities, since they are inevitably shaped by the urban conditions to a form different from that found in the forest. The popular idea of planting trees as individual specimens is a further inconsistency, since the form of open grown trees is not "natural" in the sense that it rarely occurs in a forest.

2-11
6-16
6-17

Trees can be trimmed into individual tree forms, or into a continuous canopy. Another pruning operation aesthetically motivated is thinning. By removing many small branches within the tree crown, more light is admitted. This is often desirable to reduce the shade density of trees like the Norway Maple or the Pin Oak tree. It is an operation that requires experienced judgment.

The conflict of trees with overhead utility lines has been overemphasized. With the exception of strong terminal branching trees, such as Pin Oaks, planted directly under the lines, there are few circumstances where careful pruning will not resolve any conflict between branches and wires. Trees and utility lines can coexist in harmony where there is a sympathetic handling of the pruning. There are instances where moving the utilities to save trees would be in the best interest of the public.

Dead tree removal is a routine function of some government agency in every municipality. It is not a costly service compared to most other street maintenance operations. In many places the major portion, if not all, of the budget for "tree maintenance" is used for the removal of dead trees and damaged limbs.

135

6-16 Clipped Casuarina trees in West Palm Beach, Florida. An example of trees that are individually "pollarded".

6-17 Clipped Plane Trees in Bristol, Pennsylvania. An example of trees that were trimmed to grow into a single monolithic canopy.

Removal of dead trees contributes to the control of certain insect and disease predators of trees, if the organic material is incinerated. This is especially important in control of the Elm diseases, for instance.

Although removing dead trees is generally a priority, replanting trees to take their place is almost never accomplished as a routine part of maintenance operations. As a result, the attrition rate from dead trees usually exceed the rate of replacement of new trees. In New York City, about 10,000 trees die every year, according to the Parks Department's estimate. This makes the average life span of a street tree in New York about seven years. Replacing dead trees with large size new trees ought to be a high priority for all municipal tree maintenance forces. The budget for this operation must include the cost of stump removal, if that is not part of the dead tree removal maintenance.

Other tree related maintenance. Most urban spaces, except parts of some large parks, require the complete removal of leaves and other droppings from trees. In the wild, this is organic forest litter. Allowing leaves to blanket the ground in large urban parks, though beneficial to trees, is impractical for aesthetic and sanitary reasons. The process of separating tin cans, dead cats, old shoes, discarded limbs, banana peels, and other detritus from the organic leaf litter is not easily accomplished. Increased mechanization makes selective rubbish removal less likely. In most urban areas, leaf removal is combined with general litter removal for the sake of economy. In heavily used spaces, leaves also effect pedestrian circulation and water flow into drain inlets.

The aesthetic values associated with fallen leaves are overwhelmed by our janitorial concerns. The importance of autumn leaves and the illimitable drama of change that deciduous trees bring are an indispensible psychological phenomenon in temperate climate cities. The price of forgetting autumn cannot be measured by any gain in maintenance efficiency.

Damage to buildings by healthy trees is uncommon and is usually associated with storm damage. Trees growing near tall buildings tend to grow away from the structure toward the light, as illustrated in Chapter 4. Roots of very large trees sometimes raise or crack paving. The propensity of tree roots to deflect sidewalks depends mostly on soil porosity and depth. Trees growing in deep, well drained soil will not damage pavement. Where trees grow in open jointed block or brick paving, the roots sometimes cause undulations which add to the textural interest of the ground surface without interfering with circulation. New planting precautions, such as adequate preparation and volume of soil mixture, and use of flexible paving materials, will prevent pavement problems caused by root growth. Certain tree species can enter leaky water or sewer pipes. Poplar or Willow trees should not be planted near susceptible underground pipes or utility lines.

Newly planted trees require more intensive maintenance than trees that are well established. Transplanted trees become established at different times, depending on the species and on local growing conditions. Soil adequacy, protection from excessive sun and wind, and sufficient maintenance are typical variables. Tree species vary widely in their recovery rate after moving. Trees such as American Beech may take as long as five years to recover their normal vigor after transplanting. The Sugar Maple and Red Oak are intermediate and the Plane tree and Honeylocust can sometimes reestablish themselves in one year.

Frequent inspection to discover and correct detrimental conditions is necessary during the initial maintenance period. Loose guys, broken branches, insect invasion, and constricting tree wrap ties are conditions that often need attention when a tree is becoming established. All of these maintenance measures are so important that clients pay a contractor to maintain and guarantee the trees he plants for at least the first year after installation.

Most planting contractors will provide a one year guarantee at extra cost, which will include the responsibility for maintenance. The guarantee normally provides for replacing a tree if it dies within one year after planting. The extra cost, which can run between ten and 30 percent of the planted price, is usually worth paying. In this way municipal and institutional purchasers can avoid the need for temporary additional maintenance forces during the period when the most extensive maintenance of new trees is required.

The price of tree maintenance. Traditionally expenditures for public tree care in American cities have not been based on realistic estimates and costs. Budgets for tree work usually cover emergency removal of dead and fallen trees and limbs. Less often, there is a modest allowance for tree pruning and what amounts to emergency spraying. In addition, there may be a pitifully small budget for tree planting on public streets.

The situation is hard to quantify. Specific amounts spent by a municipality for basic tree care, as opposed to clearing and removal operations, are difficult to identify. The appropriations for work that is directly beneficial to living trees are included with expenditures that involve dead tree removal and other non-tree related maintenance tasks. Often it is part of a highway or sanitary department budget. Figures from a 1965 survey of street tree budgets for selected cities show expenditures for street tree maintenance ranging from $.67 to $9.80 per tree, with an average expenditure of $2.47 per tree. (Hatcher) These amounts were spent for normal tree care and removal, and would not cover the expenditures of an extensive emergency spray program or clearing after a severe storm. Most tree service contractors would regard $10.00 per tree per year as too little to adequately maintain city trees, where the average age is over 50 years. Fifteen dollars per tree is a more realistic figure. However, the actual need could vary by more than 100 percent from year to year.

If we contrast this with a conservative estimate of tree worth, it seems a small amount to pay to protect a valuable investment. For example, if we use the International Shade Tree Conference method and evaluate a mature tree at nine dollars per square inch of trunk cross section, a 20 inch diameter tree would be worth 2,800 dollars. This is substantially less than the cost to replace a tree of this size. At 15 dollars per tree, the annual maintenance cost would be less than the average American family spends to keep its television set running.

A rational approach to formulating a budget for civic tree maintenance would be to inventory all municipally owned trees, noting their age, location, size, species, and condition. Local arborists could then provide approximate figures for the annual cost per tree for a specific level of maintenance, taking into account the condition of the inventoried trees. (Grey and Deneke)

Tree management. Urban silviculture encompasses three essential operations that are referred to as *tree management:* establishing trees, maintaining trees, and removing trees. Important design aspects of establishing trees were discussed in the previous chapters; tree maintenance and removal have been discussed in the first part of this chapter. The aspects of tree management discussed so far relate to typical municipal governments as they function today. It will be useful to look at the broader implications of a tree management program as it should be organized for the improvement of cities.

The urban tree network requires a *tree management division* of the minicipal government that has equal footing with transportation, utilities, and sanitation in the operation of the city. The basic function of this division or department would be to operate a comprehensive program of planning, design, planting, maintenance and removal, integrated with the other operations of the city. Ten years ago the idea of giving trees a status at least equal to sewage and garbage was unthinkable. Our pathetic attempts at planting trees in cities still reflect the old attitude. An organizational structure of the kind proposed here recognizes the biological necessity of trees in cities, and the new attitude of people toward the natural environment.

In a municipal management system we gain the ability to use maintenance and removal as design tools. Here are two examples of techniques that are available to the urban designer under a management program.

Trees are planted close together in a pattern designed for later modification by removal of selected trees. The advantages gained by such a plan are: stronger immediate visual impact, increased rate of growth in height, more upright tree trunks with high branches, and protection by mutual shading of bark and root systems of the young trees. The plan and perspective illustrations, Figures 6-18 and 6-19, show just one of the many possible pattern changes. The time lapse between initial planting and thinning will depend on various circumstances such as species, age at planting, location, and intended form. If the initial planting of Red Maple trees shown diagramatically in Figure 6-18 were installed at four inch caliper size, with adequate soil, and were well maintained, removal of the interstitial trees would occur ten years later.

6-18
6-19

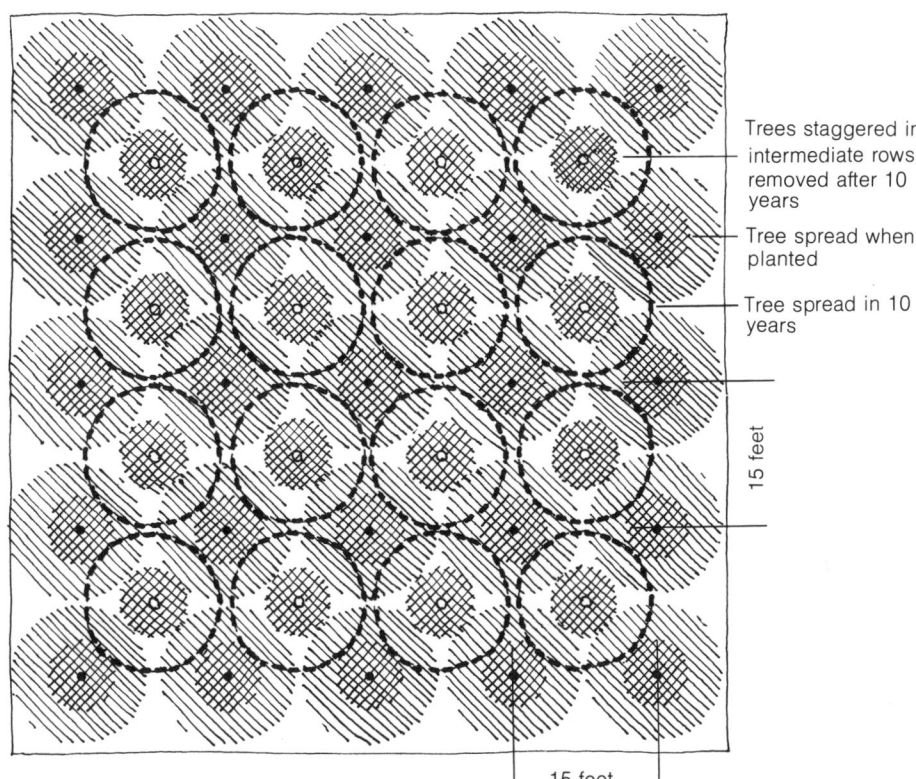

Trees staggered in
intermediate rows,
removed after 10
years

Tree spread when
planted

Tree spread in 10
years

15 feet

15 feet

6-18 Plan: Planned thinning. One example of how trees can be planted in a closely knit pattern designed so that, as trees grow, the pattern can be opened up by removing designated trees. This type of strategy can be used to increase the branch height of trees and provide a more immediate visual effect.

6-19 Perspective: Planned thinning. Trees to be removed are shown by outlines. Were it not for pedestrian circulation, the trees could initially be much closer together than shown. Trees benefit by mutual shading and protection when they are planted close together. The slower rate of growth may be more than compensated for by the initial tree mass achieved.

A more experimental planting technique available under a tree management program is the addition of new trees beneath an existing canopy of older trees. This method aids the transition from older unhealthy trees to young trees. In some instances this could involve the use of a tree type that, in forest communities, would replace the older trees on the site by natural plant succession. The dominant species is more tolerant of shade and would grow up under the existing trees. As knowledge is gained about the behavior of plant communities in an urban habitat, this could become a more sophisticated device for improving city parks with trees.

The most extensive benefit to cities from *tree management* would result from the exploitation of over-planting and later thinning to take advantage of the natural forest regeneration process. It is based on knowledge that has been utilized by foresters for over a century in cultivating timber trees. Trees are allowed to grow in dense groves until they reach an age when they will benefit by a "release cutting," which is a forester's term for selective thinning. An adaptation of this same process to urban conditions could prove of immense benefit in restoring the number of trees needed to make the city wholesome. The spectacle of tree groves throughout the metropolis would create a striking contrast to the spindly twigs that occasionally appear in lonely isolation within our urban centers.

Opportunities

The significant obstacles to using trees effectively in cities and towns are tractable. More trees are not planted in urban situations because it is believed that they will not grow. The argument is circular. More trees are not growing in urban situations now because they are not properly planted. The conclusion is: in urban habitats biologically fit for human beings, large trees can be grown, if there is public enlightenment and technical understanding. Full public perception of the value and cost of trees can lead to more realistic policies on tree planting. Negative regulations which limit trees can then give way to regulations that actually require the use of trees in urban spaces. Our fear of trees can be conquered.

The physical impediments to good tree growth can be cured by adopting sound techniques. There are five essential rules:

1. Provide an adequate depth and spread of prepared growing medium to accommodate the root system below ground level, with positive subsoil drainage.

2. Plant durable types of trees that are over four inches in diameter in sufficient quantity to form a self-protecting grove.

3. Protect tree roots from compaction, salt, and dog abuse.

4. Plant trees in locations that receive an average of at least three hours of direct sunlight each day during the growing season.

5. Provide a basic maintenance program that satisfies the specific needs for the locality and tree type.

If we are to make full use of current technical knowledge and build cities that are a true measure of our modern capabilities, large scale planning and implementation by public agencies are necessary. A *tree management program* that incorporates design with tree planting and maintainence is a practical way to enrich cities.

References

Laws of New Jersey Pertaining to Shade Tree Commissions. New Jersey: New Jersey Federation of Shade Tree Commissions, 1969.

Beatty, Russell, and Heckman, Craig. *Urban Tree Survey Summary.* (unpublished) University of California, Berkeley, 1978.

Gutman, Robert, and Landry, Jean. *Tree Ordinances in the Bicentennial Year.* (unpublished paper) Princeton University, New Jersey.

Manual of Tree Planting Standards. Illinois: Department of Streets and Sanitation, Bureau of Forestry, Parkways and Beautification, 1977.

Grey, Gene W., and Deneke, Frederick J. *Urban Forestry.* New York: John Wiley and Sons, 1978.

Report of the President's Council on Pennsylvania Avenue. *Pennsylvania Avenue*. Washington, D.C.: U.S. Government Printing Office, 1964.

Stout, Benjamin R. *Studies of the Root Systems of Deciduous Trees*, Black Rock Forest, Bulletin #15. Mass: Harvard University Printing Office, 1956.

Flemer, William. "Container Trees for Use in Landscaping", *Better Trees for Metropolitan Landscapes*, Symposium Proceedings, USDA Forest Service General Technical Report NE-22. Washington, D.C.: U.S. Government Printing Office, 1976. (pp. 185–193)

Seelye, Elwyn E. *Data Book for Civil Engineers, Design*, Third Ed. New York: John Wiley and Sons, Inc., 1960.

Zion, Robert. *Trees for Architecture and the Landscape*. New York: Reinhold, 1968.

Patterson, James. "Soil Compaction and its Effects Upon Urban Vegetation", *Better Trees for Metropolitan Landscapes*, Symposium Proceedings. (pp. 91–100)

Davis, Donald and Gerhold, Henry. "Selection of Trees for Tolerance of Air Pollution", *Better Trees for Metropolitan Landscapes*, Symposium Proceedings. (p. 61)

Smith, William and Gerhold, Henry. "Capability of Metropolitan Trees to Reduce Atmospheric Contaminants", *Better Trees for Metropolitan Landscapes*, Symposium Proceedings. (pp. 49–59)

U.S. Department of Agriculture, Forest Service. *Our Air*. Washington, D.C.: USDA.

Loomis, Robert C. and Padgett, William. *Air Pollution and Trees in the East*. USDA Forest Service, 1975.

Dodge, Bernard O. and Rickett, Harold W. *Diseases and Pests of Ornamental Plants*. New York: The Ronald Press Co., 1948.

Dirr, Michael. "Salts and Woody-Plant Interactions in the Urban Environment", *Better Trees for Metropolitan Landscapes*, Symposium Proceedings. (pp. 103–110)

Pirone, P. O. *Tree Maintenance*, Fourth Ed. New York: Oxford University Press, Inc., 1976.

Cathey, H. M. and Cambell, L. E. Security lighting and its impact on the landscape. *Journal of Arboriculture*, 1(10): 84 (1975).

May, Robert M. The evolution of ecological systems. *Scientific American* 239: 160–175 (1978).

Hatcher, O. "Scope of Shade Tree Care in Region 5 of the International Shade Tree Conference". *Proceedings of International Shade Tree Conference* 41: 114–119 (1965).

International Shade Tree Conference. *Shade Tree Evaluation*. Illinois: International Shade Tree Conference, Inc., 1970.

A nobler vision

7

Tree management and urban planning

The renewal and enrichment of public open spaces with trees hinges on a very practical question. Who will carry through such an important and far reaching program? The advantages of having a separate division of municipal government, devoted exclusively to the culture of trees have been discussed. Let us now consider the formation of an appropriate mechanism for the broad planning responsibilities of an urban municipality. An outline of the responsibilities and tasks involved in beneficial tree planning is presented here in schematic form to show its relationship to other government tasks.

Responsibilities. The tree management agency, a division of the city parks department, would have the mission of establishing, maintaining, and removing trees. Planning responsibilities would be shared with the city planning department, which would prepare the city-wide master plan for parks and open spaces. The *tree management* division would prepare the master tree plan and work with the parks department on detail design involving trees. The details of organization would vary with the way the government is structured. However, the essential tasks to be shared by these agencies are as follows:

1. Developing a positive written public policy with respect to tree planting, maintenance, and removal.
2. Establishing urban design criteria for trees.
3. Preparing and publishing a municipal tree plan as part of the master plan.
4. Preparing standards and regulations for tree planting.
5. Carrying out and administering the plan and regulations.

Public policy statement. The basis for tree management would be an adopted declaration of public principles about trees in relation to needs, attitudes, and public welfare. It should reflect the value that citizens and civic leaders place on trees in urban design, and an appropriate degree of commitment. In a community where trees are considered very important, a goal provision could perhaps be a continuous canopy of trees along all streets in the municipality and installation of shade trees in all parks and public open spaces. It might even establish a hierarchy of master plan components, showing the importance of trees in relation to other items. In tone and purpose the statement should be inclusive rather than restrictive.

Urban design criteria.   A series of general statements is also needed, more definitive than the policy statement, to provide consistency and thoroughness in preparing the Municipal Tree Plan. For example, the criteria might include the following:

1. Plant trees that reach a mature size of over 40 feet in height within public street right-of-way and as near to the curb as the root ball permits.

2. Plant street trees on the south side of the east-west streets no closer to the buildings than one-third of the adjacent building height.

3. Plant street trees no further apart than 25 feet on north-south streets and 30 feet apart on east-west streets.

4. Provide at least four feet of prepared topsoil depth and 500 cubic feet of prepared topsoil for each tree that is planted in paved areas.

The urban design criteria for trees should generally be part of a comprehensive set of criteria governing urban design in the municipality. They would enumerate aesthetically sound planning principles for urban tree use, cultural necessities for plant growth, and operational requirements of the municipality, such as movement of vehicles and people. It is by this process, rather than by chance, that priorities can be established in locating trees, utilities, and other urban service structures. Obviously each city, town, and maybe precinct will vary its criteria to suit local climate, building height, latitude in relation to solar angles, and other local variables that affect how trees are best utilized for effective design. These criteria are constructive rather than restrictive. Guildlines are based on reasoned principles or measured determinants.

It is counter-productive for a municipality to set arbitrary guidelines limiting planting. For example, setting a minimum spacing between trees limits the number of trees that can be planted and can interfere with good design. However, setting a maximum distance between trunks assures that there will be enough trees to improve the city noticeably. It also assures better tree survival and necessary latitude in design.

Municipal tree plan. This is a map showing existing trees, where new trees should be planted, and what type of tree should be planted for each area, block, or street. Prepared as part of the master plan for the municipality, this is an important urban design document, not included in many municipal plans. Stress should be placed upon sound aesthetic criteria, as well as plant culture and municipal operating requirements. The plan must achieve unity for the city by limiting and organizing different species or else it will have little value. Any arborist or competent observer of nature can name trees that are culturally suitable for planting. The crucial need in every city of the United States is for a strongly organized arboreal pattern.

Municipal design regulations. These should be projected from the urban design criteria in support of the Tree Plan and should not be a series of prohibitions that restrict tree use. The broad purposes of these regulations are:

1. To encourage the use of more shade trees.

2. To develop unity in the overall street and open space pattern.

3. To promote good cultural planting practices.

4. To preserve trees and control practices harmful to trees.

In the few cities that have design regulations encouraging planting, they are part of a broad ordinance that regulates new building development. For example, the New York City Zoning Ordinance incorporates standards and requirements for trees as part of a special amendment dealing with urban open space. The purpose of the amendment is to improve the quality of open space (resulting from a height bonus allowed developers in return for providing open space at the ground level of tall buildings). Standards are set for widening sidewalks, for plazas that require seats, special materials, trees, and other amenities. The regulations direct the number, size, spacing, and location of trees in relation to the area, configuration, and orientation. An important part of this ordinance requires large trees at planting and sets a minimum acceptable volume and depth of planting soil for each tree.*

* Detail design requirements of this zoning ordinance amendment are available in publication entitled "New Life for Plazas," New York City Planning Commission, May 1975

Administering the plan. This task is best accomplished by a tree management division of the municipal government, and not as an ancillary function of another specialized department. The situation of trees in the government structure reflects the public perception of their usefulness and importance. The government agencies that perform urban design services should be organized so that the tree planners have a staff position as important and effective as transportation and utility planners. The tree management division, in carrying out its responsibilities of design and planning, will have the advantage of being able to integrate the tree maintenance and removal efforts of the city into the new designs. This is rarely, if ever, accomplished now because of incorrect structuring of responsibilities in city government.

The technical design staff of the tree management and planning agencies, the landscape architects, city planners, and architects, must enlarge the scope of their efforts to revegetate our urban areas by dealing with trees in appropriately large units. Building design should encompass the entire site. The use of trees should influence the building design, just as building design influences where trees should go. The space between buildings is as important as the space within buildings. If planting becomes an accepted, standard part of every site plan, it will become as indispensible as utilities, drainage systems, and pavement.

The urban region and trees

City and region. The context of the city in its regional landscape is important because the city can be either enhanced or compromised by surrounding development. There is an interdependence of parts in every system, whether the system is man-made, such as the highway network, or natural, such as the land drainage pattern. The urban and rural parts must accommodate one another. Seen from the air, the pattern of trees in a metropolitan region tells at a glance how well the city and countryside operate together.

The suburbs represent a failure of human spirit—a reluctantly accepted compromise—that no amount of tree planting can assuage. The contrast of the current treelined streets of Levittown with the image of the new development 20 years ago, provides a convenient diversion. Neither the unlimited ecological cost nor the social isolation produced by such inefficient land use can be vindicated by replanting trees. The quintessential value of reforesting cities lies in the need to humanize moderate density living to save land.* There is a need, widely recognized by planners, for a different kind of diversity in the regional land use pattern from what we find in typical suburban density development. The immediate adjacency of city and town to forest and meadow is an ideal with such universal appeal and instinctive good sense that it justifies reevaluation of our sacred assumptions about property rights and development. The planners of Great Britain have recognized the value of this concept in their Green Belt zoning laws. Limiting further fragmentation of the landscape is inescapable. Therefore we must agree on national goals to limit the size of cities, keep natural areas intact, increase gross density of new development, and allow people to live near their place of work. In nonurbanized areas, every new highway and ground level transportation system absolutely decreases the plant and animal species diversity within the natural region. The total damage done to forest, soil, and stream by highways permeates every strata and ecological niche of the land to an extent that is unassessable in its magnitude. The loss of surrounding forest hurts the city even more than the absence of trees in the urban center.

New town efforts. Optimism prevailed among conservationists and planners in the 1960's that large scale building with good planning might provide a new alternative to the problem of urban sprawl. Unfortunately the recent attempt at

* Moderate densities here refer to between 25 and 50 dwellings per acre accommodated with low and medium rise residential structures that make good communal use of the land. There are a number of low rise housing prototypes that permit densities up to 90 units per acre and satisfy many current social demands, including in-town automobiles. (Institute for Architecture and Urban Studies)

building new towns in the United States such as Reston, Virginia, or Columbia, Maryland, produced a land use pattern that is indistinguishable from the post World War II suburbs. The orthodox new town mixture of scattered, low single family houses and casually placed higher density groups of houses on curvilinear streets does not form an integrated pattern of buildings and trees that define open spaces. The major failing of these new developments, to provide high density populations, is traceable to the building prototype and assumptions about what type of houses would have been marketable. A bolder building form incorporated with more intensive use of trees would have allowed a higher density without compromising the land form or the visual scale. Even where an effort was made to design building and landscape together, the full spatial potential of trees was never exploited. An often praised example, the first Lake Anne Center at Reston, might have used trees as a superb transitional device to amalgamate building, plaza, forest, and water edge. Instead, the background of existing trees provided an excuse not to plant trees where they could do the most good, in shading the water edge pavement and the central plaza. The opportunity was lost to structure the open space near the buildings with trees. Even an arcade of trees planned as an extension of the store fronts was left out in the execution. This open plaza without trees unsuccessfully mimics the Mediterranean piazza, but in a more hostile climate.

Columbia, Maryland, provides another example of low density development on a massive scale that is dependent on automobile transportation, even for local shopping and recreation. Trees provided no design challenge in this conventional suburban development pattern, and indeed, there were no exemplary results. The unfortunate aspect of new community efforts like Columbia, Reston, Woodlands, Lysander, and Irvine, was not so much the failure to produce better planning techniques, such as innovative tree use, but the utter failure to provide higher density prototypes for future development. This failure is inextricably linked to the economics of speculative development in this country. The new town efforts that were urban in character, notable Cedar Riverside in Minnesota, and Roosevelt Island in New York, did not exploit trees imaginatively in a way that would make these living materials a fundamental design determinant. On the whole, new town experiments of the 1960's and early 1970's ignored the opportunity to incorporate biological criteria in their basic planning and followed conventional speculative development models regardless of density.

Development and tree pattern. The best hope for our immediate future is to rehabilitate our existing cities by the reintroduction of water, trees, and clean air. As of today, we do not have the economic mechanism to finance environmentally sound, land conserving forms of new development. With the revival of cities as functional and cultural nuclei, the preservation of wild and cultivated landscapes can be assured. It is this clear separation of urban and rural landscape that alone can offer a totality of human experience. The suburban land pattern does not fulfill our deep, shared perceptions of "city" and "country."

Our objective should be a completely integrated assembly of structures, trees, movement systems, and water. In this organic regional pattern, large scale reforestation would accompany the construction of other physical elements and assure the environment for their success. The economical and ecological benefits of forest farming make large tree planting projects appear feasible. (Sholto) It is in this regional context that the ecological principle of plant *diversity* makes sense, not at the level of the city block. At the regional scale, the use of trees would exhibit a highly structured diversity. From the air, the tree pattern would reflect the land use and transitions between developed and wild land. Center city, high and low density urbanized land, agrarian land, and forest would each have its discrete arrangement and composition of trees. The appropriate tree pattern for the downtown would never be confused with the native forest, because their aesthetic expression is as different as their cultural requirements.

A transition to an ecologically stable regional land pattern will complement the restoration and enhancement of cities. These restored urban centers will serve as models to demonstrate the effectiveness of biologically sound planning and design. Keeping the cities and towns intensively urban and curtailing the development of undisturbed land is an essential basic premise. Some other characteristics of this regional land development pattern might be:

1. A complete, continuously linked system of forests spanning the range of scale from regional preserves to narrow treelined streets.

2. Net residential densities that permit human interaction and civilized commerce at travel speeds of no more than 20 miles per hour, with a maximum trip of 15 minutes for normal daily activities.

3. Gross residential densities that allow access to a complete range of cultural interaction without traveling longer than 30 minutes on public transit facilities.

4. An urban reticulum of lakes, canals, and ponds to replicate the natural water system in an aesthetically appropriate urban way and provide irrigation for trees.

5. Land use arrangements that exploit the solar benefits of trees and allow more extensive man-made solar collection systems to localize energy production and eliminate megalithic power transmission line structures. The resulting tree cover pattern would reflect building orientation, height and setbacks for tree growth, as well as the amount and orientation of solar collection surface.

6. Inter-city transit systems, suspended above or tunneled below the ground to allow continuous uninterrupted land areas to be preserved in their natural state. This would prevent further fragmenting of land into smaller and smaller islands as now results from highway expansion.

7. Intra-city transportation for people based on free use of bicycle technology and small scale, low power vehicles that complement but do not compete with the bicycle.* Human feet and wheel chairs are also more compatible with these pedestrian scaled machines, and give the disabled a genuine share in the conviviality of a city. The movement of walkers in cities should be at ground level, where people can enjoy the life of the city, experience weather, and know the season.

8. Freight moving constantly in tubes or guideways below or above ground level to eliminate parking space requirements and pedestrian conflict.

9. Water for human use as a major determinant of population dispersal. In grossest terms this could be expressed as person per square mile per average annual inch of rainfall. Then, based upon per capita water consumption, irrigation, regional stream flow requirements, and adequate reserves for drought, a biologically stable limit on population could be determined for each watershed.

10. The highest social priorities given to public open space and the related biological necessity of an urban environment fit for plant—and therefore human—vitality. This necessitates air and water quality standards maintained at levels that support healthy forest growth.

* The bicycle has more advantages for human mobility in cities than any vehicle yet devised. Not only is it the most energy efficient machine for moving people, but it can move ten times the volume of traffic under city conditions that automobiles do with a single occupant in less time, and requires about one-twentieth of the storage space of a car. Trees and people on bicycles complement each other, the one providing shade, scale, and lane separation, and the other producing only beneficial effluent, carbon dioxide, for tree growth.

Cities and trees

The evolving city/forest. There are numerous examples in European cities and more limited, scattered examples in this country of trees used to reflect and reinforce the geometry of the man-made city. These examples represent an approach to urban open space design that is both symbolically and functionally sympathetic to expressing human creativity. The historic design form that has been endlessly repeated in our cities now seems naive and inappropriate. We see less of a relationship to natural plant communities in the studied random tree arrangements of the romantic park than in more organized man-made patterns. Pastoral landscapes no longer symbolize the good, honest agrarian life that was falsely imagined to exist a century ago.

The inevitable direction of change in our attitude toward the use of trees in cities is salutary. We will have greater freedom in urban design to evolve city forms that represent our age. The form of our metropolitan areas can begin to reflect the biological requirements—the symbiotic associations—that express the harmony of man and nature. Change, even evolutionary change, is sometimes impeded by the slowness with which we assimilate new non-technical knowledge. Surprisingly, one of the impediments to reforesting cities is lack of technical knowledge. Our standards for tree planting are based on an outdated historic style and the influence of pastoralism. How better can we explain the preference for the open grown tree form among plant scientists who develop our tree planting methods?

The gradual appreciation of the value of trees in the biosphere reinforces the aesthetic justification for more trees in cities. As our institutions change to reflect this understanding, trees will become more important than bricks in building cities. These concepts of urban forestry and tree management are now frequently being discussed.* In retrospect, it is surprising how long it has taken our culture to act upon such an obvious need—trees as an inseparable part of the urban structure.

*The second annual National Urban Forestry Conference was held in Washington, D.C. in November, 1978.

Coherence in design. If it were necessary to select one single over-riding principle to guide the use of trees in cities, it would be the establishment of a unifying order. Cities, with all of their unrelated little pieces cry out for order. There is a desperate unequivocal need for coherence based on continuity, rhythm, repetition, and linkage. Trees alone satisfy this need. There is the need and potential for a quiet and pervasive order that arises from the power of art working with the cosmic forces of nature. Bringing into the city, the forest concepts of unity and coherence, through the natural principles of plant adaptability, density, and species uniformity, is the hope and the promise of trees in urban design. The resulting geometric tree pattern is the collaborative expression of evolutionary forest and rational thinkers.

New design criteria. The density of trees in cities is a truer numerical measure of the health and well being of the city than the population density. A city with 800 persons per acre with trees in the spaces presently usurped by automobiles could be far more liveable and functional than another city with 100 persons per acre in the conventional land use arrangement where the "open space" is given over to the needs of transportation. In fact, in a well designed city, higher population density will be a direct result of more usable open space and compatible transportation based on metabolic energy (greatly enhanced by the bicycle). The discovery of the paradox that the more we accelerate speed, the more time we spend in travel, can now serve as a lesson to city planners in viewing density and dispersal. (Illich) The quintessential interdependence of people, forest, and benign technology sets radically different criteria for urban design. These criteria can provide the basis for imaginative planners to reforest the city without suburbanizing or compromising its essential density.

Visions and revisions. Modern projections of future cities have eliminated trees as part of the city. These proposals give complete ascendency to scientific technology. The technocratic concepts of Buckminster Fuller and Palo Solari separate the man-made environment from the evolutionary habitat of trees and people. Their proposals signify a further chilling step toward the surrender of man's native abilities to the expert and the machine, because of their appealing promise of utilitarian ease. By increasing our dependence on technology, they promote the myth that physical work is undesirable for people.

A more appealing approach for designing cities would give great importance to biological criteria concerned with the dimensions and growth requirements of trees. The promise of a more humanistic order for cities rests on physical design determined by solar angles, seasons, human metabolism, soil structure, and forest patterns that are genetically part of our being. Intuitively this approach seems right, because as living organisms we adapt readily to biological communities. We are genetically attuned to a natural environment that has been modified by human toil. The redesign and construction of these cities can only be wrought by human understanding and sensitivity. Then technology can be used to enhance rather than destroy creative life. It is inevitable, because of our biological heritage, that the creation of an ideal human habitat will restore forests.

The necessity of understanding the city as part of a larger natural region has been inhibited by the same obstacle that stifles regional planning—municipal boundary lines. The resulting absurd mosaic of unrelated land use plans is reflected eventually in the fragmented tree pattern. The view from the air demonstrates why planning on a natural land form basis is so much more logical than the current "practical" way. The regional tree pattern will continue to be the most highly visible expression of the land use structure. It will be either a desultory spattering of green, or a web of green threads that radiate from city centers and merge into the regional forest. The nucleus of these life-giving strands will determine which pattern describes the industrial city of the year 2001.

We can have cities that are made of buildings, water and trees, utilizing concepts and materials that are as old as evolution. Cities where people walk and bicycle through arabesques of trees will reinstate the street level for human activity. In these places, the geometry of man will be perceived as the expression of a society where art governs the use of scientific knowledge. What now seems an unattainable utopian world will grow from the rediscovery of human toil to create excellence rather than to increase quantity. The view from the air will reveal the intricate juxtaposition of rural farm patterns and subtly organized forest communities bordering on crystalline mosaic patterns of trees and buildings. From other corners of the galaxy, this planetary pattern will perhaps be admired as the supreme expression of successful evolution.

References

The New York City Planning Commission. *New Life For Plazas*. New York. May 1975.

The Institute for Architecture and Urban Studies. *Another Chance for Housing: Low Rise Alternatives*. New York: The Museum of Modern Art, 1973.

Sholto, J., and de J. Hart, Robert. *Forest Farming*. London: Watkins, 1976.

Illich, Ivan. *Toward A History of Needs*. New York: Pantheon Books, 1978.

Common and botanical names of trees mentioned in the text

Acacia	Acacia species
Ailanthus (Tree of Heaven)	Ailanthus altissima
American Arborvitae	Thuja occidentalis
American Beech	Fagus grandifolia
American Elm	Ulmus americana
American Holly	Ilex opaca
American Linden	Tilia americana
Amur Cork	Phellodendron amurense
Angsana	Pterocarpus indicus
Aspen	Populus tremuloides
Baldcypress	Taxodium distichum
Black Cherry	Prunus serotina
Black Locust	Robinia pseudoacacia
Black Olive Tree (Oxhorn bucida)	Bucida buceras
Black Spruce	Picea mariana
Boxelder Maple	Acer negundo
Bradford Pear	Pyrus calleryana "Bradford"
California Pepper Tree	Schinus molle
Callery Pear	Pyrus calleryana
Camphor-tree	Cinnamomum camphora
Casuarina	Casuarina equisetifolia
Catalpa Tree	Catalapa speciosa
Cherry Laurel (Laurelcherry)	Prunus laurocerasus
Chinese Elm	Ulmus parvifolia
Coconut Palm	Cocos nucifera
Crape-myrtle	Lagerstroemia indica
Dawn Redwood	Metasequoia glyptostroboides
Dedfree Elm	Ulmus americana "Dedfree"
Desert Willow	Chilopsis linearis
Emerald Queen Maple	Acer platanoides "Emerald Queen"
English Oak	Quercus robur
Eucalyptus Tree	Eucalyptus species
European Larch	Larix decidua
Flowering Cherry Tree	Prunus species
Flowering Dogwood	Cornus florida
Ginkgo	Ginkgo biloba
Golden-rain Tree	Koelreuteria paniculata
Groenveldt Elm	Ulmus hollandica "Groenveldt"
Hawthorn	Crataegus species
Hemlock (Canadian Hemlock)	Tsuga canadensis
Honeylocust (Common Honeylocust)	Gleditsia triacanthos

Horsechestnut	Aesculus hippocastanum
Horsetail (Beefwood)	Casuarina equisetifolia
Indian Laurel	Ficus retusa
Jacaranda	Jacaranda acutifolia
Japanese Larch	Larix leptolepis
Japanese Pagoda Tree	Sophora japonica
Japanese Tree Lilac	Syringa amurensis "japonica"
Kentucky Coffee Tree	Gymnocaldus dioicus
Larch	Larix
Laurelcherry (Cherry Laurel)	Prunus laurocerasus
Littleleaf Linden	Tilia cordata
Live Oak	Quercus virginiana
Lombardy Poplar	Populus nigra var. italica
London Plane	Platanus acerifolia
Madras Thorn	Pithecellobium dulce
Mexican Fan Palm	Washingtonia robusta
Modesto Ash	Fraxinus velutina "Modesto"
Mountain-ash	Sorbus species
Norway Maple	Acer platanoides
Norway Spruce	Picea abies
Olive Tree	Olea europaea communis
Oriental Plane	Platanus orientalis
Palo Verde (Blue Palo verde)	Cercidium floridum
Rain Tree	Enterolobium saman
Red Maple	Acer rubrum
Redmond Linden	Tilia americana "Redmond"
Red Oak	Quercus borealis
River Birch	Betula nigra
Royal Palm	Roystonea regia
Russian Olive	Elaeagnus angustifolia
Saga	Adenanthera pavonia
Sargent Cherry	Prunus sargentii
Sassafras	Sassafras albidum
Saucer Magnolia	Magnolia soulangeana
Scarlet Oak	Quercus coccinea
Scotch Pine	Pinus sylvestris
Silver Linden	Tilia tomentosa
Silver Maple	Acer saccharinum
Southern Magnolia	Magnolia grandiflora
Spanish Oak	Quercus falcata
Sterile Mulberry	Morus alba vars.
Strawberry Tree	Arbutus unedo
Sugar Maple	Acer saccharum
Sweet Gum	Liquidambar styraciflua
Sycamore	Platanus occidentalis
Sycamore Maple	Acer pseudoplatanus
Thornless Honeylocust	Gleditsia triacanthos inermis (and vars.)
Tree of Heaven	Ailanthus altissima
Tulip Tree	Liriodendron tulipifera
Washington Hawthorn	Crataegus phaenopyrum
Weeping Willow	Salix babylonica
White Ash	Fraxinus americana
White Oak	Quercus alba
Yellowwood (American Yellowwood)	Cladrastis lutea
Zelkova	Zelkova serrata

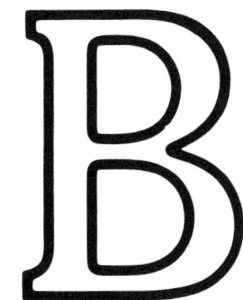

Descriptive information about photographs of exemplary tree use

The following comparative data will supplement selected photographs. The intent is to provide general information about how trees grow under certain limited conditions. The descriptions are derived from a variety of sources including drawings, files, the author's sketch pad, memory, field measurements and in some instances simply considered judgment. Where information is unknown and cannot be reliably estimated, it is left out. The table is not intended as a source of precise data.

1. Figure number of illustration.
2. Page number of illustration.
3. Geographical place.
4. Year in which picture was taken.
5. Brief description of subject.
6. Common name of tree species. Where significant for design the particular type or variety is noted. See Appendix A for Botanical names.
7. Diameter of the tree: Trees over 8 inches measured at breast height—4½ feet above ground (DBH) in inches. Tree 8 inches or less measured 12 inches above the ground (caliper) in inches.
8. Spacing: The distance in feet between trees in a line where only one figure is given. Where there are two figures, the first is the distance in feet between rows and the second is the typical distance between trees within each row. Stagger rows are noted under comments.
9. The age of the trees in years from seedlings to the date of photograph. Since historical data for most trees is difficult to uncover, the figure given is usually estimated from the trunk diameter taking into account site conditions, growth rate of the species, and known historic information.
10. Comments include information of possible interest to design professionals, and where known, landscape design credits.

The purpose of providing comparative data about exceptional tree use in urban spaces is to assist designers in planning for trees. These examples provide a starting place for learning about the growth habits and visual effects of urban trees. The factual data show why most rules-of-thumb about tree spacing, type and location are misleading. The large disparity in habit of growth for urban trees in various situations makes such generalizations meaningless. The designer who uses trees must know about the possibilities and not just the limitations. An extensive compilation of comparative data about visually successful tree use would make a valuable replacement for the popular generalizations that hamper rather than guide design with trees.

Figure	Location	Date	Description	Type
1-1	Brooklyn, New York	1977	Cadman Plaza Park, N.Y.C. Parks Department	London Plane
1-2	Philadelphia, Pennsylvania	1976	Benjamin Franklin Parkway, view northwest from 16th Street	Plane
1-18	Charlotte, North Carolina	1973	Residential street	Willow Oak
1-21	Houston, Texas	1973	Main Street at Rice University	Live Oak
1-27	Rome, Italy	1966	Along the Tiber River	Plane
1-32	Ashville, North Carolina	1973	Biltmore Estate view down central axis	Tulip Tree
1-33	Ashville, North Carolina	1973	Biltmore Estate side view of trees	Tulip Tree
1-34	Ashville, North Carolina	1973	Biltmore Estate view under trees	Tulip Tree
1-35	Manhattan, New York	1978	Central Park view north of the "Mall"	American Elm
1-36	Manhattan, New York	1978	Central Park, tree grove	Sycamore
1-48	Oak Park, Illinois	1977	Oak Park Center Mall	Pin Oak
1-49	London, England	1977	View along the "Embankment"	London Plane
1-51	Mexico City, Mexico	1979	Paseo de la Reforma	
1-52	Mexico City, Mexico	1979	Boulevard at Chapultepec Park	
1-53	Canton, China	1977	A city street	Poplar
1-57	Singapore	1970	A city street	Rain Tree
2-2	Manhattan, New York	1976	Bryant Park	Oriental Plane
2-3, 4	Houston, Texas	1973	City Hall Park	Live Oak
2-5	Philadelphia, Pennsylvania	1969	Delancey Street Park	Thornless Honeylocust
2-6	Singapore	1971	Cannaught Drive, the Padang	Rain Tree
2-7	Chicago, Illinois	1977	Central District Filtration Plant	Thornless Honeylocust
2-8	Philadelphia, Pennsylvania	1973	Independence Mall, 3d Block	Thornless Honeylocust
2-9	Chicago, Illinois	1977	Chicago River Park	Redmond Linden
2-10	Chicago, Illinois	1977	Grant Park	American Elm
2-11, 12	Bristol, Pennsylvania	1976	Grundy Park	London Plane
2-13	Savannah, Georgia	1973	Park near waterfront	Live Oak
2-14	Singapore	1970	Park along Canal Street	Madras Thorn
2-15	Cambridge, Massachusetts	1968	Memorial Drive	Sycamore
2-16	London, England	1977	The Mall	London Plane
2-17	Philadelphia, Pennsylvania	1977	Benjamin Franklin Parkway	Sycamore
2-18	Palm Beach, Florida	1977	Street with Palm Trees	Coconut Palm
2-19	Palm Beach, Florida	1977	Royal Palm Way	Royal Palm

Type	Diam.	Spacing	Age	Comments
London Plane	11	20 x 20	42	Planted 1951; 3½″ caliper, design: Clarke & Rapuano
Plane	21	30	100	50′ to 60′ tall
Willow Oak	38	25		
Live Oak	25	15 x 30	70	Planted by Rice University in 1916
Plane	40	18	100+	
Tulip Tree	40	240 x 40	100+	Planted about 1890, plan by F. L. Olmsted Sr. with Morris Hunt
Tulip Tree	40	25 x 40	100+	Same
Tulip Tree	40	25 x 40	100+	Same
American Elm	26	66 x 45	60	Originally planted 1860, plan by Olmsted and Vaux
Sycamore	37		120	Planted about 1870, plan by Olmsted and Vaux
Pin Oak	6	11 x 22	20	Planted in 1975, design: Joe Karr
London Plane	14	30 x 20	50	
	17	45		
	8	20		
Poplar				Recent planting
Rain Tree	19	25	20	Planted about 1965, 10″ caliper
Oriental Plane	16	20 x 20	62	Planted 1934, 5″ caliper, 25′ tall
Live Oak	18	20	70	
Thornless Honeylocust	5	17 x 20	18	Planted 1966, design: Philadelphia Department of Recreation/Collins and DuTot
Rain Tree	42	25		
Thornless Honeylocust	5	8 x 12	24	Planted 1967, design: Dan Kiley
Thornless Honeylocust	7	12 x 18	28	Planted 1962, design: Dan Kiley
Redmond Linden	7	21	25	Planted 1976, design: Joe Karr
American Elm	18	12 x 18	50	
London Plane	16	20 x 20	50	Planted 1928
Live Oak	25	25 x 25	65	
Madras Thorn	28	35	25	
Sycamore	40	45 x 40	140	
London Plane	11	25 x 25	25	
Sycamore	22	30	100+	
Coconut Palm	—	25 x 20		
Royal Palm	—	24 x 20		

Figure	Location	Date	Description	Type
2-20, 21	Columbus, Indiana	1973	Cummins Engine Company	Plane Tree
2-22	Manhattan, New York	1977	West 81st Street	Plane Tree
2-23	Trenton, New Jersey	1977	Lamberton Road	Sycamore Tree
2-24	Philadelphia, Pennsylvania	1978	Delancey Street	Plane Tree
2-25	Philadelphia, Pennsylvania	1978	Panama Street	Ginkgo
2-26	Tempe, Arizona	1973	Arizona State walkway	Mexican Fan Palm
2-27	Versailles, France	1966	Chateau Gardens	Maple Trees
2-28	Boston, Massachusetts	1977	Faneuil Hall Market	Thornless Honeylocust
2-29	Manhattan, New York	1976	Lincoln Center	London Plane
2-30	Manhattan, New York	1975	Rockefeller University	London Plane
2-31	Berkeley, California	1970	University of California	Eucalyptus
2-32	Manhattan, New York	1978	Stuyvesant Town	London Plane
2-33	Manhattan, New York	1978	Stuyvesant Town	London Plane
4-2	Manhattan, New York	1976	Bryant Park	Oriental Plane
4-3	Princeton, New Jersey	1978	Witherspoon Street	Plane
4-4	Brooklyn, New York	1978	South Portland Avenue	Plane
4-6	Princeton, New Jersey	1978	Battle Road	Plane
4-15	Cleveland, Ohio	1978	Board of Education Building	Sycamore
4-16	Cleveland, Ohio	1978	Board of Education Building	Sycamore
4-17	Cleveland, Ohio	1978	Board of Education Building	Sycamore
4-18	Princeton, New Jersey	1978	Battle Road	London Plane
4-23	Chicago, Illinois	1978	Grant Park	American Elm
4-24	Chicago, Illinois	1978	Grant Park	American Elm
4-42	Philadelphia, Pennsylvania	1978	Delancey Street	Plane Tree
4-43	Kingston, New Jersey	1977	Dirt Road	Pin Oak
4-44	Philadelphia, Pennsylvania	1978	Independence Mall, third block	Thornless Honeylocust
4-45	Brooklyn, New York	1978	Fort Green Park	Ginkgo
4-46	Princeton, New Jersey	1977	Battle Road	London Plane
4-47	Washington, D.C.	1976	The Federal Mall	American Elm
4-48	Arnheim, Holland	1964	Tree Tunnel	European Beech
5-4	Philadelphia, Pennsylvania	1978	Vine Street south side	Ginkgo
5-5	Princeton, New Jersey	1978	Library Place street trees	Red Oak
5-6	Deal, New Jersey	1978	Morgan Avenue	Plane
5-7	Brooklyn, New York	1978	Cumberland Street at Ft. Greene	Horse-chestnut
5-10	Philadelphia, Pennsylvania	1978	Independence Mall, third block	Thornless Honeylocust

Type	Diam.	Spacing	Age	Comments
Plane Tree	8	12 x 25	25	Planted 1962, design: Dan Kiley
Plane Tree	19	24 x 20	55	
Sycamore Tree	38	12 x 35	90	
Plane Tree	20	22 x 12	55	
Ginkgo	14	12 x 18	65	
Mexican Fan Palm	—	30 x 30	57	Planted at 6' in 1916, 90' tall
Maple Trees	28	12 x 12	100+	
Thornless Honeylocust	8	25	25	
London Plane	9	10 x 10	28	Planted 6" caliper in 1965, 18' x 18' x 42" planters over garage, design: Dan Kiley
London Plane	16	20 x 20	45	Design: Dan Kiley
Eucalyptus	32			
London Plane	13	20 x 20	40	Residential area, 12 story buildings
London Plane	12	10 x 20	37	Three staggered rows in semi-circle
Oriental Plane	16	20 x 20	62	Planted 1934, 5" caliper, 25' tall
Plane	11	24	30	Planted in 9' wide sidewalk, 42" from curb.
Plane	19	25	60	
Plane	26	20	65	Trees vary from 20" to 36" DBH.
Sycamore	17	10 x 15	55	
Sycamore	17	10 x 15	55	
Sycamore	17	10 x 15	55	
London Plane	32	20	65	
American Elm	18	12 x 18	50	
American Elm	18	12 x 18	50	
Plane Tree	20	12	55	
Pin Oak	18	20 x 18	40	
Thornless Honeylocust	7	12 x 18	28	Planted 1962, design: Dan Kiley
Ginkgo	10	7 x 7	50	Approximately 50' tall
London Plane	26	40 x 20	65	
American Elm	24	50 x 50	55	Eight rows planted in 1930
European Beech	33	10 x 6		
Ginkgo	13	28 x 24	75	
Red Oak	30	12	100	Trees average 70' tall
Plane	22	30 x 20	55	
Horse-chestnut	21	18 x 30	80	
Thornless Honeylocust	7	12 x 18	28	Planted 1962, 5" to 11" caliper, design: Dan Kiley

Figure	Location	Date	Description	Type
5-11	Burlington, Vermont	1971	Summit Street trees	Horse-chestnut
5-13	Savannah, Georgia	1973	Park near waterfront	Live Oak
5-14	Chicago, Illinois	1977	Grant Park	American Elm
5-15	Richfield, Connecticut	—	Main Street	Sugar Maple
5-16	Oak Park, Illinois	1977	Oak Park Center Mall	Pin Oak
5-17	Philadelphia, Pennsylvania	1978	Independence Mall, first block	Sweet Gum
5-18	Princeton, New Jersey	1977	Battle Road	London Plane
5-19	Princeton, New Jersey	1978	University Engineering Building	Thornless Honeylocust
5-20	Queens, New York	1978	Flushing Meadows Park	Norway Maple
5-21	Tucson, Arizona	1973	University of Arizona	Olive Tree
5-22	Fredonia, New York	1969	State University of New York	Larch Tree
5-24	Singapore	1970	Canal Street Park	Madras Thorn
5-25	Singapore	1970	Street Trees	Casuarina
5-30	Burlington, Vermont	1971	Summit Street	Horse-chestnut
5-33	Queens, New York	1978	Flushing Meadows Park	Plane
5-34	Brooklyn, New York	1978	South Portland Avenue	Plane
5-35	Princeton, New Jersey	1977	Battle Road	Plane
5-36	Deal, New Jersey	1978	Almyr Avenue	Plane
5-37	Fredonia, New York	1972	State University of New York	Lombardy Poplar
5-39	Manhattan, New York	1967	Paley Park	Thornless Honeylocust
5-41	Brooklyn, New York	1977	Cadman Plaza Park	London Plane
5-42	Brooklyn, New York	1977	Cadman Plaza Park	London Plane
5-43	Brooklyn, New York	1977	Cadman Plaza Park	London Plane
5-44	Oak Park, Illinois	1975	Oak Park Center Mall	Pin Oak
5-45	Oak Park, Illinois	1975	Oak Park Center Mall	Pin Oak
5-46	Chicago, Illinois	1977	Chicago River Park	Redmond Linden
5-47	Houston, Texas	1973	Rice U.: President's house	Live Oak
5-48	Houston, Texas	1973	Main Street	Live Oak
5-49	Boston, Massachusetts	1977	The Arbor Way	Red Oak
5-50	Cleveland, Ohio	1978	The Public Mall	Sycamore
5-51	Cleveland, Ohio	1978	The Public Mall	Sycamore
5-52	Cleveland, Ohio	1978	View from the Public Mall	Sycamore
5-53	Philadelphia, Pennsylvania	1978	Benjamin Franklin Parkway	Plane
5-54	Philadelphia, Pennsylvania	1967	E. River Drive, Fairmont Park	Plane
6-1	Columbus, Indiana	1972	Cummings Engine Co.	Plane

Type	Diam.	Spacing	Age	Comments
Horse-chestnut	16	30	65	
Live Oak	25	25 x 25	65	
American Elm	18	12 x 18	50	
Sugar Maple	29	15	80	
Pin Oak	6	11 x 22	20	Planted 1975, design: Joe Karr
Sweet Gum	14	27 x 24	35	Planted 1955, design: Harbeson, Hough, Livingston, Larson
London Plane	26	40 x 20	65	
Thornless Honeylocust	10	24 x 32	30	
Norway Maple	13	36	30	Planted in 1963
Olive Tree	18	20		
Larch Tree	6	12 x 15	18	Planted 1967, design: Dan Kiley
Madras Thorn	31	30	25	
Casuarina	16	20	15	60' tall
Horse-chestnut	16	30	65	
Plane	14	30 x 36	25	Planted in 1963
Plane	19	25	60	
Plane	26	40 x 20	65	
Plane	22	20	55	
Lombardy Poplar		6 x 8	20	Planted 1964, 40' tall
Thornless Honeylocust	8	12 x 12	35	Design: Zion and Breen
London Plane	11	20 x 20	42	Planted 1951, 3½" caliper, design: Clarke & Rapuano
London Plane				
London Plane				
Pin Oak	6	11 x 22	20	Design: Joe Karr
Pin Oak				
Redmond Linden	7	21	25	Design: Joe Karr
Live Oak	27		75	
Live Oak	25	15 x 30	70	
Red Oak	28	40/20–50	90	Six rows
Sycamore	10	24 x 24	28	
Sycamore	10	12 x 15	28	Staggered rows, over garage structure
Sycamore	10	24 x 24	28	
Plane	17	24 x 25	80	50' to 60' tall
Plane	30	25	90	80' to 90' tall
Plane	8	12 x 25	25	Planted 1962, design: Dan Kiley

Figure	Location	Date	Description	Type
6-2	Manhattan, New York	1976	Lincoln Center	London Plane
6-3	Washington, D.C.	1977	Capitol Parks Townhouses	London Plane
6-6	Manhattan, New York	1978	Stuyvesant Town	London Plane
6-7	Philadelphia, Pennsylvania	1978	Cypress Street	Plane
6-8	Philadelphia, Pennsylvania	1978	Delancey Place	Plane & Norway Maple
6-9	Washington, D.C.	1978	Pennsylvania Ave. at FBI Building	Littleleaf Linden
6-12	Washington, D.C.	1975	L'Enfant Plaza	Norway Maple
6-15	Bronx, New York	1976	Melrose Apartments	London Plane
6-16	Palm Beach, Florida	1977	Street trees	Casuarina
6-17	Bristol, Pennsylvania	1976	Grundy Park	London Plane

Type	Diam.	Spacing	Age	Comments
London Plane	9	10 x 10	28	Planters 18' x 18' x 42" over garage, 1965, design: Dan Kiley
London Plane	10	20	30	Planted 1963, design: Dan Kiley
London Plane	13	30 x 30	40	Planted about 1948
Plane	16	20	48	
Plane & Norway Maple	15	20	45	
Littleleaf Linden	6	20 x 30	25	Staggered rows; 10' x 10' tree grates, design: Dan Kiley
Norway Maple	6	15 x 12	20	
London Plane	4	10 x 14	16	Planter over structure, 48" soil depth, design: Arnold Associates
Casuarina	8	18		Trees pollarded
London Plane	16	20 x 20	50	Clipped as mass, 45 feet tall

Bibliography

Bacon, Edmund. *Design of Cities*. New York: Viking Press, Inc., 1967.

Barnett, Jonathan. *Urban Design as Public Policy*. New York: Architectural Record Books, 1974.

Bernatsky, Aloys. *Tree Ecology and Preservation*. New York: Elsevier Scientific Publishing Co., 1978.

Caro, Robert. *The Power Broker*. New York: Alfred A. Knopf, 1974.

Chadwick, George. *The Park and the Town*. New York: Frederick A. Praeger, 1966.

Chapin, Raymond, and Kozel, Philip. *Shade Tree Evaluation,* Research Bulletin 1074. Ohio Agriculture Research and Development Center, March 1975.

Cole, Rex Vicat. *The Artistic Anatomy of Trees*. Philadelphia, Pa.: J. B. Lippincott, 1925.

Colvin, Brenda. *Land and Landscape*. London: John Murray, 1970.

Corner, E. J. H. *Illustrated Guide to Tropical Plants*. Tokyo: Hirokawa Publishing Co., 1969.

Corner, E. J. H. *Wayside Trees of Malaya,* Second Ed. Singapore: Government Printing Office, V. G. Gatrell—Government Printer, 1952.

Cranz, Galen. Changing roles of urban parks. *Landscape* 22 (Summer 1978).

Crowe, Sylvia. *Tomorrow's Landscape*. London: Architectural Press, 1956.

Dice, Lee R. *Natural Communities*. Ann Arbor, Michigan: University of Michigan Press, 1952.

Dober, Richard. *Environmental Design*. New York: Van Nostrand Reinhold, 1969.

Dodge, Bernard, and Rickett, Harold. *Diseases and Pests of Ornamental Plants*. New York: The Ronald Press Co., 1948.

Doxiadis, Constantinos. *Ekistics*. New York: Oxford University Press, 1968.

Elias, Thomas, and Irwin, Howard. Urban trees. *Scientific American* 235: 110–118 (Nov. 1976).

Fabos, Julius. *Frederick Law Olmsted, Sr.* Amherst, Massachusetts: University of Massachusetts Press, 1968.

Fairbrother, Nan. *The Nature of Landscape Design.* New York: Alfred A. Knopf, 1974.

Fein, Albert. *Frederick Law Olmsted and the American Environmental Tradition.* New York: George Braziller, Inc., 1972.

Feininger, Andreas. *Trees.* New York: Viking Press, 1968.

Flemer, William III. *Shade and Ornamental Trees in Color.* New York: Grosset and Dunlap, Inc., 1965.

Forest Cover Types of North America. Washington, D.C.: Society of American Foresters, 1962.

Grey, Gene W., and Deneke, Frederick. *Urban Forestry.* New York: John Wiley and Sons, Inc., 1978.

Guthiem, Fred, and Washburn, Wilcomb. *The Federal City: Plans and Realities.* Washington, D.C.: Smithsonian Institute Press, 1976.

Halprin, Lawrence. *Cities.* New York: Reinhold, 1963.

Harlow, William, and Harrar, Ellwood. *Textbook of Dendrology Covering the Important Forest Trees of the U.S. and Canada.* New York: McGraw-Hill Co. Inc., 1941.

Hartmann, Frederick (ed). The metro forest. *A Natural History Special Supplement,* Nov. 1973.

Hecksher, August. *Alive in the City.* New York: Charles Scribner's Sons, 1974.

Hecksher, August. *Open Spaces.* New York: Harper and Row, 1977.

Horn, Henry S. *The Adaptive Geometry of Trees.* Princeton, New Jersey: Princeton University Press, 1976.

Jellicoe, Geoffrey, and Jellicoe, Susan. *The Landscape of Man.* New York: Viking Press, Inc., 1975.

Jacobs, Jane. *The Life and Death of Great American Cities.* New York: Random House, 1961.

Loomis, Robert, and Padgett, William. *Air Pollution and Trees in the East.* USDA, Forest Service, 1975.

Lyon, Lyttleton, and Buckman, Harry. *The Nature and Properties of Soils,* Fourth Ed. New York: Macmillan Company, 1943.

Marx, Leo. *The Machine in the Garden*. New York: Oxford University Press, 1964.

McArthur, Robert. *Geographical Ecology, Patterns in the Distribution of Species*. New York: Harper and Row, 1972.

Muirhead, Desmond. *Palms*. Arizona: Dale Stuart King, Publishers, 1961.

Mumford, Lewis. *The City in History*. New York: Harcourt, Brace and World, Inc., 1961.

Mumford, Lewis. *The Condition of Man*. New York: Harcourt, Brace and World, Inc., 1955.

Nadel, Ira Bruce and Oberlander, Cornelia Hahn. *Trees in the City*. New York: Pergamon Press, 1977.

Newton, Norman T. *Design on the Land*. Massachusetts: Harvard University Press, 1971.

New Towns. *Architectural Record,* December 1973.

Olmsted, Fredrick Law, Sr. *Forty Years of Landscape Architecture: Central Park,* Edited by Fredrick Law Olmsted, Jr. and Theodora Kimball. Massachusetts: M.I.T. Press, 1973.

Payne, Brian and Strom, Steven. The contribution of trees to the appraised value of unimproved residential land. *Valuation* 22(2): 36–45 (1975).

Peet, Louis Harmon. *Trees and Shrubs of Central Park*. New York: America Printing House, 1902.

Peets, Elbert. *On the Art of Designing Cities*. Cambridge, Massachusetts: M.I.T. Press, 1968.

Pirone, P.O. *Tree Maintenance,* Fourth Ed. New York: Oxford University Press, Inc., 1976.

Reed, Henry and Ducksworth, Sophia. *Central Park, A History and Guide*. New York: Clarkson N. Potter, Inc., 1967.

Reps, John. *The Making of Urban America*. Princeton, New Jersey: Princeton University Press, 1965.

Repton, Humphrey. *The Art of Landscape Gardening*. Boston: Houghton Mifflin Co., 1907.

Rudolfsky, Bernard. *Streets for People*. New York: Doubleday and Co. Inc., 1964.

Santamour, Frank Jr., Gerhold, Henry, and Little, Silas (eds). *Better Trees for Metropolitan Landscapes,* USDA Forest Service General Technical Report NE-22. Washington, D.C.: U.S. Government Printing Office, 1976.

Schmidt, Peter. *Back to Nature, The Arcadian Myth in Urban America*. New York: Oxford University Press, 1969.

Scully, Vincent. *American Architecture and Urbanism*. New York: Praeger Publishers, 1969.

Seymour, W. H. *Small Urban Spaces*. New York: New York University Press, 1969.

Shepherd, John and Jellicoe, G. A. *Italian Gardens of the Renaissance*. New York: Charles Scribner's Sons, 1925.

Sholto J., and de J. Hart, Robert. *Forest Farming*. London: Watkins, 1976.

Sitte, Camillo. *City Planning According to Aristic Principles*. New York: Random House, 1965.

Smith, Alice U. *Trees in a Winter Landscape*. New York: Holt, 1969.

Soil—The 1957 Yearbook of Agriculture, USDA. Washington, D.C.: The U.S. Government Printing Office, 1957.

Stroud, Dorothy. *Capability Brown*. London: Country Life Ltd., 1950.

Stroud, Dorothy. *Humphrey Repton*. London: Country Life Ltd., 1962.

Sutton, S. B. (ed). *Civilizing American Cities—Olmsted Writings*. Massachusetts: M.I.T. Press, 1971.

Trees and Forests in an Urbanizing Environment, A Symposium. Amherst, Massachusetts: M.I.T. Press, 1968.

Tunnard, Christopher, and Pushkarev, Boris. *Man-Made America*. New Haven: Yale University Press, 1963.

Tunnard, Christopher, and Reed, Henry. *American Skyline*. New York: The New American Library, Inc., 1956.

Walker, Theodore. *Perception and Environmental Design*. Indiana: PDA Publishers, 1971.

Walker, Theodore. *Plan Graphics*. Indiana: PDA Publishers, 1975.

Weddle, A. E. (ed). *Techniques of Landscape Architecture*. New York: American Elsevier Publishing Co., Inc., 1967.

Wilson, Brayton F. *The Growing Tree*. Massachusetts: University of Mass., 1970.

Wyman, Donald. *Trees for American Gardens*. New York: Macmillan Co., 1970.

Zevi, Bruno. *Architecture as Space*. Translated by Gendel Milton. New York: Horizon Press, 1957.

Zion, Robert. *Trees for Architecture and the Landscape*. New York: Rinehold, 1968.

Index

Index

Nature—agrarian: 43, civilized: 43, man and nature: 41, pastoral: 67, uncultivated: 43.
Newark, New Jersey: 5, 6, 7.
New Haven, Connecticut: 5.
New London, Connecticut: 5.
New towns: 145, 146.
New York, City of: 5, 16, 19, 26, 36, 51, 67, 88, 103, 120, 122, 123, 124, 136, 146. Parks department: 49, 111. Zoning Ammendment of May 1975: 144. Zoning Resolution of 1961: 51.
New York, State of—University at Fredonia: 102. Niagra Falls: 26.
Niagra Falls, New York: 26.
Nomenclature: 79.
Norway Maple: 79, 88, 89, 93, 95, 111, 114, 123, 125, 127, 135.
Norway Spruce: 111.

Oakland Museum, California: 26.
Oak Park Center Mall, Chicago: 105, 106.
Oak: 85, 99, 111. See also English Oak, Pin Oak, Red Oak, Scarlet Oak, White Oak, Willow Oak.
Odd tree types: 102. Dwarf trees: 54, 102. Columnar trees: 73. Vertical trees: 70.
Olive tree: 14, 87.
Olmsted, Frederick Law Sr.: 16, 17, 19, 21, 40, 67, 110, 111, 113, 114, 116.
Open grown tree form: 12, 47, 48, 74, 148.
Ordinances, tree planting: See Regulations and standards.
Oriental Plane Tree: 49.
Ornamental trees: See Flowering trees.

Palm Beach, Florida: 33.
Paley Park, New York: 103, 123.
Palo Verde: 88.
Paris: 2, 15, 83.
Parks: See also individual names of parks. Large urban parks: 58, 65, 66, 67, 71.
Paseo de la Reforma, Mexico City: 23.
Pastoral landscape: 16, 110, 148. Pastoral ideal: 17. Pastoral nature: 67.
Paving: 67, 74, 83, 97, 130, 133, 137. Tree grates: 130.
Paxton, Joseph: 16.
Pedestrian mall: 11, 42.
Pennsylvania Avenue, Washington, D.C.: 125, 126.
Persians: 13.
Pest Control: 98, 99, 133, 134.
Philadelphia: 2, 8, 30, 35, 51, 80, 88, 108, 109, 122, 125, 129.
Photosynthesis: 95.
Phototropism: 50, 95.
Piazza Navona, Rome: 22.
Pin Oak: 62, 85, 87, 94, 104, 105, 106, 113, 115, 131, 135.
Plane Trees: 2, 8, 14, 62, 63, 65, 83, 84, 85, 87, 88, 89, 90, 96, 99, 100, 103, 104, 107, 108, 109, 115, 116, 120, 123, 124, 125, 133, 137. See also London Plane Tree, Oriental Plane Tree, Sycamore.
Planning and design: 122, 138, 147, 149. See also Tree Management. Development pattern: 146. Public spaces: 66. Regional pattern: 146, 147. Urban design criteria: 143.
Plant community: 43, 47, 66, 110, 139, 147.
Plant ecology: 12, 39.
Planters, raised: 8, 54, 128, 129.
Plant Hardiness Zones: 92, 99.
Pollutants: 49, 90, 94, 131. See also Air quality.

Poplar: 137. See also Lombardy Poplar, Silver Poplar.
Princeton, New Jersey: 4, 63, 83.
Poussin, Nicolas: 16.
Prospect Park, New York: 16, 116.
Providence, Rhode Island: 5.
Pruning: 81, 135, 136, 137, 139, 140.

Railroad stations: 5.
Rain Tree: 25.
Random tree arrangement: 37, 42, 57, 58, 147, 148.
Range of tree types: 41, 92.
Red Maple: 41, 63, 79, 89, 90, 94, 96, 97, 138.
Redmond Linden: 105.
Red Oak: 83, 89, 96, 106, 107, 113, 114, 137.
Regulations and standards: 121, 122, 144. See also Tree Management.
Renaissance villa garden: 14.
Reston, Virginia: 146.
Rice University, Houston Texas: 124.
River Birch: 114.
Rockefeller University, New York: 36, 124.
Roman Empire: 13.
Romantic tradition: 12, 40.
Rome: 13, 22, 23, 14.
Roosevelt Island, New York: 146.
Root systems: 48, 54, 94, 127, 128, 137. Girdling roots: 132. Root zone: 94, 127, 128, 130.
Rosa, Salvatore: 16.
Rousseau, Jean-Jacques: 17.

Salt Lake City, Utah: 10, 51.
Salts, to melt snow: 49, 132.
Sassafras: 96.
Savannah, Georgia: 2, 32.
Scale: 11, 12, 27, 37, 39, 44, 53, 54, 59, 63, 67, 70, 76, 81, 91, 110, 124.
Scale models: 75, 76.
Scarlet Oak: 131.
Scotch Pine: 111.
Shade tolerance: 95.
Sheperd, Alexander Robey: 122.
Sidewalks: 50, 54, 124, 125.
Silver Maple: 95, 114.
Silver Poplar: 111.
Singapore: 24, 25, 30, 32.
Society of American Foresters: 111.
Soils: 93, 94, 127, 128, 130, 132. Soil compaction: 95, 130, 132. Soil drainage: 95. Soil depth: 54. Fertilizing: 134. 134.
Solar angle: 52, 123.
Spacing of trees: 51, 53, 55, 58, 61, 62, 63, 123.
Spatial order: 42. Composition: 58, 59, 60, 61, 71, 73. Continuity: 37. Proportion: 12. Rhythms: 22.
Species diversity: 40, 93.
St. Mark's Square, Venice: 22.
Streets: 50, 53, 55, 97, 122, 123, 124, 125. Manhattan cross streets: 124. Street orientation: 51. Street trees: 51, 53, 54, 56, 62, 121, 122.
Suburban development: 26, 145.
Succession—plant: 66, 92, 116, 139; forest: 48, 114.
Sugar Maple: 62, 84, 86, 95, 111, 130, 133, 137.
Sunlight: 51, 123, 124.
Sweet Gum: 85, 86, 89, 97, 111, 131.
Sycamore (Plane): 13, 99, 107, 108, 111, 113.
Sycamore Maple: 114.

Technology: 26. Abuse of technology: 13, 25, 94, 122.
Tempe, Arizona: 35.
Thames, The Embankment: 22.
Thoreau, Henry David: 17.
Thornless Honeylocust: 63, 103, 107.
Tiber River, Rome: 14.
Traffic sight distance: 54, 56.
Transplanting—cost of: 120. Size of trees: 63. Tolerance: 96.
Tree height: 82.
Tree Maintenance: 66, 95, 98, 131, 133, 134, 136, 137, 138, 140. See also Pruning, Soils, Water and Pest Control.
Tree Management: 98, 114, 133, 138, 139. See also Tree Maintenance and Regulations & Standards. Government agencies for tree management: 143, 145. Municipal design regulations: 144. Municipal tree plan: 143, 144, 145. Urban planning: 143.
Tree of Heaven: See Ailanthus.
Trenton, New Jersey: 4, 5, 11, 34.
Tropical Cities: 25.
Tuilleries Garden: 15.
Tulip Tree: 18, 89, 90, 91, 95, 97, 130, 134.
Tulsa, Oklahoma: 2, 3.

Union Station, Washington, D.C.: 5, 7.
Utility lines: 51, 54, 122, 123, 135.

Vancouver, British Columbia: 122.
Varieties of trees: 80, 82. See also Flowering trees & Odd tree types. Clones: 103. Cultivars: 79.
Vaux, Calvert: 16, 18, 21, 67.
Vaux-le-Vicomte: 15.
Venice: 22.
Venturi, Robert: 42.
Versailles: 15, 16, 35.
Visual presentation techniques—drawings: 74, 75, 76; holography: 76; models: 75.

Washington, D.C.: 5, 7, 63, 70, 71, 99, 120, 125, 126, 128. Georgetown: 125.
Water: 94, 127, 130, 133, 147.
Waterfront: 5.
Weeping Willow: 111, 113.
West Palm Beach, Florida: 2, 3, 136.
White Oak: 96, 114.
Willow: 137. See also Desert Willow, Weeping Willow.
Willow Oak: 7, 89.
Wilmington, Delaware: 5, 6.

Zion and Breen: 103.
Zones, plant types: See Plant Hardiness zones.
Zoning Regulations—New York: 51, 144. Green Belt Zoning Laws: 145.

WITHDRAWN

JUN 0 3 2024

DAVID O. McKAY LIBRARY
BYU-IDAHO

RICKS
DAVID O. McKAY LIBRARY
REXBURG, IDAHO 83440